CONFUCIANISM AND CHRISTIANITY

儒与耶

秦家懿博士著

CONFUCIANISM
AND
CHRISTIANITY

A COMPARATIVE STUDY

JULIA CHING

KODANSHA INTERNATIONAL
Tokyo, New York & San Francisco
in cooperation with
THE INSTITUTE OF ORIENTAL RELIGIONS
Sophia University, Tokyo

Distributed in the United States by Kodansha International/USA, Ltd., through Harper & Row, Publishers, Inc., 10 East 53rd Street, New York, New York 10022. In South America by Harper & Row, International Department, 10 East 53rd Street, New York, New York 10022. In Canada by Fitzhenry & Whiteside Limited, 150 Lesmill Road, Don Mills, Ontario. In Mexico and Central America by HARLA S. A. de C. V., Apartado 30–546, Mexico 4, D. F. In the United Kingdom by Phaidon Press Limited, Littlegate House, St. Ebbe's Street, Oxford OX1 1SQ. In Europe by Boxerbooks, Inc., Limmatstrasse 111, 8031 Zurich. In Australia and New Zealand by Book Wise (Australia) Pty. Ltd., 104–108 Sussex Street, Sydney 2000. In the Far East by Toppan Company (S) Pte. Ltd., Box 22, Jurong Town Post Office, Jurong, Singapore 22.

Published by Kodansha International Ltd., 2–12–21 Otowa, Bunkyo-ku, Tokyo 112 and Kodansha International/USA, Ltd., 10 East 53rd Street, New York, New York 10022 and 44 Montgomery Street, San Francisco, California 94104. Copyright in Japan 1977 by Kodansha International Ltd. All rights reserved. Printed in Japan.

LCC 77–75962
ISBN 0–87011–303–8
JBC 1014–785804–2361

First edition, 1977

For
W.T. deBary
(*in honor of his vision for education*)
and
Heinrich Dumoulin
(*for his life of dialogue with other religions*)

CONTENTS

Foreword

Confucianism and Christianity is the third in a series of books published under the auspices of the Institute of Oriental Religions of Sophia University, Tokyo. The first two books, written by H. Enomiya-Lassalle and Heinrich Dumoulin, dealt with Christianity in dialogue with Buddhism; the present book deals with Confucianism and Christianity.

One need not be a prophet to declare that the theology and religious thinking of the next century will be preoccupied with the meeting of the great religions. Already we see great growth in mutual understanding and cooperation between Buddhism, Christianity, Hinduism, Islam and Judaism. Hopefully, this trend towards union will continue, and the great religions will serve the modern world, providing it with the spiritual values it so greatly needs.

It is our hope that this series will make some contribution to the Western understanding of Eastern religions and to the Eastern understanding of Christianity.

William Johnston
Director
Institute of Oriental Religions
Sophia University, Tokyo
March 1977

ACKNOWLEDGEMENTS

I wish to record here my gratitude to all those who have helped and encouraged me, in one way or another, to write this book. I shall venture to mention some names, while acknowledging that my indebtedness extends to many others also, whose names may not appear. I should like first of all to mention the names of certain Asians, specialists in the field of Chinese philosophy: Wing-tsit Chan, T'ang Chün-i and Okada Takehiko, each of whom has encouraged me in this endeavor even though some of them are not Christians. I think also of others who have a more committed concern for Christianity: of Searle Bates, Thomas Berry, Tilemann Grimm, Douglas Lancashire, James Martin, Yves Reguin and D. Howard Smith. I remember also with special gratitude those persons who have read draft chapters in earlier forms, and whose advice has led me to their complete revision. I refer here to W.T. deBary, David Dilworth, Hans Küng and John E. Smith. I remember also those who have looked at the later drafts: Norris Clarke, Edmund Leites and Hans Küng. Hans Küng deserves special mention for helping me to decide to write this book according to theological perspectives, and for suggesting certain general orientations. I do not wish to forget my friends in Hongkong who have a special concern for the evolution of Asian theologies: especially Peter Lee, Lee-ming Ng and Philip Shen. I would also like to remember other friends in Brussels-Louvain, Parig Digan and Jan Kerkhofs. At our "China Consultations," Confucianism was less a topic of discussion than Marxism, but I learned much from these all the same, and at least some of it went into the making of this book. And then, I remember with affection and respect Heinrich Dumoulin, whose original invitation to me to write this book started the whole thing rolling.

I should also like to thank the editors and staff of Kodansha International for their kind cooperation. And I must mention here that Chapter Two: "Confucianism: A Critical Reassessment of the Heritage," and Chapter Four: "The Problem of God," appeared earlier in slightly modified form in *International Philosophical Quarterly*, in March 1975 and March 1977, respectively.

There is also my family, or, should I say, families: both the Christians, the non-Christians, the post-Christians, and the atheists, including, of course, the Confucians and the Buddhists. Each has helped in a special way to provoke my thinking.

It is my place here to say, Thank You, one in all.

The mistakes, however, of information and interpretation, should be attributed solely to me, and not to any of these kind persons.

J.C.

Introduction

APOLOGIA PRO LIBRE

Confucianism and Christianity. Is the former a philosophy or a religion, or both? And is it compatible with the latter? Such were some of the questions posed by missionaries in China over three hundred years ago. And they have never been adequately answered. The times, of course, have changed. There are people who now consider them no longer worth asking. And yet, Confucianism and Christianity remain *living* traditions, even if each sees its own survival somehow threatened. These will remain, in my opinion, important questions for a long time to come, not only to the student of comparative philosophies and religions, but also to the theologian concerned with a proper understanding of Christianity itself.

THE PROBLEM OF DEFINITION

"Confucianism" is actually a misnomer for a tradition which is known in the country of its origin as the School of the Scholars, or *Literati*, that is, a broad, intellectual tradition based on the continuing interpretation of a body of writings known as the Classics. These revered writings include works of various genres: poetry, purported historical documents, divination oracles and accompanying interpretations, annals of a feudal state, and certain ritual texts.[1] The very diversity of these texts has allowed for a plurality of methodologies and interpretations, even within the cultural circles where they exercised the greatest influence: in China, Korea, Japan and Vietnam (known earlier as Annam). It is a tradition which transcends and includes philosophical and religious concerns, since it is one which experienced a long evolution before the entry of such more technical terms as "philosophy" and "religion" into the Sino-Japanese vocabulary.[2] And it may be useful to recall that where Christianity is concerned, philosophy and theology did not become clearly separated from one another at least until the time of the Renaissance, and perhaps later.

In this light, I believe it accurate to say that Confucianism represents a tradition of human wisdom—which is what philosophy in East Asia signifies to a large extent. Thus, it differs from Christianity, which is first and foremost a revealed religion. However, contemporary scholars like Wing-tsit Chan, a Chinese philosopher, Joseph Kitagawa and Ninian Smart, historians of religion, agree with the earlier Max Weber in discerning a strong religiosity at the heart of the Confucian tradition. After all, both Confucianism and Christianity have exercised decisive influence in shaping the beliefs, moral codes and behaviors of large populations in the East and the West. A comparative study of Confucianism and Christianity should therefore not only be possible but also fruitful.

THE PROBLEM OF METHOD

Granted the viability of such a study, one might ask further, by what method? In the United States, Eastern religious philosophies are taught and studied in one of three different university departments: Philosophy, Religious Studies (sometimes Theology), and East Asian Languages and Cultures. This is in itself illustrative of the problems of definition and method that confront every scholar. How should a book like this be written, and for which audience?

The comparative philosopher has a vested interest in the transcultural comparison of ideas and problems of a speculative nature. The student of religion may be himself or herself a philosopher, a historian, or a social scientist. To this day, however, comparative philosophy, or religion, remains a frontier region rather than a discipline in itself, and those engaged in opening up the frontier are regarded as possible dilettantes who dare to do the nearly impossible.[3] Depth of knowledge and breadth of perspective are considered almost as mutual exclusives. The East Asian specialist is usually alarmed at the *naiveté* of those philosophers and religionists who attempt to interpret Eastern traditions without possessing the necessary linguistic skills, while the comparative philosopher or religionist—a somewhat rare specimen of the scholarly breed— is dismayed at what appears to be a "ghetto spirit" among the

Orientalists. Moreover, both tend to be disdainful of the missiologists, who, as theologians, pursue an openly pragmatic and sectarian
interest in desiring to further the number of religious conversions.
Methodologies fluctuate, therefore, depending not only on the
definition of such a tradition as Confucianism as either philosophy,
religion, or—for most Sinologists—culture, but also on the vested
interests of the disciplines themselves. But the problem of method
is further complicated—or, perhaps, simplified—by the situation
in which the author of this book finds herself: an East Asian who
has studied in both East and West, and who is at present living
and working in the West. The dilemma becomes one of identification—with the East or the West. Joseph Kitagawa has expressed
this sense of dilemma well, and has also pointed a way out:

> An Easterner coming to settle in the West faces a number of
> alternatives. He can consciously remain an Easterner and try
> to interpret Eastern religions from this perspective. Or he can
> identify himself with the West and study Eastern religions as
> a Westerner . . . in so far as his method [is] . . . concerned.
> Or again, he can choose to stand in a borderland, being
> conscious of . . . both sides but . . . refusing to be drawn into
> either side . . . . The writer has chosen still another alterna-
> tive, and a more difficult one. . . . He has tried to identify
> himself with the West without losing his identity with the East.[4]

I have attempted to resolve my personal East/West dilemma in
a manner which is much like his—emphasizing, like him, that this
is more a matter of aspiration than of achievement. I am thankful
for my dual background, and hope to put it to good use. But where
Kitagawa has kept a mainly social focus, oriented to the phenomenon of the believing community in the East Asian religions, my
own is more problem-oriented. I regard myself as doing the work
here of a comparative historian of ideas and doctrines—with the
understanding of the word *doctrina* in the broad sense of "teaching."[5] I have also kept an open theological horizon, with the aim
of initiating religious dialogue between the two living traditions.
I argue that I am drawing my methodology from the nature of the
traditions being studied, proceeding, in each case, from the sacred
books and classical texts to the development of philosophical
interpretations and their present-day relevance. The vastness of the

scope precludes comprehensive treatment, and my priority is always placed upon a clearer exposition of Confucianism with reference to certain themes common to itself and Christianity. I regard Christianity as a religious tradition grounded in the New Testament teachings, known to me through contemporary exegesis, both Protestant and Catholic. And I consider Confucianism to be likewise based on classical texts—the so-called Five Classics and Four Books.[6] I seldom refer to the many notable works of Confucian textual commentaries except to clarify certain ideas, but I give real importance to the movement of thought called Neo-Confucianism, in which form the Confucian tradition has come down to the present. This method seems suited to the study of both traditions which have their origins in a reverence for *the word*, first spoken and then written down in texts that are revered as deposits of divine revelation in one case, and instructions of sages in the other. I have given some attention to semantic analysis seeking to determine the pristine meanings of certain keywords, before going on to discuss the evolution of their meanings as well as the institutionalization of this process of interpretation. I consider exegesis to be crucial to a correct understanding of Christianity as well as of Confucianism. And I hope that this method will help to clarify the common themes in the two traditions while contributing to a broader, hermeneutical task of rendering *meaningful* the work of exposition and interpretation.

THE THEOLOGICAL HORIZON

As a book which concerns itself with Confucianism and Christianity, or rather, a study of Confucianism in the light of certain perspectives borrowed from Christianity, this is not the first work of its kind. Missionary-scholars such as James Legge and W.E. Soothill have produced, many decades ago, studies of Chinese religions which include Confucianism. The more recent publications of D. Howard Smith also make use of a thematic approach which presupposes a knowledge of the Christian religion.[7] But this is, I think, the first study of Confucianism done in the light of a clearly contemporary understanding of Christianity, with a manifest intention of promoting more intellectual dialogue between the two traditions. My main focus remains Confucianism. I offer an examination of the internal structure of Confucian thought in view of suggesting ways by which each of the two traditions might be better understood in the light of each other. I present a comparative study, but I have no intention of judging either tradition according to any predetermined, hierarchically oriented, system of values. I believe also that I have pondered many times over the questions discussed in this book, and always as a Chinese with a nonChristian background, who considers herself both Christian and non-Christian, and attempts a dialectical integration of the double heritage.

In this sense, I present this book to all those who have some interest in Confucianism as a religious tradition. I hope that my historical sense and systematic treatment of the subject matter, based as it is on the reading of many primary sources, will serve the Sinological circles in resolving some of the problems which are still regarded as unsettled and unsettling: such as, is the Confucian tradition theistic, atheistic or pantheistic? I have taken some pain to show how such problems are to be resolved in the *total* context of the Chinese tradition, rather than by taking a part to be the whole. I trust also that my book will confirm the judgments of those comparative religionists who have always pointed out the religious horizon of Confucianism and offer a starting-point for philosophers interested in comparative thought. I should also like to provoke more interest in the subject among contemporary theologians, in both East and West.

Indeed, more Christian theologians are taking notice of "world religions," a subject which hitherto has been relegated mainly to the smaller circles of comparative religionists and missiologists. In the last few years, such notable summaries of Christian teachings as the *Neues Glaubensbuch* (1973), prepared by an ecumenical team of theologians, Hans Küng's *Christsein* (1974), the Lutheran *Erwachsenen Katechismus* (1975) as well as W. Bühlmann's *Wo der Glaube lebt* (1975), all make some mention of the subject and, one after the other, give it a greater importance.[8] But such attention is yet limited in scope and depth. The theological circle, the orientalist circle, and the circles of comparative philosophers and religionists remain largely aloof, each from the other. One can only hope that the increased attention given to "world religions" is a sign of things to come—a deeper and more serious interest in mankind's manifold ways of finding the divine and of giving expression to religious experience. This is all the more important in an age when an increasing number of the young, coming from Western and Christian backgrounds, especially in the United States but also in other parts of the world, shows an absorbing and enduring interest in the so-called Eastern philosophical and religious traditions. This interest can yield a broadening and enriching effect on such persons. But it requires the assistance of specialist guidance.[9] And it calls for more concerned attention on the part of those scholars with a declared interest in the problems of the world today, who claim for Western Christianity a role which is yet vital and relevant. In the last analysis, for theologians living in a world known to be of such religious diversity, the only honesty and relevance will come when they examine their own religious heritage in the light of those of others—of the rest of mankind. And this is all the truer at a time when theology is taking the path of the human to reach the divine.

The Plan of the Book

I have chosen also to begin with the concrete encounter between Christianity and Confucianism (Chapter One). This does not take place so much at international conferences, although these have their usefulness and should be encouraged. This had a historical existence and continues to have existential importance. The Jesuit interpretation of the Chinese tradition which later became known as Confucianism began a task that has been continued in various ways by other interpreters, whether Western or Chinese, believing Christians or confirmed agnostics. The controversies surrounding the translation of specific terms, such as God, and the question of the compatibility of Confucian rites and Christian faith, outlined for us, several hundred years ago, the similarities and differences inherent in certain "common themes" and the subtleties of implications for both sides. I have especially included a chapter on critical reassessment of the Confucian heritage (Chapter Two), as its very survival appears to be challenged today, and yet, upon this question of its viability rests the importance—or lack of importance—of such a study as this one. I would like to note here that this critical reassessment was completed in late 1974, when the intellectual and political developments in China had not yet clearly indicated what was—and is—yet to emerge, from the anti-Confucius campaign. One can only hope that such a politicized event may not represent the authentic spiritual pulse of the Chinese people.

Only after having grounded my study in the historical encounter, with its continuing legacy of ambiguity, and in the critical situation in which Confucianism finds itself today, do I move into more speculative issues. Here, I begin with the problem of man and of man's ability to transcend himself—in theory as well as *praxis* (Chapter Three). The problem of conscience comes in as the ground of self-transcendence. The notion of community also comes in, as the Confucian conscience has always had a clearly social focus, which offers also a direction for self-transcendence, with an ideal of the sage as a man of affairs. The theoretical rationale for this transcendence-dimension leads to the problem of an Absolute or God (Chapter Four). Here, as in the following chapter which deals with prayer, meditation, mystique and cult (Chapter Five), the exposition is made with the assistance of such heuristic principles—taken from Friedrich Heiler's book on Prayer[10]—as the prophetical and mystical religions, with their respective emphases on a personal deity or a transcendent Absolute, and on varying practices of prayer as dialogue with God or of meditation leading to the mystical experience of oneness with all things. I contend that early Confucianism bears a greater resemblance to Heiler's archetypal "prophetical religion" with belief in a supreme, personal deity, as extant prayers in the Classics continue to attest, while later Confucianism approaches what may be called "mystical religion" in which a transcendent and yet immanent Absolute takes the place of God. My concern is always to make manifest certain similarities between the two traditions without overlooking basic differences. I do not wish to use such concepts as prophecy or mysticism to argue for greater merit for Confucianism, and I make use of them always with a knowledge of the limitations of such analogies. Besides, it is my contention that Christianity is constituted by the belief in the God of Jesus Christ, whereas ethical values—rather than belief in God—determine who is Confucian. And, just as Chapters Four and Five form a kind of unit, so do Chapters Three and Six, where the discussion of the *praxis* of self-transcendence continues in the direction of political relevance (Chapter Six). This problem has always been a conscious and integral part of Confucian teachings, and has become increasingly recognized by Christians today as part and parcel of Christian responsibility.

Our confrontation of the present always leads to a future, and it is this concern that has prompted me to conclude the study with an Epilogue, in which I discuss the issue of Asian theologies in the light of the dialogue between Confucianism and Christianity. I use the plural, theologies, to indicate my preference for pluralism, both theological—on the level of reflection—and religious—on the level of practice. I do not look forward to a world faith, although I see the possibility of certain universal elements emerging from particular world religions, and contributing to a more common recognition of a set of shared beliefs. But I cannot accept, for example, a theory of "radical displacement,"[11] according to which a convert must break with his or her cultural past in order to become a Christian—because Christianity used to be considered by its adherents to be the only way to salvation.

I acknowledge a clear theological horizon indicated throughout this study, but I wish also to express indebtedness to the work of many others who followed a different approach, such as that of *Religionswissenschaft* or history of religions. I have sought to base my theological reflections upon the interpretations of both Protestant and Catholic theologians, without entering into controversial issues which do not belong to the scope of such a book. But I address this book not merely to the theological circle, but also to all others who have some interest in comparative philosophy and religion, as well as in Sinology. And then, while I refer mostly to Chinese Confucian scholarship,[12] I do not forget the immense contribution made also in Japan and Korea, and even elsewhere. My intention is not to write an exhaustive study, nor do I pretend to resolve certain controversial problems. I only hope that the extent and depth of certain common themes found in both

Confucianism and Christianity will open real horizons of thought and reflection through this book, intended as an introductory study. Introduced to Europe by Jesuit missionaries in the seventeenth and eighteenth centuries, Chinese philosophy—mostly in the form of Confucianism—made a real impact upon European intellectual circles, especially in the Age of Enlightenment, the cultural legacy of which we are all heirs. At the same time, Confucianism also became the occasion for some heated religious controversies, surrounding such questions as the compatibility of Confucian rites with Christian beliefs. Today, however, Christian intellectuals and missionaries appear to have largely neglected the study of Confucianism in a newly discovered enthusiasm for Buddhism.[13] I do not wish to discourage any such interest. I regard it as very useful and even necessary for those who desire to understand their own religious heritage in greater depth to do so against a broader, comparative perspective, taking into account the entire human heritage in its manifold variety. But I also consider Confucianism to be more compatible with Christianity than is Buddhism, because of a more pronounced, shared ethical concern. Besides, Confucianism does not lack spiritual depth. Indeed, contact with Buddhism has served historically to expand its spiritual horizons. It may even be said that Confucianism has transformed Buddhist spirituality and mysticism for its own purposes, integrating its central, ethical concern with a deeper dimension of interiority. Like Christianity, Confucianism possesses both an "inwardness," based on proper regard for the self, for its dignity and its ability to transcend its limitations, and an "outwardness," based on a real respect for social and even mondial responsibilities. Moreover, as I have labored to make manifest, Confucianism has also a definite vertical dimension, rooted in its openness to the transcendent. I consider, therefore, a better knowledge of Confucianism a valuable vantage point from which to re-evaluate the Christian heritage and to speculate a little about its future. Such knowledge should contribute not only to a Christian sense of self-understanding, but also to the continuing task of building genuinely Asian theologies.

My advocation of Confucianism is not entirely uncritical. On the one hand, I have sought to expound Confucian *ideas* of human perfectibility and the ideal polity, of man's openness to the divine and his harmony with nature. On the other, I have also pointed out certain difficulties: those related to the fossilization of ideas and ideals, and those contingent on historical contexts and conditions. I could have dwelt at greater length, for example, on the relatively low position of women in the Confucian system. But I consider what I have said adequate for a work such as this one. Moreover, in explaining how Confucianism and Christianity could learn from each other, I am of course maintaining that neither is perfect. In discussing man and society, God and Absolute, prayer and mysticism, I have also indicated certain difficulties with Christianity: difficulties that are also contingent on time and culture.

After having enunciated my presuppositions, I should like also to clarify certain practical points. My scriptural references are usually to the Revised Standard Version (Catholic edition) of the Holy Bible (London, 1966) in English translation. My references to the Confucian Classics are usually made to James Legge's translation of the Chinese Classics (Oxford, 1893), although I often make adaptations according to a reading of the original Chinese texts. At times, I have also made use of translations by other scholars, as indicated in my footnotes, sometimes also adapting from them. I have also kept to the Wade-Giles system of romanization of Chinese words, as it is the best known among English-reading Sinologists. I have given, within the text itself, the Chinese word, and in some cases the character, of certain principal technical terms. I have not, however, provided Chinese or Japanese titles in the bibliographical notes, since I believe that they would be known to specialists and of little importance to the non-specialist. A Chronological Table as well as an Index-Glossary are included at the end of the book.

Many people have encouraged me in the writing of this book; some have offered positive advice and support. I am grateful to all, and mention a few names in the Acknowledgements. I look forward also to the help, support, and criticism of my readers. I hope that there will be among them comparative philosophers and religionists, theologians, Sinologists and Orientalists, as well as a more general public concerned with the challenge of inheriting a world heritage which includes Confucianism and Christianity. I know that I cannot satisfy everyone. Some will question

my generalizations, while others will desire more detailed information. But I hope at least to be able to provoke some thinking, and
to learn personally from those who are thus provoked.

JULIA CHING
Yale University
New Haven, Connecticut
November 1976

NOTES

1. The formal names of these Classics are the Book of Odes (or Poetry), the
Book of Documents (or History), the Book of Changes, the Spring-Autumn
Annals, and the Book of Rites. They have all been attributed to Confucius, as
editor or chief author, although the authenticity of such is dubious. These
"Five Classics" probably had their origins in groups of texts predating Confucius (551–479 B.C.) and acquired their present forms during the centuries
which followed his death.
2. The words philosophy (*che-hsüeh*; 哲学) and religion (*tsung-chiao*; 宗教) came in
to the Chinese vocabulary in the late nineteenth century, when they were introduced with translations of Western works—and then through the intermediary
of Japanese translators. Before that, all intellectual traditions—Confucianism,
Taoism, Buddhism and others—were designated "Teachings" (*chiao*) or
"Schools of Thought" (*chia*). It is interesting to note that the Sanskrit vocabulary also lacked such technical terms as "philosophy" and "religion," and
relied on the term *Dharma* to designate traditional teachings.
3. A work which seeks to explain the nature and methodology of "Comparative
Philosophy" deserves to be better known, although its author is better acquainted with Indian than with East Asian philosophy: Paul Masson-Oursel, *La
Philosophie Comparée* (Paris, 1923). The work of such journals as *Philosophy East
and West* are to be commended for promoting interest in comparative philosophy.
4. Joseph M. Kitagawa, *Religions of the East* (Philadelphia, 1968), Foreword,
p.12.
5. Richard McKeon, "Philosophy and Theology, History and Science in the
Thought of Bonaventura and Thomas Aquinas," *Journal of the History of Ideas*
36 (1975), p. 387.
6. The "Four Books" refers to the Analects of Confucius, containing recorded
conversations of the master with his disciples, the Book of Mencius—Mencius'
recorded conversations—the Great Learning and the Doctrine of the Mean.
The last two works are chapters taken out of the Book of Rites and given a
special importance from about the tenth century on.
7. I refer here to such works as James Legge's *The Chinese Religions* (London,

1881); W.E. Soothill's *The Three Religions of China* (Oxford, 1923) and then to D. Howard Smith's *Chinese Religions* (New York, 1968) and *Confucius* (New York, 1973). But there exist also many other books on Confucius and Confucianism. Some of them will be referred to in the course of this study.

8.   Of these books, the *Neues Glaubensbuch* has appeared as *The Common Catechism: A Book of Christian Faith*, edited by Johannes Feiner and Lukas Vischer, translated by David Bourke and others (New York, 1975); Hans Küng's *Christsein* appears in English as *On Being a Christian* (New York, 1970).

9.   R. C. Zaehner discusses some of the dangers inherent in misinterpreting Eastern religions. See *Our Savage God* (London, 1974), especially the Introduction.

10.   Friedrich Heiler's book, *Das Gebet* (München, 1921), has an English translation *Prayer*, edited by Samuel McComb (London, 1932). I shall be referring to these in Chapters four and five.

11.   Hendrik Kraemer emphasized "radical displacement" as condition for conversion to Christianity in *The Christian Message in a Non-Christian World* (Zürich, 1940). Already, William E. Hocking, who had a vision of a "world faith" emerging, disagreed with Kraemer in his own book, *Living Religions and a World Faith* (New York, 1940), ch. 3.

12.   I have confined myself to Chinese Confucian texts and their exponents in the development of the main themes. But I do not mean to overlook the contributions of Japanese and Korean thought and scholarship. I have chosen to limit myself, on account of my greater familiarity with the Chinese side, and also to give more clarity and consistency to the main discourse.

13.   The Buddhist tradition and the Hindu tradition are worlds in themselves and deserve respect and careful interpretation. I should merely like to point out that R. C. Zaehner, in *Our Savage God* (referred to in note 9), has pointed out certain difficulties arising from the ethical ambivalence of some of their teachings, and has also hinted at a greater compatibility between Christianity and Confucianism. This is noteworthy coming from a comparative religionist with special knowledge of Indian religions, who also professes openly the Christian (Catholic) faith.

Confucianism and Christianity

Chapter One

THE ENCOUNTER

Introduction

This study sets out to offer an examination of some common themes of Christianity and Confucianism, with the aim of provoking more interest in and further study of "the other side" by Christians and Confucians, as well as by all who take an interest in these two traditions. As such, it will begin with some clear definitions of what I consider to be Christianity on the one side and Confucianism on the other.

Some of the issues which first became controversial during the encounter of the Jesuit missionaries with Confucian civilization concerned the translation of the word "God," and accommodation of Confucian rituals. They will be discussed here in a historical context. The problems they represent will re-emerge as theological issues in some of the other chapters—particularly in Chapter Four, which is concerned with the Problem of God, and in Chapter Five, which touches upon the question of rites and sacraments. In this way, I hope to show that these important theological problems have historical roots in earlier missionary encounters, and still remain vital—in fact, have acquired new meaning—in light of our contemporary consciousness of the need for inter-cultural and inter-religious dialogue. It is with such a consciousness and in the hope of contributing to this dialogue that I am writing this book.

What is Christianity?

And so, what do I mean by Christianity? Do I refer here to the original teachings of Jesus Christ, or to later developments of doctrine throughout two millenia, to institution(s) or to more spontaneous groupings which make up today's Jesus movement, to

3

everything that is *good*—as Christians are wont to use the word "Christian"—or to something specific and particular? And *also*, can this word accept or tolerate a hyphenated meaning: can there be a Confucian Christianity, a Buddhistic Christianity, and so on?

Clearly, to be able to write a book on the subject of Christianity and Confucianism, I must have some idea of their *differences*. Otherwise, there will be no room for comparative analysis. I cannot accept the use of the term "Christian" to designate all that is good and virtuous. This is too presumptuous: like calling good Buddhists anonymous Christians, when they, on their part, can just as well call good Christians anonymous Buddhists, should they think that doing so could save them. For me, Christianity refers to a religion that is historic and contemporary. It is Semitic in origin, and later became Hellenized and Latinized, after which it spread to Europe north of the Alps, developing, all the while, a philosophical formulation that was for a long time bound, first to a Platonic and neo-Platonic, and then to an Aristotelian-Thomistic tradition. Christianity refers to *both* its Latin—Roman—and Greek Orthodox forms, the latter spreading especially among the Slav peoples of eastern Europe, and keeping more to the Platonic formulations, while the former became almost identified to western and central Europe, until exploration discoveries carried it to other continents as well. Christianity also refers to the developments following the Reformation of the sixteenth century, with its many divisions and with the theological developments that followed them. Christianity refers to the institutional churches which confess the name of Jesus Christ, even if they differ among themselves on certain points of dogmatic, cultic and structural-institutional expressions. Christianity also refers to individual or "communal"[1] Christians, who, for some reason or other, prefer to dissociate themselves from the institutions, but remain faithful to certain essential beliefs and to the way of life ordained by these beliefs. And then, last but not least, Christianity refers to the Christianity of the future—that which will have weathered all the present crises, to be born of these very crises, as well as of a dynamic dialogue with the non-Western world religions and cultural traditions, with their basic insights into God and man, their more *diffused* forms of structural expressions, and their revived vigor in the world of today. In all these definitions, the one essential condition which differentiates a follower of Christianity from a non-Christian or a post-Christian is his/her free and conscious confession of Jesus Christ in his/her beliefs and behavior.

The question of hyphenated Christians is more complex, but, with time, will become more common. Judaism, Islam and Christianity have all been regarded as exclusive religions, where Hinduism and Buddhism, Confucianism, Taoism and Shinto, have been recognized as more consciously syncretic. Conversion to Christianity, a decisive step in a person's life, has long been considered to bring with it a *rupture* with the past, particularly if that person has been a believing Jew, a Moslem, or a Buddhist. Indeed, Christian exclusiveness carried itself over to sectarian differences. A Protestant becoming a Catholic might not need a second baptism, but, until Vatican II, usually received a *conditional* one and made a public renunciation of his former "errors."

Christianity, of course, was always a "hyphenated" affair—having absorbed and, to some degree, transformed the beliefs of Greece and Rome, of the Germanic tribes of Europe as well as of the native Indian tribes of Central and South America. But this has not always been properly acknowledged or analyzed. Today, however, in an atmosphere of greater mutual tolerance, first among the various Christian communions themselves, and then among all religious believers, the walls of exclusiveness are gradually eroding. Although no one calls himself a Protestant and Catholic at the same time, almost everyone prefers to call himself simply a Christian, to underline the important similarities rather than to emphasize the minor differences. Relations between Christians and Jews, Christians and Moslems, seem to be improving, although the exclusivist tradition at the heart of these three great religions is such that "hyphenation" does not naturally result from dialogue, except perhaps among those Christians who are ethnically Jewish or Arab.

But dialogues between Christianity and the religions of South Asia and the Far East have another potential. In the measure that Christianity abandons much of its former triumphalism and exclusivism, there seems possibility for the development of such forms of religious life as Hindu Christianity or Zen Christianity. Confucian Christianity has even a greater potential. Confucianism and Christianity are, in my view, more compatible than

Hinduism and Christianity, or Zen Buddhism and Christianity. This view will be developed in the course of this book. Suffice it for me to say here that I see a certain future for hyphenated Christianity, provided that certain essential conditions are fulfilled.

This can be better understood if we return to the core of Christianity, to belief in Jesus Christ and his message. It is not within the scope of this book to deal with this at length. I wish merely to say that I consider belief in Christ as the revelation of God, a belief expressed by a way of life in accordance with the spirit of the Gospels, as *the* essential characteristic of Christianity. There can be no hyphenated Christian in cases of persons who do not fulfil this condition. And there can only be hyphenated Christianity where the *other* religion—Zen Buddhism, Confucianism, *etc.* —allows for this central belief without offering any ground for fundamental conflict. In other words, in the life of the Zen Christian or Confucian Christian, the Buddha and Confucius can remain as models for behavior and as sources of inspiration, but only as secondary to Jesus Christ, whose life and teachings are *normative* for all forms of Christianity.

Jesus Christ is the decisive norm for Christianity and the Christian way of life. The Christian message is not Jesus' teachings *plus.* It can only be *his* teachings. And Christian theology must be an elucidation of these teachings. True, Christian theology can have its philosophical dimension even though Jesus was not a philosopher. And Christian theology can also have—it *must* also have—a dimension of prayer and spirituality, including the elaboration of those forms of prayer and the spiritual life which may not be found in the Gospels themselves. For theology is also man's *response* to God's revelation, on the intellectual and moral levels, as well as on a personal and existential level, as man's quest for God in his own soul. And it is on all these levels that dialogue takes place between Christianity and the other forms of religious belief and religious life.

Jesus Christ is *more* decisive for Christianity than Confucius is for Confucianism. This will become clearer with later explanations of what I mean by the word "Confucianism." For purposes here, I wish to give this as a reason why I have chosen to examine certain Confucian themes in the light of Christianity—as Jesus

Christ has taught it. Generally speaking, I shall say little of the developments which followed, except in the realm of prayer and spirituality—where the personal and subjective takes on a special importance. As a rule, I shall also refer to the teachings of Jesus as they are understood today, with the help of contemporary scientific discoveries, progress in the various related disciplines, and the independence and openness that no longer allow themselves to remain inhibited by past taboos in theological inquiries. This is all the more necessary in my perspectives, since I am writing for readers of our own times, in view of inviting them to learn more about *both* Christianity and Confucianism, and with the hope that such studies will lead to creative understanding and renewal, for *both* sides.

What is Confucianism?

What do I mean by Confucianism? This is not an easy question to answer, and yet, upon such answer depends much of the usefulness of any criticism against Confucius and Confucianism. The term "Confucianism" is obviously ambiguous. It signifies an ideology developed by a man of the name Confucius. Yet, if we compare it to the term "Christianity"—or better, to the French equivalent, *christianisme*—we find that the man Confucius did not have a role that is nearly as decisive as that claimed by Jesus Christ for his own mission and teachings. "Confucianism" is actually a misnomer, a Western designation of a Chinese tradition. The Chinese themselves have usually preferred *Ju-chia*(儒家) or *Ju-chiao* (教), the school or teachings of the scholars, to "Confucianism" or *K'ung-chiao* (孔教), the more general term. Confucius himself never made exclusive claims as a teacher, calling himself rather a "transmitter" of the teachings of ancient sages. But even for the Chinese, this native designation, *Ju*, has different connotations. It refers to Confucius himself and the ethical teachings he transmitted to the later ages. It refers also to the entire development of the so-called Confucian tradition, throughout the centuries. This includes the metaphysical strands which became prominent from the eleventh century on. And it may frequently refer, to the uncritical mind—even among the educated—to the twentieth century Confucian "vestiges:" to the ethical teachings concerning political loyalty, filial piety, female chastity, and justice or righteousness, or to the "Confucian" social structure, in which these teachings had become imbedded. It is especially as such an intellectual and social establishment that Confucianism came under fire during the early twentieth century, in 1916 and during the May Fourth Movement of 1919 and its aftermath. It is also to this establishment of the past, "Confucius & Sons," that today's critics point back, saying that the "ghost" of the Confucian establishment is still "lurking around," even though the political state has espoused Marxist ideology.

If the term "Confucianism" remains ambiguous, another term, "Neo-Confucianism," is even more so. In the West, it usually refers to the Confucianism that developed after the T'ang (618–907) and Sung (960–1279) dynasties, with its greater metaphysical interests which were in part derived from encounters with Taoist and Buddhist philosophies. Some confusion arises from the fact that not all later Confucians were metaphysicians. Indeed, many scholars of the Ch'ing dynasty (1644–1911) were consciously anti-metaphysical, and yet remained Confucian, as were also many contemporaries of the great metaphysicians themselves. In China, the term Hsin-ju-hsüeh (新儒学) (New Confucianism) was in use especially during the years of the Sino-Japanese war (1937—45), to designate the same development in Confucianism and to encourage its modern revival. In this sense, it is also used in Taiwan, where the government continues to speak out for a Confucian revival.

For my purposes here, I shall use the term "Confucianism" to refer to the entire Confucian tradition, but particularly to those aspects which distinguished the beginnings of the tradition and are especially associated with the name and memory of Confucius himself. And I shall use the word "Neo-Confucianism" to refer to the philosophical-metaphysical movement that emerged during the Sung and Ming (1368–1644) dynasties and was considered orthodox state philosophy until the end of the Ch'ing dynasty in the early twentieth century.

Is Confucianism a religion, or is it a philosophy? Is it not merely a body of practical moral teachings—prescriptions and proscriptions largely with relevance to social behavior? These questions have been asked again and again, and frequently so, by the critics of Confucianism. For our purposes here, I shall offer an understanding of Confucianism by using such vocabulary—after carefully defining the usage of specific terms.

If by "religion" is meant an institutional church in its classic Western form—such as Roman Catholicism, with its organized hierarchy and priesthood, a clearly defined system of dogmas and moral precepts, a solemn and public cult and a sacramental system, then premodern Confucianism can be said to possess some of these traits and not others. Confucianism had a public cult: as mentioned, this was occasion for controversy. Confucianism had a sacrificial cult of veneration for Heaven and for ancestors, and it allowed for sacrifices of incense and foods even to "semi-deified" historical personnages, including Confucius himself. But it had no organized priesthood outside of the recognition of the emperor himself as a "high priest," the only person qualified to sacrifice to Heaven, and the heads of families as mediators between the ancestral spirits and the living. Civic leaders were the usual presiding figures at ceremonies held in Confucian temples throughout China, although the descendants of Confucius himself had a special place—as government-appointed sacrificial officials at Ch'ü-fou, the sage's native place. And so, Confucianism had a secular priesthood, which was not clearly separated from the rest of society. It did not have monastic orders. In fact, Confucian emphasis on family life and progeny was in principle opposed to clerical or monastic celibacy, while Confucian teachings of social responsibility abhorred any self-imposed isolation from society unless it was motivated by social protest. Confucianism was—and still remains, wherever it is found—a secular religion.[2]

Where dogmas and morals are concerned, Confucianism identified the two in its teaching of *jen*(仁)—the virtue of humanity, a universal virtue underlying all the particular ones regarding the five moral bonds, father-son, ruler-subject, husband-wife, elder and younger brother, and between friends. *Jen* is what makes a man truly human, by making him a perfect man, a sage. The virtue of *jen* was given a metaphysical and even cosmic dimension during the Chinese Middle Ages, Sung and Ming dynasties, as *jen* became identified with the cosmic life force itself. Confucianism is essentially a humanism, with its focus on the real and potential greatness of man—since every man can become a sage.[3] Confucian humanism remains committed to the social order. A sage is not only one with Heaven and Earth and all things, he is especially a man *for others*. He is the one who is first to worry about the world's worries, and last to enjoy its pleasures.[4] This does not mean he is solely devoted to what resembles the Protestant work ethic. The Confucian finds his joy in his harmony with nature, and in his own humanity—in *jen*. He does not seek to abound in good works in this life, to save himself in the next. He has rather a realized view of eschatology. Here on earth, the future life is not his primary concern. It will take care of itself.

When compared to Christian dogmas and morals, this secular and human orientation of life leaves a vacuum for the supernatural as such. Not that the Confucian denies the supernatural. The Confucian rites express explicitly what Confucian philosophy teaches, although in a somewhat ambiguous language, a world of the beyond, with which man can communicate. The Lord-on-High or Heaven of the classical texts resembles the Christian God. The semi-deified sagely personages, including Confucius himself, are rather like Christian saints. Ancestral spirits remain difficult to classify, as they are not all proven moral giants. But the very veneration given them expresses a belief in the afterlife, and a solicitude for these spirits. And Confucian optimism regarding man's goodness has been interpreted as a religious *faith*, a faith in man rooted ultimately in a faith in an invisible order, the order of Heaven, immanent yet transcendent, even in the language of the Neo-Confucians. Confucianism also took seriously certain crucial moments in human existence, such as coming of age, marriage and death, giving them a "sacramental" dimension through its own ritual symbolisms.

If Confucianism could be called a secular religion, it could, with better reason, be said to possess a strong religiosity, at the very heart of its spiritual doctrine—that of sagehood. Sagehood offers a model of self-transcendence, and the way to sagehood—by self-cultivation, a process which acquired an ascetic dimension especially during the Sung and Ming dynasties—was formulated as a way of self-transcendence, with clear religious dimensions. Confucian sagehood was not described, as with Christianity, in terms of justification from sin by grace, but rather, as the realization of the immanent principle of innate human goodness. Confucian self-cultivation said little, if anything, of prayer and penance as did Christian asceticism. But its focus on inner reverence, on quiet sitting—the Confucian way of meditation—and on the unity between man's interior life and his exterior activity, bespeak a way of *lay spirituality*, of union between contemplation and action, which within Christianity itself is usually a preoccupation for monastic orders only—of those whose moral striving offers a model of "vicarious sanctity" for the rest of the believers.

And what about Confucianism as a philosophy? Does it also offer, as the Christian religion, a philosophical formulation of its teachings? Would it be better described as simply a body of moral teachings or prescriptions, of do's and don't's, closely resembling the Ten Commandments?

We come here to a question of the "popular" image of Confucianism. A cursory reading of the Analects yields a picture of Confucius as a teacher of moral behavior: of benevolence, justice, and filial piety. The emphasis on the five moral relationships gives such teachings a strongly hierarchical orientation, and the virtues recommended take on a tone of conformity and passivity, as social mores destined for the support of a ruling elite. Such an interpretation of Confucianism would distort its inner meaning, just as an exclusive identification of Christianity and the Ten Commandments—most of which are formulated in negative terms—would leave out of its picture the image of Jesus Christ himself, and his principal teaching of love of God and neighbor, the basic underlying commandment.

Confucianism resembles Christianity in the fact that it is basically a teaching about a way of life—of self-transcendence through moral striving. Philosophical elaboration came later for both ways. Philosophical formulation enlarges the intellectual horizon in some directions while narrowing it in others, by binding the original teachings to a definite speculative system. In this sense, Neo-Confucianism resembles medieval Scholastic Philosophy—without taking on the dogmatic orientations which early Semitic and Hellenic Christianity already possessed. In its rigid form as state orthodoxy, Neo-Confucianism remained a humanism, but a fossilized one, sacrificing the real human being to theoretical teachings of virtue, and fostering hypocrisy rather than authentic moral striving. In its worst form, Scholastic Christianity did the same—by giving importance to human existence exclusively in terms of finding happiness in future life.

Basically, whether Confucianism should be considered a religion, a philosophy, or something in between, is irrelevant to an attempt of reassessment. Such intellectual classifications may well carry emotional overtones—according to the persons who use them. For example, missionaries in China have singled out for attack a lack of religiosity in Neo-Confucianism, but Marxist critics have done just the opposite. For them, Neo-Confucianism is abhorrent *on account of* its religiosity, which they have discovered in its teachings on self-cultivation. On such matters, it may be better to recall to mind the absence of both words—religion *and* philosophy, in the classical Chinese vocabulary. Confucianism represents rather a teaching (*chiao*; 教) that has both religious and philosophical dimensions.

THE HISTORICAL ENCOUNTER

What did Christians know of Confucianism and Confucians of Christianity? The earliest extant records on both sides are blank on this subject. Where Europe was concerned, the more common and negative tendency was to see the people in East Asia as pagans and idolators, because they were "non-Christians." The occasional and more positive viewpoint was to imagine the East to be a land of wise men, of learned philosophers and astrologers—possibly in part a vestige of the story of the Magi in the Gospel of Matthew, chapter 2. A third and in-between tendency was to look upon the Chinese people as quasi-Christians, or at least, as including among them a Christian community, under the rule of the near-immortal—because always evoked, during a course of centuries—Prester John of legendary fame. It was this last tendency that served as a moving force to bring the earliest "missionaries" to China, in search of a Christian Cathay.[5]

The Chinese, on their side, were just as ignorant of Europe and its religion. The people of China considered their own country to be the center of the world. For them, the "West" was the home of the Buddhist religion. Even after Portuguese traders and travellers had settled in Macao in the sixteenth century, the Chinese tended to regard them as believers in a "Buddhist sect."

Such early mutual ignorance is in itself instructive. Each of the two great civilizations of Western Europe and Eastern Asia understood the other in terms of its own self-knowledge. There appeared no strong reason on either side to deepen such mutual acquaintance as did exist. So it was at least until the Jesuit missionaries came to China in the sixteenth and seventeenth centuries. Western intellectual curiosity and religious zeal and expansionism finally led to the discovery of China's native philosophico-religious traditions.

The Jesuits are rightly considered the earliest known Europeans to have discovered Confucianism. They became its earliest interpreters to Europe. True, long before Jesuits could have dreamt of going to China—long before the Society of Jesus was founded— other Christian missionaries from the West had preceded them. We know of the Nestorians in the seventh and ninth centuries, from extant historical remains, including a stone tablet unearthed in the early seventeenth century—during the time of Matteo Ricci's presence in China—recounting the arrival in T'ang China of the monk Alopen, probably from Persia.[6] In the thirteenth century, when the Franciscan friars came to Mongol China, there were yet Nestorians there, although they were no longer actively missionary. The Franciscans gave China its first Catholic archbishop, John of Montecorvino, who resided in the city of Cambaluc (Peking), and supposedly baptized six thousand people. But the Franciscan interlude proved even more short-lived than the Nestorian, and neither of these groups appeared to have paid much attention to Confucianism as a Chinese religion or philosophy.[7] Marco Polo, who also visited Mongol China and stirred Europe with accounts of his experiences there, made no mention of Confucianism, being content with describing the Chinese as pagans.[8]

Europe, therefore, did not seem to know of Confucius and his teachings until the seventeenth century, following the reports and writings of the Jesuit missionaries. But this belated discovery made profound impact on the European intellectual world. By that time, Europe was no longer a united Christendom, even in name.

Europe had become both Protestant and Catholic in religious beliefs, and these differences were frequently coextensive with national frontiers. Europe was also experiencing profound social and intellectual changes, following scientific discoveries—Copernicus, Galileo, Newton—and geographic expansions—Christopher Columbus, Vasco da Gama and others. These events made possible the Jesuit mission to China and East Asia. They also prepared the intellectual elite for a new age of rationalism and a questioning of Christian beliefs and values. Quite ironically, the Jesuit interpretation of Confucianism contributed in part to this growth in rationalism and secularism.[9]

The Jesuit Interpretation of Confucianism

When the Jesuits first went to China,[10] they knew more of Buddhism than Confucianism, and made their first efforts of missionary accommodation by dressing as Buddhist bonzes and using a vocabulary borrowed from Buddhism to teach the Christian Gospel. This was natural, considering that Buddhism offered more religious parallels with Christianity than did Confucianism, at least to the superficial observer. Popular Buddhism, as the missionaries would have encountered, was obviously a religion with doctrinal teachings and deified figures, with beliefs in a future after death, with a compassionate outlook for humanity and an example of monastic asceticism. It was for this same reason that the Chinese themselves regarded Christianity also as another Buddhist sect. But Matteo Ricci thought otherwise. His early experience in China proved to him that the dominant value system was not Buddhism, but Confucianism. Besides, he devoted long years to the study of Chinese and of Confucian classics, and became persuaded that there was more compatibility between Christianity and Confucianism, particularly the early teachings of Confucius himself, with reverence for a supreme being and sublime moral exhortations. Confucianism did not pronounce on the future life, and lacked dogmatic structure. But this was all the more congenial to Christian missionaries, who believed that they could supply for the void.[11] Buddhist doctrines of *samsāra* and *nirvāna*, on the other hand, presented knotty problems for Christian theologians who conceived of human life in a linear rather than cyclic pattern, and who saw life after death as fulfilment rather than emptiness. And so, Ricci removed his bonze's garb, and changed into the robes of a Confucian scholar. It was a calculated move, made for reasons of expediency as well as of convictions. From then on, where the Jesuits were concerned, Buddhists were idolators whereas Confucians were potential allies and converts. As Ricci expressed it in his famous Catechism, *T'ien-chu shih-yi* (The True Idea of God),[12] the Confucian Classics contained allusions, albeit in an inchoate manner, to such Christian notions as God and a future life. These insights had become obscured with the passing of time, partly because of Buddhist influences and partly because of justifiable Confucian reactions to certain Buddhist excesses. But the Classics remained the sacred books of Confucianism, so that a rediscovery of the true and original teachings of Confucius himself would contribute to an understanding and acceptance of the Christian Gospel.

Was Ricci justified in his persuasions? This question arose less out of any particular attraction among missionaries to accommodate Christianity with the alternative religion—Buddhism—but more out of doubts regarding Ricci's favorable interpretation of Confucianism. The concrete issue was that of the Confucian rites. Should Christian converts be allowed to continue offering worship to ancestral spirits, and to the spirit of Confucius himself? Did these rituals signify deification of the persons concerned, or were they merely a symbolic token of veneration? And how about the Chinese terminology for the divine: were such terms as *Shang-ti* (上帝; Lord-on-High) and *T'ien* (天; Heaven) adequate vehicles for the expression of the Christian belief in God?

The Rites Controversy and the debate over terms divided the missionaries in China as well as Japan into two opposing camps. Those working among the educated classes—mostly Jesuits—preferred accommodation, while others, Franciscans and Dominicans, evangelizing the illiterate masses, cried out against it, quite understandably, as the uneducated frequently gave a religious meaning to those rituals which the educated regarded as primarily commemorations rather than worship. Besides, popular Confucianism, as the "masses" understood it, was much more influenced by ideas of popular Buddhist and Taoist religions. Even with the more privileged classes, the accommodating Jesuits had their problems. The prevailing Neo-Confucian metaphysics has given the early Confucian term for the supreme being, Heaven, a largely metaphysical content. Heaven has become the dual Heaven-and-Earth, the universe, to which the Neo-Confucian soul sensed itself attuned and in harmony. But, for the Christian believer, was this not pantheism replacing an earlier theism? And besides, there were the terms of *li* (理) and *ch'i* (気)—metaphysical principles which could have materialist connotations to the Christian seeking for a clear enunciation of spiritual substance and of the immortality of the soul. Were not the Jesuits deceiving themselves by insisting upon the existence of a purer form of Confucianism, which was to be found only in books, rather than among men?

It is against such polemical perspectives that we should evaluate two events: the manner in which Jesuit writers sought to interpret Confucianism to their European readers, and the controversies which led eventually to the papal decisions condemning the Confucian Rites. The Jesuits were eager to promote a favorable impression in Europe of Confucian religious teachings, to further their own end of missionary accommodation. They did not quite foresee that their enthusiastic eulogies of a non-Christian religious and philosophical heritage of such historical antiquity would also serve the purposes of those intellectuals in Europe who were looking for reasons to discredit the established forms of Christianity itself in favor of deism and rationalism. On the other hand, Christian accommodation of Confucian teachings and rituals could not be so simply accepted and carried out. The encounter between Christianity and Confucianism was in fact a meeting between two traditions of orthodoxy: that of post-Tridentine Catholicism, which considered that no one could be saved outside the Church, and that of Neo-Confucian state philosophy, which saw no need for salvation, as it had no doctrine of original sin. There was enough openness on both sides to allow dialogue to develop, and conversions to occur, as a number of Chinese embraced the Christian faith while remaining Confucians. But such accommodation would not have continued long even without outside intervention, unless theoretical justification was developed under the form of theological reflection. And this was rendered impossible by the Papal decisions against the Confucian rites, the ensuing religious persecutions in China, as well as the suppression of the Society of Jesus. Only in our own days has this been called for, when the situation has been altered drastically.

For a time, the Christian missions prospered, in Japan[13] as well as in China. It has been estimated that 750,000 Christians could be counted in Japan in 1605, about four per cent of the whole population—and that in spite of the edict of proscription issued in 1587 by the shogun Toyotomi Hideyoshi. In China, by 1700, there were allegedly 300,000 baptized Christians, and the Jesuits at court were hopeful that the Manchu emperor, K'ang-hsi (r. 1662–1723), might himself become a Christian. But the prosperity was short-lived. In Japan, the shogun Ieyasu Tokugawa banished all missionaries in 1614. The terrible persecutions under him and his successors showed the grave mistrust—religious as well as political—that Japan's rulers had for Christianity, a foreign religion associated with Europeans and with—so it sounded to Confucian ears—superstitions. The Tokugawa shogunate did its best to propagate Confucian teachings, while also wiping out Christianity. In China also, the intermissionary conflicts as well as Rome's intervention in the Rites controversy compromised the cause of Christianity. Political reasons, including intrigues at court, complicated the situation further. Ensuing persecutions brought an end to the great age of the China missions, until, by 1800, all former gains appeared to have been lost.

The fourth attempt to evangelize the Confucian world took place in the late nineteenth century, when the missionaries returned in the wake of traders and conquerors. This time, their position was compromised by their political protector, and they in turn compromised their converts. It was the result of Western triumphalism, born of the success of the scientific and industrial revolutions and the possession of a superior technology: a triumphalism at once racial, political, religious and cultural. And it spelt havoc for the Confucian culture. Christian missionaries, both Catholic and Protestant, were largely responsible for the lowered prestige of Confucianism during the late nineteenth and early twentieth centuries. Christian missionaries and their Chinese converts stood for Westernization and modernization. With a few isolated exceptions, Christian missionaries regarded themselves as bearers of a superior evangelical message of salvation for pagan sinners living in religious darkness and ignorance, and without the benefits of Western material progress. They were scarcely conscious that such an outlook issued out of a century of rationalism with anti-Christian presuppositions, and that the development of these presuppositions in a new and militant ideology—Marxist dialectical materialism—would soon sweep away any gains they could make during a hundred years or more. This fourth attempt to evangelize the Confucian world found that the fall of Confucianism would lead not to conversion to Christianity, but to the triumph of an alternative way of life: Marxist socialism, at least in mainland China, North Korea and Vietnam. Outside of these areas, Christian missionaries could continue to evangelize, in a milieu of Confucian and Buddhist vestige influences. It was here that Christianity made its greatest number of converts in the recent decades among former Confucians. It is also here that today there is more readiness for missionary accommodation. The successes of Marxist atheism and secular materialism have chastened Christians and Confucians alike. In Hongkong, Taiwan, South Korea and Southeast Asia, the number of Christians has grown steadily, amid the Chinese "diaspora"—at least until very recently.

One interesting question about Christian converts from Confucianism remains: are these persons more Christian, or more Confucian? Unlike the converts from Buddhism, they no longer have to abandon their "rituals"—the Rites Controversy is no longer a vital issue. It has been resolved, less by the Roman decree of 1939, allowing for Christian participation in rituals honoring the ancestors and Confucius, but by the accelerated process of secularization in Confucian societies. Ancestral rites are less and less practised, all the more so as the *emigrés* from China to Southeast Asia and beyond did not bring their ancestral tablets to their new homes. But the comment of a Chinese pastor serving a large group of interdenominational, overseas Chinese Christians in Sydney was revealing. According to him, this community of Christians—Protestants—most of whom had left China during the recent two or three decades, is essentially Confucian in outlook, desiring a morally upright life for themselves and their families, and coming to church to find mutual support and solidarity. He could have added, that they also found consolation in a common belief in God, and in a common prayer service. For it is here that Christianity has something to offer to an "uprooted Confucian community."

The Terms and Rites Controversies

Christian missionaries—Jesuits and others—went to the Far East primarily to preach the Gospel. Their contact with a highly sophisticated Confucian culture with its own view of man and the universe and its own ritual expressions of beliefs posed the problem of cultural encounter. Should the unique claims of Christianity regarding man and his salvation be safeguarded by a rejection of any possibly rival doctrine; should they rather be permitted to come to terms with the native traditions, through a genuine encounter involving impartial intellectual debates and discussions; or should they merely seek to borrow from the native traditions a suitable vocabulary as vehicle of expression for Christian truths? Such questions led to two heated controversies that had crucial consequences for the history of Christianity in the Far East. I refer here to the Terms and the Rites controversies.

The first question concerned the translation into Chinese of the Latin term for God, *Deus*.[14] Here the Jesuits grappled with problems similar to those encountered by Buddhist missionaries in China many centuries earlier—those of rendering philosophical and theological concepts of one religious and intellectual tradition into the language of another. The Buddhists had settled for *ko-yi* (格義),[15] a method by which a selection was made of Chinese words from classical texts offering meanings that approached those of the original Pali or Sanskrit. Even then, they were obliged sometimes to use transliterations for certain technical terms as *nirvāna* (*nieh-p'an*; 涅槃) and *samsāra* (*sheng-ssu*; 生死)—in the latter case, making use of the Chinese words meaning life and death, which signify rather well the idea of the cycle of transmigration. Such a method presupposed a conciliatory attitude toward the Chinese philosophy itself and led to a lengthy process of cultural assimilation during which Indian Buddhism became Sinicized, so that Buddhist dominance from the sixth to the tenth century—the "Buddhist conquest of China"[16]—has sometimes been described as the Chinese conquest of Buddhism. But where Buddhism took as its point of departure the existential sorrows of human life, and developed different schools of thought that could be interpreted as theistic, pantheistic or atheistic, Christian missionaries regarded the revelation of God as their central teaching, and sought especially for a suitable term which could translate the meaning of the Latin *Deus*.[17] They were embarrassed to find in the Chinese language a multitude of terms each of which could be used to refer to a supreme being while frequently containing other meanings as well: *Shang-ti* (上帝; Lord-on-High), *T'ien* (天; Heaven), *Shen* (神; Spirit), *T'ai-chi* (太極; the Ultimate). The problem was rendered all the more complex as the usage of some of these terms in the early Confucian Classics tended to signify a greater degree of transcendence and personhood while the later Neo-Confucian commentaries interpreted the same words in a much more metaphysical sense, emphasizing the mutual near-identity of the Absolute and the Universe, in an integrated, "organismic" philosophy of immanence. Besides, the usage of the selfsame terms on the popular level, through the influence of Buddhist and Taoist religions, was even more diverse, bringing in strands of what appeared to be animist and polytheist beliefs. The Jesuit missionaries who worked mainly with the educated gentry followed the example of Matteo Ricci in an effort of cultural accommodation. After examining the Chinese classics, they argued between *Shang-ti* and *T'ien*, and settled publicly for *T'ien-chu* (天主; Lord of Heaven), Lord also of whatever Heaven may represent to the Chinese, while continuing occasionally to refer to the Lord of Heaven as Lord-on-High or Heaven. Even there, controversy arose, first among the Jesuits themselves and then among a larger missionary circle, including other orders, many of whom opposed the Jesuit method of accommodation. Ricci's appointed successor, Nicolas Longobardi, superior of the Jesuit missions in China and Japan, questioned the prudence of using even *T'ien-chu* because of the prevalent Neo-Confucian intellectual milieu and its understanding of *T'ien*, proposing rather the setting aside of all Chinese terms with their ambiguities of meaning, and the adoption of the term *Deus* in Chinese or Japanese transliteration. The experience in Japan was all the more painful as the first Jesuit there, in the mid-sixteenth century, Francis Xavier, had earlier used the Shingon Buddhist term *Dainichi*. He later adopted *Deusu* (*Deus*)[18] only to find Buddhist bonzes referring to it as *Dai-uso* or a big lie. In course of time, missionaries vacillated between using Lord of Heaven in Chinese characters or *Deusu* in Japanese syllabary, settling for the latter. The Three Persons of the Trinity were rendered as *Deusu Patere, Deusu Hiiryo* and *Deusu Supiritsu Santo*, in an effort to safeguard doctrinal accuracy. Such actions emphasized the foreign origin of the Christian religion and caused converts to think of themselves as believers in a foreign god, whose teaching they did not really understand, as it was given in the "language" of European scholasticism, full of *other* transliterations, including *persona* (person) *susutanshiya* (substance), *garasa* (grace) and even *hiidesu* (faith).[19]

In Korea, the God-language presented less of a problem than in China or Japan, in part because Christianity was introduced there through the medium of Chinese priests and Chinese books, for the first time, probably in the early seventeenth century. Besides, the Korean language always had its own term for a supreme being endowed with personality attributes: *Hananim*, the God of their indigenous beliefs, originally associated with their mythical ancestor, Tangun.[20]

The Terms Controversy became itself engulfed by the larger Rites Controversy and was "decided" by intervention of Rome, whereby Catholic missionaries were instructed to abide always by the term *T'ien-chu*, neglecting therefore the other terms of *T'ien* or *Shang-ti*, in order to avoid confusion in the minds of converts or prospective converts. The controversy, however, was revived during the middle and later part of the nineteenth century by a new generation of China missionaries, this time the Protestants especially. The eventual decision among the Protestants to adopt the term *Shang-ti* as God, and the continued Catholic adherence to *T'ien-chu*, has signified, in the minds of many Christians even today, the coexistence of two religions, that of the Lord of Heaven (Catholic) and that of Christ (*Chi-tu*; 基督) or the Protestants, each with its own God. In Japan, the situation has ameliorated as both Protestant and Catholic missionaries today tend to favor the use of the term *kami* (Japanese version of the Chinese *Shen*, 神). In Korea, both Protestants and Catholics invoke *Hananim*, although Catholics also call upon the Lord of Heaven *(Chung-ju)*.

The Confucian "Rites" refer to a whole range of practices.[21] These included the sacrifices to Heaven, performed annually by the emperor alone, the public rites directed to Confucius himself twice a year in spring and autumn, other rituals incumbent on scholar-officials involving the veneration of the spirits of mountains and rivers, believed to have protective powers over the local region, and especially the "city-gods" *(ch'eng-huang*; 城隍), semi-deified figures of history given an official status for their continued interest in this world and in the common welfare of the local populace. There were also the family rites—ancestral ritual offerings on anniversaries of births and deaths as well as funeral and mourning ceremonies, celebrated in the presence of ancestral "tablets" where names are inscribed or in front of the bodies of the deceased. In the Confucian world-view and life-view, the rites had an important significance, the very word *li* or ritual meaning also propriety or correctness of behavior. Besides, they also had important cosmic and social meaning, being connected with the seasonal changes, with government administration and with the entire educational system, as well as with clan life.

The problem was, do these rituals represent beliefs that are incompatible with Christian faith? Is Confucius or are the ancestors being considered as deified beings to whom worship is due? And if not, why should incense, and on occasions, sacrificial animals, be involved, since in the West such usage signifies a divine object of worship? Should Christian converts be allowed to continue participating in these rites, or must they give up such practices, thus signifying their rupture with their own cultural past, their family traditions and ancestors, and also compromise their own education and public career—since regular participation in certain public rituals is obligatory for students and officials?

The opponents of the Confucian rites point out the ambiguity of meaning associated with these practices, because of the use of incense, sacrificial foods and ancestral tablets. They say that the cult given to the local spirits is reminiscent of animism or pantheism, while that rendered to Confucius and the ancestors suggests, at least in the popular mind, if not also in the mind of the educated *literati*, a certain status of deification given to the persons honored, making cult participants idolators. Should Christian converts be allowed to continue in such practices, they might seem to regard the Christian God as an addition, perhaps, to a familiar pantheon.

The Rites Controversy began as intermissionary debates and developed into mutual accusations that were brought to the attention of the Sacred Congregation of the *Propaganda Fides* and of the Pope in Rome, on the one side, and of the Chinese court and Emperor K'ang-hsi, a personal friend of the Jesuits, on the other. Rome's decision was to ignore the interpretation openly declared by the Chinese emperor on the meaning of the Rites—that Confucius was honored as a teacher, not a god, that sacrificial offerings to the dead were intended as memorial services rather than worship, that ancestral tablets represented a focus for filial attention and devotion, and no more, and that *T'ien* and *Shang-ti* were identifiable, not with the physical heaven, but the Lord of Heaven and Earth and all things. Instead, the opposition views were those that shaped Rome's final decision: that the ancient Chinese were idolators and the modern Chinese, atheists, that the Confucian Classics themselves, and even the Jesuit works published in Chinese, taught doctrines contrary to Christian faith, that ancestral rites were illicit because they were offered to spirits of ancestors and so involved idolatry and superstition, that Confucius himself was a public idolator and a private atheist, and should not be venerated by Christians as a saint. And so, the Papal decree, *Ex quo singulari* (1742), intervened "definitively"—by condemning the "Chinese rites."[22]

The Terms and Rites controversies are important in our considerations firstly because the decisions of Rome entailed several centuries of adverse developments in the missions of the Far East. Secondly, throughout the decades of debates and uncertainties involving the missionaries and Europe—the theological faculty of the University of Sorbonne, the European philosophers Leibniz, Wolff, Voltaire and others, and the Holy See—the interpretation of the Chinese themselves, of the Court and of the intellectuals, made little difference to those who finally helped to contribute to the unfortunate decision against the Rites and cultural accommodation as such. I refer here also to such Chinese as the great scholar convert of the Jesuits, Hsü Kuang-ch'i (1562–1633) and the first Chinese bishop, Lo Wen-tsao (*alias* Gregory Lopez)[23] a Dominican friar himself but a sympathizer of the "Jesuit" view on the Rites question. Lo suffered the harassment of his own religious superiors and confreres who tried to keep him in confinement because of his stand. His consecration as Bishop of Nanking was delayed until 1685, nearly two years after the patents had arrived from Rome. Up to modern times, the Rites Controversy remained an emotional issue among missionaries in China, and the 1939 decree permitting Christians to take part, with reservation, in certain rites, was not promulgated until later, when the Chinese had virtually lost interest in these practices due to more urgent issues of war and national survival. True, a belated attempt has been made in the name of cultural accommodation, by the building of churches in Chinese architectural styles, and by permitting usage of incense-sticks and the like in Christian cult. But these developments came too late, and would have little meaning for converts, most of whom come from a Westernized milieu. They even tend to create confusion in the minds of those who remain followers of native religions, Buddhist or Taoist, or who continue to be Confucians in sympathy. They tell us that no external accommodation could bring lasting or meaningful results. The expressions of accommodation must represent an encounter in depth, and the encounter itself has to differ from that of the sixteenth century. Today, it is no longer a question of Christianity and Confucianism, or even of Christianity and the non-Christian religious tradition. The historical scene has changed drastically, and many elements of *secular* Western thought have influenced the mentality of the peoples of the Far East. I refer here to the importance of Western secular humanism—both liberal and socialist—which evolved in agnostic or militantly atheistic circles, and which have come to represent Westernization in Asia, whether in the form of a political state and ideology, or of educational theories and practices.

Anti-Christian Polemics in China and Japan

Anti-Christian polemical writings give expression to the difficulties of the people whom missionaries were seeking to evangelize, while also revealing missionary difficulties in their evangelizing task. They represent the mutual fears, misunderstandings
and rejections. At times, they also express individual traumas,
rivalries and jealousies. Interestingly, the anti-Christian writings
in the China[24] and Japan of the seventeenth and eighteenth centuries converge in attacking Christianity for its allegedly anti-
rational teachings, its "superstitions." This was largely a Confucian argument, made against a religious sect which its critics
considered to be both akin and inferior to Buddhism. It is evident
in the earliest anti-Christian work known to us, the *P'o-hsieh chi*
(Preface, 1640), a collection of about sixty essays and memorials
to the throne compiled by about forty late Ming scholars, both
Confucians and Buddhists. The arguments they mustered resembled those found in earlier Confucian polemics against Buddhism
itself. Besides appealing to common sense and reason—pointing
out the absence of proof for Christian dogmatic assertions—
their writers also made use of the argument of authority. They
referred both to the authority of the Confucian Classics, as well as
to that of the state, since Ming codes forbade individuals from directly communicating with Heaven—judging this to be a usur-
pation of the emperor's right as the lone mediator between Heaven
and the rest of mankind. Later, pre-modern anti-Christian writings usually followed the same lines of argument, considering Christianity to be another form of Buddhism, while also comparing it
unfavorably with Buddhism and Taoism. This was true also of
Japan. The well-known *Ha-Deusu* (Refutation of Deus)[25] was a
treatise written by Fabian Fukan (1620), an ex-Buddhist novice,
turned Jesuit brother, and later apostate from Christianity. Fabian
had earlier published, quite ironically, the first Christian apolo-
getical work in Japanese, *Myōtei mondō* (1605), in which he had
refuted Buddhism, Confucianism and Shinto, and explained Christian teachings. In his later, anti-Christian work, he sought system-
atically to prove that *Deus* was not what the missionaries said
he was: almighty, all merciful, and so on. He made use of Bud-

dhist as well as Confucian allusions, giving concrete, historical comparisons, including references to the arrogant and superior manner of the European missionaries toward their Japanese converts. The Confucian scholar, Arai Hakuseki (1657–1725), who acted for a time as inquisitor for the Tokugawa shogunate in the persecution of Christians, also gave his reasons for opposing the Christian religion. He said that he found it to be an imitation of Buddhism, teaching absurd doctrines as creation, fall, heaven and hell. He also added that the concept of *Deus* was incompatible with the Confucian teaching of *ri* (in Chinese, *li*; 理).

And so, in spite of the Jesuit effort of accommodating Christianity to the Confucian mentality in China, and of attacking Buddhism as an inferior religion, Christian missionaries found that where many Confucians were concerned—both in China and Japan—Christianity itself resembled popular Buddhism in its doctrinal teachings, and was compared unfavorably with it and with philosophical Buddhism. In the Confucian-Christian encounter, the Confucian critics of Christianity thought that they had reason on their side, against an apparently superstitious religion which derived its premises from alleged divine revelation, rather than be contented with given human experience.

In the mid-nineteenth century and after, the reintroduction of Christianity into the Far East, with the support of Western military technology and political pressure, provoked another series of anti-Christian polemics and manifestations. Western victories on the battlefield and in diplomacy did not immediately persuade the Chinese or Japanese that Western ideas and values are superior to traditional Asian wisdom. Rather, in both China and Japan, the reaction was in terms of learning from Western science and technology while keeping Eastern ethics and scholarship.[26] Later, repeated humiliations, including the failures of anti-foreign and anti-Christian political manifestations, especially the Boxer Rebellion in China (1900), convinced first the Japanese, and then the Chinese and Koreans, that there was need also to learn from the Western scientific spirit and from ideas of liberal democracy. Religion and Christianity were regarded as irrelevant. Besides, a new generation of critics repeated with firmer conviction some of the older arguments—that Christianity was an alien religion, the religious expression of foreigners intent upon dominating the countries of Asia, not only politically and economically but also ideologically. And then, equipped with better knowledge of Western principles of reason and science, they were also able to point out certain contradictions between science itself and the claims of Western Christianity. In Japan the early Meiji openness to Western ideas, including Western religion, gave way gradually to antipathy. The Meiji Imperial Rescript on Education (1890) emphasized Confucian values. The philosopher, Inoue Tetsujiro, as well as others, favored Confucianism and attacked Christianity for teaching ideas of universal love and the like that were incompatible with the virtues of loyalty and filial piety, explicitly taught by the Imperial Rescript itself.[27] In the early decades of the twentieth century, especially around the time of the May Fourth Movement, 1919, in China, many leading intellectuals considered *all* religions, traditional and modern or Western, as irrational and superstitious. They cited Western thinkers: eighteenth century *philosophes* like Voltaire and Holbach, scientists like Darwin and Lamarck, social revolutionaries like Bakunin and Marx. They repeated the anti-religious arguments of the West, affirming a new confidence in logic and clear thinking, and rejecting the theory of the soul's immortality and the Biblical myths, adding that religious views were frequently found to be exalting God at the expense of man.[28]

Anti-Christian polemics are still heard today in the socialist countries of East Asia. They include the same appeal to science and logic against religion and superstition. They also emphasize missionary involvement with imperialist power politics. And they add to these arguments Feuerbach's theory of religion as psychological projection, and Marxist arguments of dialectical materialism. In the non-socialist countries and regions, these polemics are less obvious. Today, the presence of Christian missions is largely accepted in Hongkong, Taiwan, Japan, South Korea and Southeast Asia. But certain attitudes have become crystallized. Among the majority of the populations, Christianity remains a foreign, Western religion, while for many intellectuals who are no longer "traditionalists"—Buddhists or Confucians—there is yet another alternative value system to Christianity: that of liberal humanism.

This allows them to prescind from particular religious commitments while offering them principles regarding man and his importance in society, that harmonize with certain "vestige" Confucian values. But here, we have arrived at another subject: that of the situation of Christianity today, in the post-Confucian world.

THE SITUATION TODAY

What is the situation today of Christianity in "Confucian" Asia? What are the possibilities for exchange and dialogue between Christianity and Confucianism, each with its way of life, its beliefs and its cult?

Certainly, the situation today is very different from what the situation was, even a few decades earlier, in the early twentieth century. At that time, there was yet an identifiable Confucian world, where certain well-known moral values attributed to Confucian teachings were enshrined in the social order, and respected by legal institutions, in the countries of the Far East. Today, the situation has changed drastically. The age of revolutions has swept across Asia, bringing with it social and intellectual as well as political changes. In mainland China, North Korea and the whole of Vietnam, it has brought in socialist governments committed to ideological revolutions. In the rest of the Far East, Confucian values still persist, but Confucianism has lost its privileged status as a teaching or philosophy. It has become only one ideology among many. In Hongkong, Taiwan, South Korea and Japan,[29] Confucian philosophy continues to be taught, but only as one subject among others—including Buddhism, Taoism and European philosophies. The Confucian cult—seasonal sacrifices—continues to take place, but largely as a memorial event without much social relevance.[30] One wonders how, without the support of political power, and in a new social order where the harmony of the five human relationships no longer prevails, Confucianism will be able to survive into the future. This is actually the subject for another chapter—Chapter Two. It suffices to say here that, having become disestablished, Confucianism is discovering its new strength as a diffused "religion." Throughout the centuries, Confucian-

ism has become so identified with the cultural traditions themselves and with the social mores and customs, that even without a
privileged status, it is surviving as an important and perceptible
part of the physical and moral landscape of East Asia. The clan
family might have disappeared to a large extent, but family solidarity and mutual concern persist, remaining the invisible cement
of the social order. Confucian Classics might have become the
object of specialized studies, but Confucian value overtones remain the subject of novels and television programs, whether for
approval or disapproval. In fact, the persistence of Confucian
values in socialist China appears to have necessitated an intensive
anti-Confucius campaign, organized by the Party government
intent upon the thorough substitution of Confucianism by another
ideology, Marxist socialism.

And what does this situation say to the Christian, about the
survival and future of Christianity in East Asia? Is it not confront-
ing the same threats there as in the West, with the increasingly
threatening challenges of secular materialism, in its liberal humanist form and as Marxist socialism? And does it not have addition-
al difficulties in Asia, on account of its alien origin, its Hellenic
philosophy, its former alliance with Imperialist powers during the
nineteenth century? Confucianism may be able to survive as part
of the cultural milieu in the Far East. But Christianity has not yet
succeeded in accommodating itself with the traditional cultures.
With the exception of Hongkong, a largely cosmopolitan city
where non-Christians also have acquired *some* understanding of
Christianity as a religion, the rest of the Far East is still puzzled by
much that it knows or ignores about Christianity.

Has Christianity a future in East Asia? This is our basic question. Will Christian missions remain in those countries where
governments permit their presence and their activities, but only
as a conspicuous minority, with a ghetto-like mentality? Will
Chinese and Japanese Christians continue to feel themselves uprooted persons, in perpetual conflict, torn between a foreign religion which draws them apart from their native cultural
ambiances, without permitting them to fully accept secular
values identified as Western, and what they know of the beliefs

and values of their non-Christian compatriots, struggling to achieve a new synthesis and balance between tradition and modernization on ideological levels?[31]

It is not our place here to investigate in detail the claims of liberal humanism and of Marxist socialism. But even a superficial examination will yield one result: that in spite of widely diverging answers, their one common concern is man, regarded either as an individual with certain inalienable rights, or as a member of a collectivity, which submerges the individual in a new entity. Now, as we know, man too, is the principal concern of Confucianism—man in society, with his duties and responsibilities, and man as individual, with his sacred, inner moral forum. For Confucian humanism resembles secular humanism and Marxist socialism in its proclamation of the importance of man, even if the expressions of this proclamation differ.

And what about Christianity? Does Christianity concern itself sufficiently with man and his life in the world, or does it emphasize only God and man's submission to God, giving priority to the future life at the expense of the present one, regarded only as a preparation for eternity?

It is with such questions in mind that I have written this book. For I know that Christianity and Confucianism can only engage in a dialogue about man. There will also be a question of God, but only in terms of man's openness to the divine and the transcendent, of God's *relevance for man*. Now since *I have written* this book, I am presuming that there is sufficient humanism in Christianity to allow such a dialogue to begin and to grow. For these reasons, I shall go on to the following chapter which concerns itself with the problem of the survival of Confucianism. I shall not speak of the survival of Christianity, as there are many books on such a subject. I wish to take, as central focus for this book, the place of man in Christianity and Confucianism, and the openness of man to the realm beyond. I hope that this book will serve as an expression of a desire: that the horizons of man, in both Christianity and Confucianism, be further explored, emphasized, and developed, that mutual dialogue be encouraged, for the sake of better mutual understanding, and that the future, for both Christianity and Confucianism, be more open.

NOTES

1. On communal Christians, see Andrew Greeley, "The Communal Catholic." *National Catholic Reporter* (November 1, 1974). See also the response of Michael Novak, "The Communal Catholic," *Commonweal*, vol. 101 (January 17, 1975), p. 321, 341.
2. See Wing-tsit Chan *et al.*, *The Great Asian Religions* (London, 1969), pp. 99–100.
3. See "A Manifesto for a Reappraisal of Sinology and Reconstruction of Chinese Culture" (1958), signed by Carsun Chang, T'ang Chun-i, Mou Tsung-san and Hsü Fu-kuan and given in English in Carsun Chang, *The Development of Neo-Confucian Thought* (New York, 1962), pp. 462–64; see also Robert P. Kramers, "Some Aspects of Confucianism in its Adaptation to the Modern World," *Proceedings of the IXth Congress for the History of Religions* (Tokyo and Kyoto), 1958 (Tokyo, 1960), pp. 332–33.
4. Fan Chung-yen expressed this sentiment in one of his essays, "Yüeh-yang-lou chi." It is referred to in Wm. Theodore de Bary, ed., *Sources of Chinese Tradition* (New York, 1960), vol. 1, p. 448.
5. See Igor de Rachewiltz, *Papal Envoys to the Great Khans* (London, 1971), ch. 1, and pp. 58–59, 142–43, 184–85.
6. For the Nestorians, see A. C. Moule, *Christians in China before the Year 1550* (London, 1930), ch. 2, and his later work, *Nestorians in China: Some Corrections and Additions* (London, 1940). See also the work of the Japanese scholar, Saeki Yoshiro, *Chūgoku ni okeru keikyo suibo no rekishi* (The History of Nestorianism in China) (Kyoto, 1955).
7. For the Franciscan mission, see A. van der Wyngaert, ed., *Sinica Franciscana* (Quaracchi-Firenze, 1929), vol. I, pp. 57–58, 346–493, I. de Rachewiltz, op. cit., ch. 4, 8, 9, 10; see also Fang Hao, *Chung-hsi chiao-t'ung shih* (History of the Relations between China and the West) (Taipei, 1953–54), vol. 3, ch. 8.
8. Paul Demiéville, "La Situation Religieuse en Chine au Temps de Marco Polo," *Oriente Poliano*, Rome (Istituto Italiano per il Medio ed Estremo Oriente), 1957, pp. 193–234; L. Olschki, "Manichaeism, Buddhism and Christianity in Marco Polo's China," *Asiatische Studien* 5 (1951), pp. 1–21; A.C. Moule, op. cit.
9. The best work on this subject is Paul Rule's unpublished doctoral dissertation, *K'ung-tzu or Confucius? The Jesuit Interpretation of Confucianism*, Australian National University, 1972. I have profitted from the many discussions I had with Paul Rule on this subject when we were together in Canberra.
10. For the Jesuit missions, see L. J. Gallagher, *China in the Sixteenth Century* (New York, 1953), G. H. Dunne, *Generation of Giants* (London, 1962), and the works of Henri Bernard-Maître, *Le Père Matthieu Ricci et la société chinoise de son temps* (Tientsin, 1937), 2 vols., "L'Eglise catholique des XVIIe et XVIIIe siècles et sa place dans l'évolution de la civilisation chinoise," *Monumenta Serica* (1935–36), I, pp. 155–67; Fang Hao, *Chung-hsi chiao-t'ung shih*, vol. 5, ch. 5, 6.
11. See Henri Bernard-Maître, *Sagesse chinoise et Philosophie chrétienne*, (Tientsin, 1935), pp. 101–17. This book, published forty years ago, remains one of the few which attempts to discuss Chinese philosophy in the light of Christian perspectives.

12.   I have used the edition with both classical Chinese and vernacular translation, done by Lucas Liu Shun-te, *T'ien-chu shih-yi* (Taichung, 1966).

13.   For Christian missions in Japan, see C. R. Boxer, *The Christian Century in Japan, 1549–1650* (Berkeley, 1950); Michael Cooper, *The Southern Barbarians: the First Europeans in Japan* (Tokyo, 1971).

14.   In the nineteenth century, the Protestant missionary and scholar, James Legge, also examined the whole question of how to render the word God into Chinese, defending especially the thesis put forward by Jesuits earlier that the Lord-on-High is the true God. See Legge, *The Notions of the Chinese Concerning Gods and Spirits* (With an Examination of the Defenses of an Essay on the Proper Rendering of the Words Elohim and Theos into the Chinese Language), by William J. Boone, D. D. (Hongkong, 1852).

15.   For *ko-yi*, see T'ang Yung-t'ung, *Han Wei Liang-Chin Nan-pei-ch'ao Fo-chiao shih* (Shanghai, 1938), vol. 1, pp. 234–38, and his article in English, "On Ko-yi, the earliest method by which Indian Buddhism and Chinese thought were synthesized," *Radhakrishnan: Comparative Studies in Philosophy*, ed. by W. R. Inge *et al.* (London, 1940), pp. 276–86.

16.   See the Chinese history of Buddhism by T'ang Yung-t'ung (no. 15, above), and a work in English, by E. Zürcher, *The Buddhist Conquest of China* (Leiden, 1959), as well as Kenneth Ch'en, *Buddhism in China: A Historical Survey* (Princeton, 1964), ch. 2–7.

17.   For the terms controversy, see Paul Rule, op. cit., ch. 4, in which he has incorporated his work on the original sources and documents.

18.   Ricci himself might also have used a transliteration for *Deus*, at least during a certain period of his missionary career, see P. Pasquale M. d'Elia, "Le Origini dell'Arte Cristiana cinese (1583–1640)" (Reale Academia d'Italia, *Studi e Documenti* 9, Roma, 1939) and the review by J.J.L. Duyvendak, in *T'oung pao* 35 (1940), 386–88. This was pointed out to me by Prof. Fang Chao-ying, who also incorporated it in his biography of Ch'eng Ta-yüeh in the Ming Biographical History Project published by Columbia University Press, 1975.

19.   See Georg Schurhammer, S. J., *Das Kirchliche Sprachproblem in der Japanischen Jesuiten-mission des 16. und 17. Jahrhunderts* (Tokyo, 1928).

20.   In this regard, see Spencer J. Palmer, *Korea and Christianity* (Seoul, 1967), ch. 1. For Christian mission history in Korea, the Catholic side is told by Charles Dallet, *Histoire de l'Eglise de Corée* (Paris, 1874), 2 vols. Supplementary information may be found in Charles A. Clark, *The Old Religions of Korea* (New York 1932), pp. 229–55. For the Protestant missions, see L. G. Paik, *The History of Protestant Missions in Korea, 1832–1910* (Seoul, 1971), Samuel H. Moffett, *The Christians of Korea* (New York, 1962). For Korean Confucianism, see Laurent Youn Eul-sou, *Le Confucianisme en Corée* (Paris, 19)The author of this book is a Catholic priest, and his work remains a standard Western language reference, although written over thirty years ago. See also K. P. Young and G. Henderson, "An Outline History of Korean Confucianism," *Journal of Asian Studies* 18 (1958), pp. 81–101 and (1959), pp. 259–76. I am also indebted to Prof. Cornelius Chang of Columbia University for information on Christianity in today's Korea.

21.   See Paul Rule, op. cit., ch. 4, 5.

22.   See A. S. Rosso, *Apostolic Legations to China of the Eighteenth Century* (South Pasadena, 1948), pp. 138–43; Paul Rule, op. cit., pp. 384–85.

23. On Lo Wen-tsao, I am indebted to Rev. Lucas Liu of Taiwan for enlightening information. See also Paul Rule, op. cit., pp. 313–17.

24. See Douglas Lancashire, "Anti-Christian Polemics in Seventeenth Century China," *Church History* 38 (1969), pp. 218–41. See also the most important anti-Christian treatise, *P'i-hsieh-chi*, written by a Buddhist, Chung Shih-sheng, and included in the collection, *T'ien-chu chiao tung-ch'uan wen-hsien hsü-p'ien* (Documents on the Eastward Spreading of the Catholic Church) (Taipei, 1966), vol. 2, pp. 905–60.

25. See *Refutation of Deus by Fabian*, translated by Esther L. Hibbard (Tokyo, 1963). See also the Japanese collection, *Kirishitan sho, Hai-Ja sho*, comp. by Ebisawa Arimichi and others, *Nihon shisō taikei*, vol. 25 (Tokyo, 1970).

26. This was urged in China especially by Chang Chih-tung, in his work *Ch'üan-hsüeh-p'ien* (Counsels on Learning), and in Japan by Sakuma Shōzan. See my book, *To Acquire Wisdom: the Way of Wang Yang-ming* (New York, 1976), Appendix II.

27. See Kishimoto Hideo, ed., *Japanese Religion in the Meiji Era*. Translated by J. F. Howes (Tokyo, 1956); Introduction and ch. 3, 4, for religion in Tokugawa Japan (Confucianism and Christianity) as well as later developments in Meiji era.

28. Chow Tse-tsung, *The May Fourth Movement* (Cambridge, Mass., 1960), ch. 12, 13. See Robert N. Bellah, ed., *Religion and Progress in Modern Asia* (New York, 1965), Epilogue.

29. Joseph M. Kitagawa, *Religion in Japanese Society* (New York, 1966), pp. 243–50; Warren W. Smith, *Confucianism in Modern Japan* (Tokyo, 1959).

30. On this subject, see Albert Faurot, "The Oldest Birthday Party: Confucian Rites are still Observed in Asia," *Asia Magazine* (May 12, 1974), pp. 18–20. For the history of the cult, see John K. Shryock, *The Origin and Development of the State Cult of Confucius* (New York, 1966).

31. See Robert F. Spencer, ed., *Religion and Change in Contemporary Asia* (Minneapolis, 1971), especially the chapters on China, Japan, Vietnam; see also, *Theological Implications of the New China* (Geneva and Brussels, 1974), prepared by Pro Mundi Vita and Lutheran World Federation, for some of the problems connected with Christianity and Chinese Marxism. My own contribution here is entitled, "Faith and Ideology in the Light of the New China," pp. 15–36.

Chapter Two

CONFUCIANISM: A CRITICAL REASSESSMENT OF THE HERITAGE

"Another of our tasks is to study our historical heritage and use the Marxist method to sum it up critically . . . . We should sum up our history from Confucius to Sun Yat-sen and take over this valuable legacy."

Mao Tse-tung on "Study"[1]

"We must on no account reject the legacies of the ancients and the foreigners or refuse to learn from them, even though they are the works of the feudal or bourgeois classes."

Mao Tse-tung, "Yenan Forum on Literature and Art"[2]

INTRODUCTION

The critical summation of past cultural legacies. This mode of intellectual inheritance has been much more characteristic of Western European philosophy and theology than of the Chinese. We know about the de-ontologizing and de-mythologizing, that these need not be destructive, and can be critically constructive. Some of us have rediscovered being and a new metaphysics. Others—or sometimes, the same ones—have found a God who is beyond theism. We recognize the sacred in the profane, and re-ligiosity in militant atheism.

And then we turn to China and the Chinese. We become aware of their past traditions of a Golden Age and cyclical thinking, of concern with legendary sage kings and the transmission of their wisdom. We find traces of a critical tendency, but usually with appeals for justification to Confucius and the pre-Confucius past. At least, this was so until the late nineteenth century and the invasion of the critical European spirit into the Chinese milieu.

34

But what happened since then? We have now a new China, with its official espousal of a critical ideology from the West— albeit in a Chinese form. We have a new political leadership which urges intellectuals and masses to make a critical summation of the past Chinese cultural tradition. And, during the past year or so, we have been witnesses to an intensive drive inside of China to criticize that dimension of the past legacy which seems to have survived best into the present: the Confucian heritage. Indeed, the sustained intensity of this anti-Confucius Campaign which lasted from August 1973 to July 1974, before gradually abating, was such as to have puzzled the seasoned Sinologist as well as the attentive China-watcher, bent on analyzing every line, word or picture emerging out of mainland China. The mystery regarding that campaign was all the greater to the average Westerner, with little or no knowledge of Confucius the man, who lived two millennia and a half ago. But even in China itself, where Confucian Classics have long been replaced by Marxist and Maoist tomes in the school curricula, it was necessary to bring meaning to the campaign by reviving a critical interest in the Four Books and in other Confucian educational tracts. Of course, in China, where politics embrace the whole of life, these were all political moves, and their precise meaning has not yet been made clear.

It is not my aim here to offer possible political interpretations for the anti-Confucius Campaign. It is rather my intention to take up the challenge that it has placed before us, and make my own critical reassessment of the Confucian heritage. I shall not, however, limit myself to Marxist ideological arguments concerning history, progress and philosophy. I prefer to begin by examining the principal known arguments which have been proposed in criticisms of Confucius and his teachings—in order to distinguish the valid from the preposterous or uncertain. My intention is less to defend or attack Confucianism, but rather to clarify some of the issues involved in any authentic intellectual reassessment, and to interpret the meaning of Confucianism for today, while pointing out also its obsolete archaic dimensions.

In making my own reassessment of the entire Confucian heritage, I wish to take into account all significant critiques, expressed before Confucianism became the official and dominant school of thought in Han China (206 B.C.–A.D. 220), after it was officially disestablished, following the abolition of the civil examinations in 1905, and then in our own times, during the recent anti-Confucius Campaign. I shall also discuss the Confucian "image" in the West—the favorable responses it evoked particularly during the eighteenth century, through the intermediary of the Jesuit interpreters of the Confucian tradition, and the much less favorable reaction of the later missionaries of the nineteenth and twentieth centuries, both Catholic and Protestant. And I shall conclude with a careful evaluation of all the main arguments for and against the Confucian heritage, with the aim of clarifying to some extent its relevance and importance for the Chinese themselves, as well as for other peoples in the Far East, who find that Confucianism remains part and parcel of their native cultures, official disestablishment notwithstanding. I hope that by doing so, some understanding will also emerge, relating to its relevance and importance as one of the world's spiritual heritages.

I am aware of some of the pitfalls involved in my approach. I am evaluating the Confucian heritage mainly in the light of the many critiques which have been directed against it. I am not myself articulating its positive merits, before the final conclusion. And yet I shall conclude on a note which is not entirely negative. For I am presuming that the readers have some knowledge already of Confucianism. And besides, the classical Confucian texts, their accumulated commentaries, and voluminous Western tomes on the subjects, are all available to those who wish to examine the evidence for themselves.

THE EARLY CRITIQUES

The earliest critiques were voiced by Confucius' contemporaries. They were on the issue of political involvement in a time of disorder. In Analects 14 and 18, we have several instances of the Master during his peregrinations, meeting hermits, who, feigning madness or pretending insolence, mocked him for seeking vainly a ruler who might use his counsel in governing the state. Confucius reacted in each case with respect and melancholy, accepting their judgments of the times as well as of himself, but expressing at the same time his urgently felt mission to attempt the impossible.[3] He would die, not as a philosopher-minister, which he had aspired to be, but as a teacher of disciples, who in their own turns, sought to influence the society of their days by some form of political service.

In the two and a half centuries following his death, Confucius' germinal ideas exerted increasing influence, as his many disciples developed the Master's teachings along several different lines. In an age of the flowering of a "Hundred Schools" of thought, such a development also provoked debate and opposition from other masters. Confucius' best-known early critics were those of the schools of Mo-tzu (468–376 B.C.), Yang Chu, the Taoists, and the Legalists.

During the time of Mencius (fourth century B.C.), the schools of Mo-tzu and Yang Chu seemed to have exerted an influence equal to that of Confucius. Mencius himself was occupied with the task of staving off criticisms of Confucius and his teachings which were being voiced by both the Mohists and the followers of Yang Chu, whom he called teachers of perverse learning which was corrupting the world.[4] In the book attributed to Mo-tzu, there is a chapter entitled "Against Confucians" in which the latter are criticized and ridiculed for their exaggerated observance of mourning and wedding rituals, for their belief in fate, their pompous imitation of the ancients in dress and manners, their passivity in politics and restraint on the battlefield. Certain criticisms are also directed against Confucius himself for having allegedly given counsel and assistance to minor feudal nobles plotting rebellion against their lords: "Confucius conceived deep plans and far-reaching schemes in the service of a traitor. He racked his brain and exhausted his wisdom in carrying out evil . . . His broad learning is of no use in deciding what is right for the age; his labored thinking does nothing to aid the people. . ."[5]

Yang Chu is much less known to us. Fung Yu-lan describes him as a recluse in the same class as Confucius' earliest recorded critics.[6] According to Mencius (7A26), Yang Chu taught a doctrine of complete individual freedom. The classic characterization of Yang Chu is that "He would not exchange a hair of his shank. . .for the profit of the whole world. . . . He despises things and values life."[7]

The better known Taoist writings, *Lao-tzu* and *Chuang-tzu*, also contain implicit and explicit attacks on Confucius and his teachings. Many of these are also directed by recluses or men in retirement against a life of active social and political involvement. With an irony which shocks as well as amuses, *Lao-tzu* and *Chuang-tzu* proclaim a return to nature as the state of perfection, satirizing Confucian ideals of sagehood and wisdom, ritual and government:

> Exterminate the sage, discard the wise, and people will benefit a hundredfold; exterminate benevolence, discard rectitude, and the people will again be filial. (*Lao-tzu*, Ch. 19)[8]

> In the age of perfect virtue, men live the same as birds and beasts. . . . In uncarved simplicity the people attain their true nature.
> Then along comes the sage, huffing and puffing after benevolence, reaching on tiptoe for righteousness, and the world for the first time has doubts; mooning and mouthing over his music, snipping and stitching away at his rites, and the world for the first time is divided. . . . That the Way and its virtue were destroyed in order to create benevolence and righteousness—this was the fault of the sage. (*Chuang-tzu*, Ch. 9)[9]

In the book of *Chuang-tzu*, Confucius is presented several times as a man searching for the Way, and asking help from Lao Tan, the alleged author of *Lao-tzu*, who tells him that it is found, not in the classical texts, but rather in the simplicity of nature. Both *Lao-tzu* and *Chuang-tzu* also give expression to the belief that the best ruler is one who governs by the way of nature, that is, by "non-action:"

> Do that which consists in taking no action (*wu-wei*; 無為), and order will prevail. (*Lao-tzu*, Ch. 3)[10]

> I have heard of letting the world be, of leaving it alone; I have never heard of governing the world. (*Chuang-tzu*, Ch. 11)[11]

Unlike the Mohists—who taught universal love and political involvement—and the Taoists—who preached a metaphysical way and individual freedom—the Legalists specialized in the art of acquiring and maintaining power. Theirs was the school of *Realpolitik*, offering theories and method of total state organization and leadership. They turned their backs firmly to the past and its examples of moral virtue which they considered as human weakness. In the best-known Legalist work, *Han Fei Tzu*, the followers of Confucius are criticized for offering teachings to the world's rulers:

> By practicing benevolence and righteousness, [these men] are trusted and given government posts. . . . If the government is conducted in this fashion, then the state will face disorder and the ruler will surely be in peril.[12]

Elsewhere, *Han Fei Tzu* compares the effect of awe and that of moral persuasion in government:

> In a strict household, there are no unruly slaves, but the children of a kindly mother often turn out bad. From this I know that power (*shih*; 勢) and authority can prevent violence, but kindness and generosity are insufficient to put an end to disorder. . . . Those who rule must employ measures that will be effective with the majority and discard those that will be effective with only a few. Therefore they devote themselves not to virtue, but to law.[13]

The Legalist philosophy is firmly pragmatic. People respond to rewards and punishment much more than to moral teachings and persuasion. A well-known Legalist parable is that of a young boy who remained intractable in his misguided ways despite parental advice, teachers' instructions, and neighbors' counsels. At the end, he was forced to change his life by the intervention of the local magistrate and the soldiers he sent out to enforce the law:

> Thus the love of parents is not enough to make children learn what is right, but must be backed up by the strict penalties of the local officials; for people by nature grow proud on love, but they listen to authority.[14]

With the help of Legalist ministers, the first emperor of the Ch'in dynasty (221–206 B.C.) was able to achieve the political unification of feudal China by 221 B.C. This was accompanied by an attempt at unification on other levels, including the intellectual and ideological. Laws and regulations, weights and measures were standardized, and the diverse forms of Chinese scripts made uniform. In 213 B.C. the emperor ordered the burning of all books except those which dealt with medicine, divination and agriculture. Allegedly, he also ordered the burying alive of 460 scholars, in order to put an end to criticisms of his rule. It is not known how many of these were Confucians.[15]

Confucianism remained underground, to be revived and then dominant during the Han dynasty, when Emperor Wu (r. 140–87 B.C.) made it the state philosophy, supported by government patronage and an official education system. But this could only happen at a certain cost to the teachings of Confucius themselves. The Confucianism that triumphed was no longer the philosophy of Confucius and Mencius. It had already absorbed many extraneous ideas coming particularly from Legalism and *yin-yang* cosmology and religious philosophy. It would emphasize—far more than Confucius and Mencius did—the vertical and authoritarian dimensions of the five moral relationships. Besides, official support spelled also official control. The future of Confucianism was determined, to a great extent, by its emergence during the Han dynasty as "a great synthetic religion into which were fused all the elements of popular superstition and state worship . . . thinly covered up under the disguise of Confucian and pre-Confucian classics, in order to make them appear respectable and authoritative."[16] It was a triumph which has been described, in some ways, as a "Pyrrhic victory."[17]

THE MODERN CRITIQUES

By modern critiques, I refer to those of the late nineteenth century and after. China was then shaken politically and psychologically by Western intrusion. Chinese intellectuals began a soul-searching questioning of the country's cultural heritage, particularly Confucianism. It was regarded as a weight and a burden—intellectual shackles on the mind, preventing the country from modernization. An early pre-Republican critic was Chang Pin-lin (*alias* Chang T'ai-yen, 1868–1936).[18] Later came Ch'en Tu-hsiu, the founder, in 1921, of the Chinese Communist Party, Lu Hsün (Chou Shu-jen), famous writer and biting satirist, and Hu Shih, student of John Dewey, leader of the Chinese vernacular movement, and a scholar equally at ease in the classical heritage.

In 1916, Ch'en Tu-hsiu—editor of *New Youth*—had yet to discover and commit himself to Communist ideology. Together with Hu Shih, Wu Yü and Yi Pai-sha, he spoke out against a Confucian *establishment*, opposing the proposal for constitutional recognition of Confucianism as a state religion or philosophy, and the enforcement of a Confucian-orientated education. Hu Shih criticized particularly the later Sung Confucianism which had become fossilized as state orthodoxy in pre-Republican days. Yi Pai-sha attacked Confucius and his disciples as "political revolutionaries" and described their teachings and scholarship as eclectic. But the strongest indictment of traditional Confucianism came from Lu Hsün, whose first short story, *The Diary of a Madman* (1918) to be followed by others equally famous, attacked the "cannibalistic" ritual religion which stifled human freedom and individual initiative in the name of passive, conformist, virtues.[19] Lu Hsün's critiques satirized the dehumanizing elements in a fossilized tradition until then inextricably bound up with a political-social establishment, concerned only with the survival of its own power interests. His anti-Confucian writings have been extolled and distributed during the recent campaign within China, and his biting criticisms of the Confucian tradition continue to find echoes also among the Chinese outside of China, especially those who have had personal experience with the disadvantages of the Chinese clan system, its authoritarianism and its tendency to stifle individual initiative. Their complaints and arguments resemble those critics of the Christian tradition, especially in the eighteenth century but also today, who assail the institutional church for the authoritarian and rigidly dogmatic stance which makes of it—albeit unwittingly—an enemy of the very human freedom and happiness it claims to defend.

Both as individuals and as a group, these modern critics of Confucianism desired intellectual and social emancipation from the fetters of a rigid orthodoxy which continued to give support to a dying social order. Generally speaking, they did not regard Confucianism as totally devoid of any merits, and they did not clearly know what they desired to have in its place. In the name of intellectual pluralism, they encouraged a positive reevaluation of the non-Confucian schools: Mohism, Taoism, and Buddhism. They also wanted new ideas from the West—but as yet, without much more openness to discernment concerning these, outside of slogans like "Mr. Science" and "Mr. Democracy." Ch'en Tu-hsiu could then see both positive and negative elements in Christianity. Hu Shih, the protagonist of liberal humanism, was and remained opposed to the substitution of one ideology for another, while Lu Hsün, always an iconoclast and never an idol worshipper, expressed himself strongly against any excessive praise of authority, whether conservative or revolutionary. But the Confucianism then coming under fire being that which was the support of the hated *status quo*, was not necessarily the teaching of Confucius himself. As Chow Tse-tsung pointed out:

> Whether the spirit of Confucius himself is precisely the same as the spirit of the later Confucianism attacked by the intellectuals still remains debatable. Confucius' doctrines are not free from ambiguities and limitations. Varying emphases or distortions will certainly paint a different Confucius.[20]

In this early period, few effective defenses of Confucianism were offered. The anti-Confucian sentiments being voiced were also expressive of the newly awakened Chinese patriotism, desirous of asserting national independence against the imperialist onslaught of the Great Powers—both Western Europe and Japan—whose strength was being associated with qualities diametrically opposed to the known Confucian values. China was looking for rejuvenation, and Confucian ideology represented the old and immovable. China turned itself to the West: to ideas of renaissance and enlightenment. It regarded the Confucian past as the "Dark Ages." This is significant for students of comparative thought. One can see a certain parallel in European intellectual history itself. During the seventeenth and eighteenth centuries, Western Europe was shaken by its discovery of Confucian China through the reports of the Jesuits, who thus contributed to the emergence of deism and rationalism, the result of polarization between intellectuals and a religious establishment. In the nineteenth and twentieth centuries, Europe, in its turn, overawed China, and gave rise to the Chinese questioning of their own heritage.

The Quest for a Historical Confucius

The *questioning* into Chinese tradition as such and Confucianism in particular involved also a *quest*—that for the historical Confucius, as distinct from the Confucius-image in popular veneration. The development in the 1920's and 1930's of a more scientifically critical historical method facilitated this task to a certain extent. The Chinese school of higher criticism was associated with names like Ku Chieh-kang and Ch'ien Hsüan-t'ung. The former was engaged in the "historical quest" aimed at pulling the sage down from the pedestal by a scientific investigation of historical circumstances in which the Confucian cult developed. According to him:

> Confucius was regarded as a gentleman (*chün-tzu*, 君子) in the Spring-Autumn Period (722–481 B.C.), as a sage in the Warring States Period (403–221 B.C.), as a pope (*chiao-chu*, 教主) in the Western Han (206 B.C.–A.D. 9) and again as a sage in the Eastern Han (A.D. 25–220). Today, he is to be regarded once more as a gentleman.[21]

Ch'ien Hsüan-t'ung enquired into the question of authorship of the Confucian Classics, rejecting the theory that these were personally written or revised by Confucius. He proposed that the lost *Classic of Music* never existed, whereas the other five Classics were rather unrelated works used by Confucius as teaching texts. Ch'ien was fervent in his doubts regarding antiquity and courageous in his readiness to differ from authoritative views. He gave himself the surname *I-ku* (疑古), "doubt of antiquity."[22]

The quest for a historical Confucius did not last long, interrupted as it was, by the Sino-Japanese War. But it probably would not have continued long, given the scarcity of certain historical data regarding the man and his teachings. Confucius was definitely a historical person like Jesus Christ after him. The attempt of some enthusiasts in the Han dynasty to divinize him never really succeeded, but left behind an aroma of sageliness that obscured the real man. The extant historical sources are not of much help. The brief references in *The Annals of Tso* (c. 300 B.C.) contain legendary material. The biography in Ssu-ma Ch'ien's *Historical Records*, written about 100 B.C., offers a contradictory chronology and absurd anecdotes.[23] The picture it presents conflicts with that given in the Master's collected sayings, The Analects, compiled probably by Confucius' disciples' disciples. The modern demythologization effort has made us more aware of these difficulties, and less certain of how much we can ever know of Confucius and his teachings. Nevertheless, the quest has been useful. It is comparable, in some ways, to that quest for a historical Jesus associated with Albert Schweitzer and others. But this particular quest was very short-lived. And the Confucian tradition still lacks an interpreter of Rudolf Bultmann's stature to make its message *meaningful* to modern man. Its *kerygma* yet stands in need of further exploration and proclamation.[24]

THE MARXIST CRITIQUES: 1950 ON

The conclusion of the Sino-Japanese War in 1945 was closely followed by the Chinese civil war and the triumph of the Chinese Communist Party. The new government of the Peoples' Republic was committed to Marxist-Leninist ideology and brought in a new phase of cultural evaluation. The new national leader, Mao Tse-tung, did not immediately rule out the merits of the past. He advocated a critical reassessment of the past, with a view to inheriting the great cultural legacy.

A Question of Methodology

The new ideology requires new norms for such critical evaluation. The principles of dialectical materialism and class struggle were applied to the analysis of Chinese intellectual history, with help of objective dialectical logic. Such an approach brings its own problems. The materialist interpretation of history regards the study of the past as a means toward the attainment of political ends in the future—the construction of a utopian socialist society. It is colored by ideas of scientific determinism, but appeals also to the importance of personal commitment to the utopian cause, and so assumes that it is man who makes history. It also involves a scheme of periodization which Karl Marx had applied to his analysis of European history and the genesis of capitalism, apparently, with no intention of transferring its validity to the understanding either of Russia or of Asia. However, during the era of Stalin's rule in the Soviet Union, this theory of a unilinear historical pattern became part and parcel of Communist ideology, and was taken over by Kuo Mo-jo in his own studies of ancient Chinese societies.[25] With this came the difficulty of the periodization of Chinese history, in terms of primitive communism, slave-owning, feudal, and bourgeois capitalist societies. The institution of feudalism posed a special problem. If medieval European feudal society is kept in mind, then China's past, unlike that of Japan, poses many difficulties. The Chinese *feng-chien*(封建) institution, the closest to the European model, began and finished very early—around the third century B.C.—and was followed by the rise and fall of dynastic cycles which lasted until the early twentieth century. And so, when can the Chinese feudal age be said to have begun, and when did it end?

The problem of periodization was particularly important in the reassessment of Confucius who lived during the Spring-Autumn Period, clearly a time of transition—but from what to what? If his age was feudal, and he himself an advocate of feudal values, he could hardly be condemned as an obstacle to historical development, granted the long duration of the "feudal" age in China before the emergence of a bourgeois society. This is all the more so since Confucius' critics usually agree that he did teach certain ideas which were "reformist" if not "progressive"—or, as some would claim, "revolutionary."

Interestingly, Kuo Mo-jo, the most venerated Chinese Marxist historian, *lauded* Confucius and his disciples as political revolutionaries, appealing for support for his arguments to those passages in the book attributed to Mo-tzu—the darling of anti-Confucians both of 1916 and today—which were most critical of Confucius. He warned against the substitution of "Confucius & Sons" with "Mo-tzu & Sons," and he was also strongly critical of the "Fascist" views of Han Fei Tzu and other Chinese Legalists. However, Kuo carefully noted at the end of his book, *Shih p'i-p'an shu* (The Ten Critiques), that he stood firmly on his position as a historical materialist, and that, while he regarded Confucius as a "progressive" in his own times, he did not regard Confucianism as being useful to modern China.[26]

While Chinese historians were obliged to cope with the problem of periodization, the students of Chinese thought were also required to deal with that of applying the materialist-idealist antithesis to the understanding of traditional Chinese philosophy. The cultural spokesman of Stalinist days, A.A. Zhdanov (d. 1948), had made his analysis of Russian intellectual history in this light, attacking with vigor G.F. Aleksandrov's work on the history of Western European philosophy.[27] Zhdanov has lost his importance in Soviet Russia, but his methodology and presuppositions remain normative for critics of Chinese philosophy in China, who continue to regard philosophy in a polemical light, giving priority especially to questions of method, of logic and epistemology. This basic starting point assumes also the importance of correct *methods* for the attainment of *correct ideas*, with approval given to knowledge derived from inductive experience and practical activities, while deductive, *a priori* methods of thinking and knowing are prejudged as leading to falsehood. Where China is concerned, an epistemologically oriented scheme is applied to largely ethical systems, with a view of deciding in *ethical* terms the merits of these systems. Idealist thinking, for example, is bad, not only because the method of knowledge involved is defective, but also because it is used to help the exploiting classes.

The problem here is, how to assign Chinese thinkers to the right categories in order to pronounce final judgments upon their teachings. The philosopher Mencius, for example, manifested mystical tendencies, and was surely an "idealist," yet his political doctrines evinced progressive ideas—even a theory of revolution (!)—, while some of the Taoists, Lao-tzu and Chuang-tzu, had incipient "materialist" notions, but represented more conservative political views. On the other hand, Hung Hsiu-ch'üan, the quasi-Christian peasant rebel of the mid-nineteenth century, as well as his followers, were clearly protagonists of the exploited classes, and have been praised as such, but their overt Christian beliefs should put them into the idealist category.[28]

If Kuo Mo-jo voiced his appreciation of Confucius—he also expressed his preference for the Ming Confucian thinker, Wang Yang-ming (1472–1529)[29] —other leftist writers did the opposite. A book vehemently critical of the entire Confucian tradition, but especially of Confucius himself, was Ts'ai Shang-ssu's *Chung-kuo ch'uan-t'ung chung-p'i-p'an* (A General Critique of Chinese Traditional Thought). It denounced Confucius for his aristocratic class origins, and his teachings as being the enemy of workers-peasants, of women, of the Chinese society and country, and of liberty, democracy and humanitarianism.[30] As Ts'ai himself mentioned, his readers were perplexed by the divergence of views among the Chinese Marxist interpreters of Confucius. For example, Hou Wai-lu, Chao Chi-pin and Tu Kuo-hsiang produced the monumental five-volume work on the General History of Chinese Thought (*Chung-kuo ssu-hsiang t'ung-shih*) completed in 1957. Hou and his fellow workers made systematic use of the Marxist approach to historical and intellectual analysis. Their work tends to be more critical of the Neo-Confucian movement of the Sung and Ming dynasties, that later synthesis of earlier Confucianism with philosophical Taoism and Ch'an (Zen) Buddhism. It labelled the Chu Hsi school as objective idealism for acknowledging an underlying metaphysical reality in the world of manifold objects, and the Wang Yang-ming school as subjective idealism, for completely interiorizing the external world. It criticized both schools for their near-monastic cultivation of religiosity and for philosophical scholasticism. It also gave quite some merit to the so-called Leftist Yang-ming school associated with the name of Wang Ken, a man of common background and little formal education.[31] But the chapters on early Confucianism reveal a positive appreciation of Confucius himself, described as a teacher who liberated education from official domination and a reformer whose social criticisms reveal progressive emphases.[32]

The Controversy over "Jen"

The lack of agreement among the scholars concerning the value of Confucian teachings emerged especially in 1962, during a conference held in Shantung in honor of the 2440th anniversary of the death of Confucius. And the academic dispute that attracted the most attention regarded a new evaluation of the Confucian virtue, *jen.*

Feng Yu-lan, Chao Chi-pin and Yang Jung-kuo all attempt to explain *jen* in terms of the four words *k'o-chi fu-li* taken from the long passage in Analects 12:1,[33] which describes the dialogue between Confucius and his favorite disciple, Yen Yüan. Feng adheres to the more usual interpretation, that *k'o-chi*(克己) refers to self-conquest, and goes on to explain *fu-li*(復禮), the restoration of propriety or ritual law, as the recovery of Confucius' own kind of "propriety"—that which applies to noblemen and commoners alike: *jen.* He places emphasis upon the "class-transcending" character of *jen* as a universal virtue, which Confucius has also defined as *ai-jen* (愛人; love men).[34]

Chao Chi-pin takes the two similar texts from the Analects but interprets them quite differently. He is, at the same time, uncompromisingly committed to class analysis, while also utilizing a philological method to substantiate his claims. He explains the words *k'o-chi* as meaning "personally realizing," and *fu-li,* as the restoration of the entire ritual system of Western Chou, which he, in turn, identifies with the slave-owning society. Giving his own modern translation and interpretation of Analects 12:1, he substitutes the word "slave-owning system" for that of *li* (propriety):

> Yen Yüan asked what is *jen.* Confucius said: "*Jen* is not an abstract notion . . . When, for one day only, you can *personally realize* (*k'o-chi*) the slave-owning system of Western Chou (*fu-li*), the whole world will return to *jen* . . ."
> Yen Yüan [then] said: ". . . Please tell me what are its concrete steps."
> Confucius said: "Look not at what is contrary to the color of the slave-owning system (*li*). . . . Listen not to what is contrary to the music of the slave-owning system . . . Say not anything that is contrary to the discussions and utterances of the slave-owning system. . . . Make sure that your eyes, ears, mouth, and body, your movements of sight, hearing,

speech, and action, all conform to the regulations of the slave-owning system."[35]

Chao Chi-pin insists that the word *jen* (人；men) in the Analects refers only to one social class: the slave-owning aristocrats. Within this class, he sees some distinction between *chün-tzu* (君子; gentlemen) and *hsiao-jen* (小人; small men), but he opposes both these categories of *jen* (men) to *min* (民; people), which for him refers to the lower classes, the slaves. He asserts that Confucius limits the meaning of love (*jen*) to the upper classes, excluding from its realm the "people" (*min*), who were only fit to be "ruled from above."[36]

Yang Jung-kuo, probably the best-known critic of Confucius today, in and out of China, takes a more historical approach to the whole question. He has consistently identified the Spring-Autumn Period with the slave-owning society, and has always argued that Confucius was a political reactionary who supported the *status quo* against the rising, land-owning feudal classes as well as mercantile interests.[37] Pointing out the occurrence of many slave revolts recorded in the *Annals of Tso* for the Spring-Autumn Period, he also quotes the criticisms voiced by Robber Chih in *Chuang-tzu* against Confucius, the social parasite who "ate without tilling the soil, dressed without weaving, playing with his lips and tongue and making up arbitrary standards of right and wrong." Indeed, as Robber Chih concluded, Confucius' crimes were exceedingly great, and the so-called sage should more aptly be called "Robber Ch'iu."[38]

Yang Jung-kuo also criticizes Confucius' epistemology, described as *a priori* idealism, and shown in Confucius' desire to determine the objective by the subjective, as given in the theory of Rectification of Names. Besides, Confucius speaks of two kinds of men who are unchangeable, those with superior knowledge, and those who are incurably foolish. This is, Yang says, the "Genius Theory."[39]

In attacking Confucius, Yang Jung-kuo also exalts his earliest critics, Mo-tzu and the Mohists, and Han Fei Tzu and the Legalists. He represents Mo-tzu as a progressive in his own time, a man of lowly origin who was against the domination of the ruling class and preached, instead of *jen*, the universal love of all men. Yang explains Mo-tzu's religious ideas by saying that for Mo-tzu the Will of Heaven (*T'ien-chih;* 天志) is a symbol of universal love, which actively opposes the teaching of Fate, and effectively hastens the liberation of slaves. According to him, Mo-tzu also speaks of ghosts and spirits—while really doubting their existence—in an effort to assert the equality of all during this life as well as afterwards.

Yang Jung-kuo interprets Legalism as a progressive school of thought advocating the correct means toward unifying and strengthening the country, and bringing in a new historical phase, that of China's "Feudal Age." He points out how Han Fei Tzu rejects both the doctrines of Fate and of Ghosts and Spirits, asserting rather the greatness of man, and his ability to conquer nature (*T'ien*). Han Fei Tzu's emphasis on law is presented as promoting the fight for liberation on the part of the slaves, even though his laws are to be made for a new ruling class.[40]

THE ANTI-CONFUCIUS CAMPAIGN: 1966–74

During the Cultural Revolution, with the rise to power of Lin Piao and the fall of Liu Shao-ch'i, the anti-Confucius movement enters a new phase. In 1966–67, newspaper articles reported the "cultural revolutions" which occurred within the Institute of History and that of Philosophy, both belonging to the Chinese Academy of Science, and each with its respective journal, *Li-shih yen-chiu* and *Che-hsüeh yen-chiu*. The attacks were especially against Wu Han, author of the historical drama, *The Dismissal of Hai Jui*, which Chairman Mao himself had decided was a veiled criticism of his own action in removing from office the former Defense Minister, P'eng Te-huai (1959). But this turmoil affected also Hou Wai-lu, allegedly a supporter of Wu Han as well as of Chou Yang, the Minister of Culture under Liu Shao-ch'i, who had organized the 1962 Conference on Confucius in Shantung. This event was singled out also for criticism, as "philosopher workers" were exhorted to give up the "stinking" manners of the intellectuals, and to become little pupils of the workers, peasants, and soldiers. Diatribes against "Confucius & Sons" appeared. These associated Liu Shao-ch'i's name with this establishment, and criticized in particular Liu's book, *How To Be a Good Communist*, for encouraging the party cadre to make use of Confucian ideas of cultivation in order to become a better Communist, and for the many references to the Four Books and to other Confucian texts.[41]

Strangely enough, when the anti-Confucian diatribes reappeared in late 1973, the name of Lin Piao, now fallen from grace, became also associated with that of Liu Shao-ch'i as well as that of Confucius. In the early months of 1974, the campaign intensified, as a series of diatribes in newspaper articles and provincial radio broadcasts accompanied an abundant literature of posters and pamphlets decrying Confucius and his teachings.[42]

It should be noted that, in 1972, Kuo Mo-jo published an article on the periodization of early Chinese history, in which he spoke about his own intellectual evolution regarding this problem, and how, with the help of Mao's utterances, he had finally been able, around 1952, to decide upon the "dividing line" between the slave-owning age and the feudal age in ancient China. According to him, this took place *between* the Spring-Autumn and Warring States periods, i.e., around 475 B.C.[43] Kuo makes no mention of Confucius in this article, but the consequences of such a published decision with regard to the anti-Confucius debate would clearly be in favor of the arguments put forth by critics like Yang Jung-kuo and Chao Chi-pin. Certainly, the anti-Confucius articles appearing in newspapers and pamphlets now take for granted the alleged fact that Confucius sided with the slave-owning class against the slaves, and prevented the early coming of China's "feudal age."

Of the more academic publications which have appeared on this subject, Chao Chi-pin's treatise on Confucius' killing of Shao-cheng Mao (*Kuan-yü K'ung-tzu chu Shao-cheng Mao wen-t'i*)[44] merits more attention. The alleged historical incident is mentioned not in the Analects, but in *Hsün-tzu* (third century B.C.), *Shih-chi* (first century B.C.) and Wang Ch'ung's *Lun-heng* (first century A.D.). According to these accounts Confucius is said to have ordered the execution of a well-known scholar-official, Shao-cheng Mao, seven days after he had himself been appointed to the position of Minister of Justice in the state of Lu (498 B.C.). Chao presents the arguments of all those throughout Chinese history who had believed in the historical authenticity of this story, as well as those who had denied it, or given a modified version of it. He arrives at the conclusion that the incident really took place, and that Confucius had killed Shao-cheng Mao for political reasons, as a representative of the rising landlord and mercantile interests of the merging "feudal society," as well as for reasons of petty jealousy— because Shao-cheng Mao was luring away his own students.

Many problems arise when one attempts to evaluate the current anti-Confucius Campaign. Where Confucius himself is concerned, today's criticisms are certainly the most vehement he has ever received, repeating as they also do, the more traditional attack levelled against himself and his teachings. The critics today judge him to have been "irrelevant" to his own time, indeed, a reactionary and counter-revolutionary who impeded the course of history, and *a fortiori*, of only negative use, if any, to our own age. His class-biased teachings can have no universal meaning, his thought was unoriginal, "eclectic," compromising, his scholarship was mediocre, and even his personal character is being assailed: he was no sage, but a hypocrite.[45]

These conclusions are now regarded as final and definitive. No effort is made to investigate further into the arguments proferred which may lead to differing conclusions. Fung Yu-lan, for example, has published a recent self-criticism (December 1973),[46] in which he acknowledged guilt for his past misrepresentations of Chinese philosophy in general and Confucius and Confucianism in particular, agreeing that the virtue of *jen* was limited in theory and application to one class (*chün-tzu*; the gentlemen, or better still, "superior men"). He has also pledged the remaining years of his life to a thorough revision, in the light of all he has learned during the Cultural Revolution, of the published portions of his books, The New History of Chinese Philosophy (*Chung-kuo Che-hsüeh-shih hsin-pien*) (1964), as well as to a more careful ideological rendition of the portions yet to be written. To quote his own words:

> The field of the history of Chinese philosophy is now going through a new revolution. Chairman Mao is personally leading and directing us. I am almost 80, and have spent half a century working on the history of Chinese philosophy. It is

my great happiness now to be able to participate in it. I am determined to follow Chairman Mao's instructions, to study Marxism and Mao's thought seriously, to reform my world view, and revise [my books].[47]

THE WESTERN CRITIQUES

Confucianism is a Chinese heritage, and the Chinese themselves must bear the chief responsibility of reinterpretation and critical inheritance. But the Chinese have learned from the critical spirit of the West, and may yet learn from the Western responses to and critiques of Confucianism.

The Western critiques of Confucianism were articulated especially during the seventeenth and eighteenth centuries, when missionary efforts brought China within the scope of the Westerner's knowledge. These responses were thus conditioned largely by religious attitudes, both of the missionary interpreters and those of the informed public and its intellectual spokesmen. The missionaries themselves were divided. Some were admirers of Chinese culture, and ready to accommodate Christian evangelization to Confucian teachings. They believed that they found in early Confucianism articulations of theist beliefs and of the immortality of the soul. They became the earliest Western Sinologists, and introduced to European readers the picture of an independent and non-Christian culture of high antiquity, with a rich and vibrant moral tradition which compared very favorably with the ethical teachings of Christianity. They generally preferred early Confucianism to that later metaphysical development known to the West today as Neo-Confucianism, which substituted a philosophical vocabulary of t'ai-chi (太極), li (理) and ch'i (気) for the earlier, anthropomorphically religious and practically moralistic one. Yet Neo-Confucianism then dominated the Chinese intellectual atmosphere, as its *corpus* of commentaries had been officially accepted as giving an orthodox interpretation of the earlier Classics.[48]

The Jesuit writers on China and Confucianism made the greatest impact in Europe, giving rise to theological controversies regarding the origin of the Chinese religions, the antiquity of the Chinese historical chronology when compared to the biblical, and the question of compatibility between Confucian rites and Christian faith. It is against such a background that the Western critiques of Confucianism are to be understood.

Two Jesuit works published in the seventeenth century fired the imagination of the European intellectuals and added fuel to the theological controversies. Phillipe Couplet's *Confucius Sinarum Philosophus* (1687), with translations and explanations of three of the Four Confucian Books, and L. LeComte's *Nouveaux Mémoires sur l'État présent de la Chine* (1696), whose extravagant praises of Chinese religious and moral teachings drew upon the book a solemn condemnation by the faculty of the University of Sorbonne in 1700, for questioning the uniqueness of the Christian revelation. But some of Europe's best minds were led to the study of China and to philosophical and theological reflections on Confucianism. G.W. Leibniz visited and corresponded with many Jesuits, including Father J. Bouvet, from whom he derived a knowledge of the Book of Changes and of Neo-Confucian philosophy. He left behind a collection of documents, *Novissima Sinica* (1697), with his own preface and a short treatise on Confucianism, *De Cultu Confucii Civili* (c. 1700), which gives his positions regarding the Chinese rites. In his letters and other writings, Leibniz shows his particular appreciation of Chu Hsi's teachings of *li* and *ch'i*, insisting that the Chinese were not materialists, but had a real understanding of God and of spiritual beings. C. Wolff shared Leibniz' enthusiasm, and expressed his own admiration for the moral and political philosophy contained in the Chinese classics.[49]

Not all missionaries, not even all Jesuits, were united in admiration for Chinese culture and Confucianism. And not all philosophers partook of Leibniz' and Wolff's appreciation of things Chinese. Nicholas Longobardi, an immediate successor to Matteo Ricci, and Antoine de Ste. Marie, a Franciscan, both insisted that Neo-Confucian commentaries must be accepted as interpreting ancient Confucian texts, and that this meant China had become a land of atheists and agnostics, with no understanding of spirit as distinct from matter. Longobardi's *Traité sur Quelques Points de la Religion des Chinois* and Ste. Marie's *Traité sur Quelques Points Importants de la Mission de la Chine* both appeared about 1701, presenting a vivid picture of the anxious discussions then going on among missionaries conscious of these problems. Of the scholars in Europe who had no direct experience of China, Fénélon wrote his *Dialogues des Morts* comparing Confucius unfavorably to Socrates, and voicing serious doubts regarding the superiority and antiquity of Chinese civilization. Nicolas de Malebranche, a synthesizer of Cartesianism and Thomism, also published a critique of Confucianism in the form of philosophical dialogue: the *Entretien d'un Philosophe Chrétien et d'un Philosophe Chinois.*[50] It was an exposition of Malebranche's own theology, with ontological and epistemological proof of God's existence, according to his theory that the world was created according to archetypes in the Divine Mind. Malebranche sought to reinterpret the Chinese notion of *li* (principle) in his own philosophical terms, converting it into the notion of a metaphysical Absolute which he preferred to that of an anthropomorphic God. Montesquieu was also more a critic than an admirer of China. He voiced the opinion, in *L'Esprit des Lois* (1748) and elsewhere, that China afforded a negative example of institutions and practices which Europeans should avoid. Even Rousseau questioned the extravagant claims of the Sinophiles, pointing out how China's alleged wise men had not been able to keep the country from waves of barbarian conquests.

Nevertheless, on the whole, eighteenth century European intellectuals were delighted with their discovery of China and Confucianism. Voltaire spoke with admiration of the country where reason and harmony reigned supreme, without the interference of superstition. First in *Essai sur les Moeurs* and then in *Histoire Universelle* (written around 1740), Voltaire attacked the historical authority of the Biblical chronology by reference to China's antiquity, and also made claims for an ethical system independent of revealed religion.[51] Jean-Jacques Rousseau made some favorable comments on China in an article on political economy (1755). His own ideas on the noble savage offer echoes of an affinity— probably unconscious—with Mencius' doctrine on human goodness. Francois Quesnay, the physiocrat, published his book, *Le Despotisme de la Chine*, in 1767, as a refutation of Montesquieu's criticisms of Chinese institutions, and a praise of enlightened despotism in China which was based on law and a rationalist philosophy.[52] Indeed, these French *philosophes* bore a real resemblance to the Chinese *literati*, since they were mostly universalists rather than specialists, with interests extending from philosophy to art and politics. But the days of unmixed admiration for the Chinese empire were rapidly passing. In the early nineteenth century, the German philosopher G.W.F. Hegel still affirms reason and order in China, as well as the wisdom contained in the Confucian Classics, but his *Philosophy of History* sounded a note of ambivalence and condescension. Hegel said that China, like the rest of the Orient, lacked the spiritual freedom and dynamism of Europe, and remained immune to change and transformation.[53]

The exchanges between Europe and China were interrupted by the decades of religious persecution following the controversial decision of Rome condemning the Chinese rites (1742). The country became reopened to missionaries only in the middle of the nineteenth century. This time, the missionaries who entered China, both Protestants and Catholics, were of a different mind from that of Matteo Ricci and his followers. According to Donald Treadgold, the Protestants regarded China as a land of idolatry and darkness, awaiting salvation and conversion. They considered it their duty to refute Confucianism, and in this they were joined by the Catholics, frequently for the same reasons, and in spite of the religious animosity which they might have felt for each other.[54]

Christian missionaries were largely responsible for the lowered prestige of Confucianism during the late nineteenth and early twentieth centuries. The missionaries and their Chinese converts stood for Westernization and material progress. The Jesuit Sinologist, L. Wieger, gives us some idea of a learned missionary's opposition to Chinese culture in general and Confucianism in particular. He refers to Confucianism as a "peevish conservative sect," which demands of its followers not charity or devotion, but a "neutrality of mind and coldness of heart."[55] His attitude was reflected by another Jesuit writer, S. LeGall, who says of Chu Hsi:

.... Beau diseur autant que philosophe détestable, cet homme est parvenu à imposer, depuis plus de sept siècles, à la masse de ses compatriotes, une explication toute matérialiste des anciens livres.[56]

There were a few exceptions. The Presbyterian James Legge came to China as a missionary, only to become a devoted student of Chinese civilization and its great interpreter for the West. His translation of *The Chinese Classics* (1861–72), in five volumes, remains unsurpassed. During a controversy over the translation of the term for "God" in Chinese, he maintained that Confucianism was "defective rather than antagonistic" to Christianity, and exhorted his fellow missionaries to study the Confucian texts:

> Let no one think any labor too great to make himself familiar with the Confucian books. So shall missionaries in China come fully to understand the work they have to do; and the more they avoid driving their carriages rudely over the Master's grave, the more likely are they soon to see Jesus enthroned in His room in the hearts of the people.[57]

This gave such offense at the missionary conference in Shanghai that his paper was excluded from the printed record. Indeed, the horror of Confucianism shown at that conference "fell little short of madness."[58]

Of the Westerners who visited China in the 1920s, the names of B. Russell and J. Dewey are especially remembered. Russell astonished his Chinese admirers by his positive appreciation of much that he found in the Chinese traditional thought systems, in Taoism, and also in Confucianism. But he pointed out the difficulty posed by the rigidity of the Confucian value system. For example, the insistence on filial piety, and the excessive strength of the Confucian family were barriers to social change and national reconstruction.[59] Dewey made similar observations. His emphasis on logical methodology as well as pragmatism increased the Chinese awareness of the inadequacies of Confucianism.[60] A later visitor and long-time resident in China, Teilhard de Chardin, a Jesuit and a scholar but not a missionary, said little that was specifically critical of Confucianism as such, but much that was depreciative of China and the Chinese as he knew them—without the benefit of knowing the Chinese language. Teilhard went to China originally in 1923 with great hope of discovering an old but vital civilization with a strong mystical tradition. Instead, during about fifteen years, his observations revealed a people whose thought was "static, turned to the past, [and bringing] . . . no contribution to the progress of humanity." He described the Chinese whom he met as pragmatic positivists and agnostics, living in a "milieu enfant . . . ou enfantile . . . ."[61]

A CRITIQUE OF THE CRITIQUES

I have discussed the critiques of Confucianism voiced by ancients and moderns, Chinese and Westerners. In examining them, one finds both concurrences and contradictions. Mohists and Legalists decry government by moral persuasion as a form of weakness, not strength; Mohists and Taoists rejoin in attacking an exaggerated, unnatural ritual observance; Taoists and Legalists express a sense of bemused scorn of the Confucian focus on ethics and virtues. Some of these arguments have been reiterated by modern critics, who exalt a government of laws above that of men, and insist upon the separation of ideology and cult from the state. But, until very recently, the moderns have described Confucius himself variously—for praise *or* blame—as a traditionalist, a reformist or a political revolutionary.

Many of these arguments show a concern for social order and good government. This was shared by all the early critics, although the Taoists and their kindred spirits warned Confucius and his followers against an inopportune seeking of office with would go counter to the natural order and harmony. This same concern was basic to much of the modern critiques of the Confucian legacy, during the time of China's encounter with the West, its social and political institutions as well as the *rationale* behind these.

The pre-modern Western critiques of Confucianism have less to do with society. They were colored by a theological outlook arising out of Christianity and its felt mission to evangelize the world. Longobardi criticized Neo-Confucianism for its seeming incompatibility with Christian beliefs, and Malebranche did similarly while giving philosophical arguments. Their concern was primarily with their own religious doctrine rather than with Confucianism.

The later Western critics join hands with the modern Chinese critiques. Russell and Dewey were concerned about China's social and political future, as were, much more so, their Chinese friends and disciples, Ch'en Tu-hsiu, Hu Shih, Lu Hsün and the others. They criticized especially the social vestiges of Confucianism, which remained an obstacle to intellectual freedom and social transformation. They knew that to survive, China had to modernize, and also Westernize. A certain rupture with the past had become necessary, on the level both of institutions and ideas. The Confucian continuum between ethical self-cultivation and conscientious government is important, even vital. But the study of Confucian Classics could not adequately prepare for a competent and dynamic leadership. The amateur ideal is not enough.[62] This had also been the warning of the ancient Legalists, who had, however, no place for political ethics. Nevertheless, just exactly in what ways Confucianism was and can be helpful or obstructive to modernization is a vast problem, which cannot be exactly dealt with here.[63]

The earlier Marxist critiques of the 1950s show a continuity with the modern critiques of the 1910's–30's, with their dominant social concern. But they also introduce a note of ideology, which is Western and parallel to the religious view of the missionaries. I refer to a Marxist analytical methodology and the presuppositions behind it. This ideological dimension and its class-conscious approach to philosophical cultural evaluation have continued into the 1960's and 70's. But a new factor has entered the picture. The recent anti-Confucius campaign has put an end to real discussion and debate. It is as if the insoluble problems regarding the historical Confucius and his authentic message, the development of centuries of tradition have been set aside, or considered irrelevant. We are presented no longer with arguments, but with foregone conclusions. This unrelenting attack upon Confucianism is all the more problematic because of the political overtones. The direction of the campaign itself has passed into the hands of the Central Committee of the Communist Party, and this in a land where Confucianism had been disestablished officially, and its influence formally excluded from schools and universities for over two decades. It appears that the established authority in today's China has been anxious to ascertain the lasting hold of Chinese Marxist ideology, and so jealously regards every trace of Confucian vestige as a possible threat. It seems also possible that the "ghost" of Confucianism had been resurrected by the authorities themselves *for* the attacks, the spontaneity and genuineness of which are suspect.

True, many Chinese have rightful complaints of an unhappy childhood spent in an authoritarian household or clan family, of student days under the instruction of Confucian teachers who instilled learning by rote, of adult experience in a society where human connections were more important than merit and talent, where an oligarchic government ruled according to human whims rather than laws. But then, are these experiences of Confucianism? Yes and No. In so far as Confucianism did emphasize a hierarchical structure of authority, these are Confucian vestiges. But since Confucianism itself has been much influenced by Legalism throughout the centuries, this is also Legalism, often in its worst form.

The official exaltation of Legalism in place of Confucianism spells clearly an intention to justify a highly centralized and authoritarian government. For this government, the new state orthodoxy is Marx-Lenin-Maoism. This new ideology is still in flux, and has already a history full of dialectical movement, of contradictions. The anti-Confucius campaign itself manifests two such contradictions: a tendency toward political and intellectual anarchism, through the indiscriminate attacks on the principles of authority and of continuity with the past, and another toward a more rigid form of ideological control. The fall of Confucianism as an ethical system is bringing about a total spiritual vacuum. The alternative is to be the new, still evolving Maoist ethic, with its emphasis on serving the people. But the new ethic still lacks complete structuring, and comes to the people, not from below, but from above. The message of Legalism is obvious. Faith in authority, that characteristic so much criticized in Confucianism, is not being assailed in itself. But the final arbiter of conscience has changed. It is now the state.

This sobering analysis has important lessons for the authentic Confucians, who always exalted the inner forum of the human conscience above all state decrees, sometimes by direct appeal to Heaven, or God, as his judge—as would also a Christian. Indeed, the situation in China recalls to the Christian's mind the effects of Legalist insertions into the official teachings of Christianity itself. The legacy of Roman law has been enforced especially by authorities, through their own corrective and penal institutions, to protect the purity of doctrinal orthodoxy. And the result has been, for Christianity, a remoulding of Christian teachings, somewhat as Confucian teachings were also remoulded, by the protective sanctions of Chinese Legalism. Truth frequently had to yield place to ideology, and authentic search and insight to obedience.

Where do's and don't's are concerned, let it be pointed out that the Confucian Golden Rule expresses, in negative language—the language of "Don't"—, the emphasis on human reciprocity which is itself rooted in faith in and respect for man: Do not do unto others what you would not wish them to do unto you (Analects 15:23). It is another way of articulating the great Confucian *do*: *jen*, the virtue which makes a man fully human. And *jen*, according to Confucius himself, is the love *of others* (Analects 12:22). Confucian precepts resemble certain of the Ten Commandments: filial piety, conjugal harmony, and the like. And the Confucian *jen* is the underlying and unifying precept, that which gives meaning to all the others, much as the First Commandment, belief in God, is the basic precept fundamental to the whole Decalogue. Do's and don't's have their place in religious and philosophical systems, rooted, as they are, in a fundamental view of reality and of human life. But do's and don't's cannot make up, all by themselves, a meaningfully integrated system of thought that offers also a way of life defined in terms of the good. In the Chinese context, Legalism represents best a system of mere do's and don't's, sanctioned by state authority, and offering no *rationale* for its precepts besides invoking this authority itself for rewarding and punishing the doers and the transgressors.

In the Chinese past, Confucianism has usually appeared as a school of moderation between certain extremes—retreat from society as advocated by Taoism and Buddhism, and complete immersion in the social and political order according to the tenets of Mohism or Legalism. Indeed, the Chinese opted for Confucianism on account of its moderation. But then, moderation is not enough for Confucianism to remain dominant. It had to compromise, to amalgamate. This was the result of state intervention, which brought in state orthodoxy—of a Confucianism much affected by Legalist norms, and absorbing Mohist and Taoist ideas, as well as Buddhist religious influences.

It is, therefore, extremely difficult, if not impossible, to do justice to a critical evaluation of Confucianism today. It is seldom Confucius and Confucianism which is under discussion. It is frequently the whole of Chinese culture, psychology, and society.

And this can also be said, *mutatis mutandis*, of Korea and Japan. Confucianism is as much a part of their cultures and societies as it is that of China and the Chinese, with like contributions and difficulties. And opposition to Confucianism, in these countries, has also been motivated by the fear of hindrance to social progress and individual liberty. In Japan especially, occasional anti-Confucian sentiments often allied themselves with nativist feelings rebelling against an alien-inspired cultural tradition.

But this does not mean one must give up the attempt at reevaluation. Indeed, the task of reevaluation has been thrust upon those of us who are concerned with the problem of cultural inheritance and transformation. For the challenge of evaluation is basically also a challenge of rediscovery, of returning to the sources of the Confucian inspiration. One may never discover the full dimensions of the historical Confucius and his personal teachings. But one can still see a certain vitality in Confucianism itself, as it is known today. There are positive sides to the family tradition and group solidarity, once the Legalist sanctions have been removed. There is merit in Confucian values, based on the centrality of human dignity, mutual concern, moral responsibilities, and an openness to the transcendent. These values invite us to a new and meaningful study of the Classics, with the help of modern scientific scholarship, of logic and of hermeneutics. This work is necessary, in order to distinguish timeless values from time-bound ones, and the relevant from the obsolete. To survive and to be of use to modern man, Confucianism must become young again, as in the days of its first gestation when it was only "one" of a hundred schools.

The Chinese responds to Confucianism as to part of his own immediate experience. Frequently, he has grown up in a Confucian-oriented clan family, and received an education with Confucian value-overtones. He reacts to Confucianism much as to himself. He is either a Confucian or an anti-Confucian. He is seldom entirely indifferent. His responses are charged with emotion, rather like the attitudes and responses to Christianity manifested by the committed believer, the theologian given to the task of reinterpreting its message, or the militant anti-clerical—and there is yet much of the *suppressed* anti-clerical in many of the self-declared indifferent post-Christians today.

There is indeed a certain identification between Chinese experience and Confucian values, that has survived the political and social upheavals. It is this lingering identification which troubles the new leadership in China, and which also gives the anti-Confucius Campaign such emotional vehemence. But is it possible for a nation to turn its back entirely upon its past—with uncritical attacks and diatribes? Is not a better alternative a rediscovery accompanied by reevaluation—not merely according to the needs of state and society, but also of family and individual, and all in the light of a broader consciousness of other human and ethical values, concurring or otherwise, which are bringing themselves to bear upon the whole human society? In the days when the process of secularization is forcing Christianity to find a new identity and sense of purpose in an atmosphere of religious and intellectual pluralism, could not the Confucian heritage also transform itself, in the face of greater odds?

And so, is Confucianism relevant? If we mean by the word sterile textual studies, a society of hierarchical human relationships excluding reciprocity, the permanent dominance of parents over children, of men over women, a social order interested only in the past and not in the future, then Confucianism is not relevant, and may as well be dead.

But if we also mean by it a dynamic discovery of the worth of the human person, of his possibilities of moral greatness and even sagehood, of his fundamental relationship to others in a human society based on ethical values, of a metaphysics of the self open to the transcendent, then Confucianism is very relevant, and will always be relevant.

And if, going further, we desire for Confucianism an openness to change and transformation, through confrontation with new values and ideas coming from other teachings—such as earlier from Buddhism—through a readiness to evaluate itself critically as well, then Confucianism is not only relevant, but in possession of a future.

True, Confucius has fallen from his pedestal, and Confucianism itself has been divested of its power and status. But the pedestal and the power ill befitted a man who called himself a student and not a sage, and a teaching that emphasized moral persuasion rather than force. And the anti-Confucius movement in China coincided in time with a better knowledge of China and Confucianism in the rest of the world, and indeed, works as a stimulus to greater understanding of a heritage that has become the target of attack in its native land. It is to be hoped that, humbled and made powerless politically, Confucianism will survive and become transformed, not as an ideology but as a spiritual influence, both in China and outside. Perhaps, the destruction of the older synthesis, forced upon it by modern science and socialization, and by the anti-Confucius Campaign, will eventually do the cause a greater good. Confucianism may need to die, in order to live again, as a new synthesis, to serve a new age—an age of pluralism with an increasing recognition of Eastern and Western heritages as heritages of all mankind.

NOTES

1. *Selected Works of Mao Tse-tung* (Peking, 1967), vol. 2, p. 209.
2. Ibid., vol. 3, p. 81.
3. James Legge, tr., *The Chinese Classics* (Oxford: 1893), vol. 1, pp. 290–91, 332–35.
4. See Book of Mencius, 3B9, 7A26, in Legge, tr., *The Chinese Classics*, vol. 2, pp. 282–83, 464–65.
5. Burton Watson, tr., *Mo-tzu: Basic Writings* (New York, 1963), p. 131.
6. Fung Yu-lan, *A History of Chinese Philosophy*, tr. by Derk Bodde (Princeton, 1952), vol. 1, p. 135.
7. Burton Watson, tr., *Han Fei Tzu: Basic Writings* (New York, 1964), p. 121.
8. D. C. Lau, tr., *Lao-tzu: Tao Te Ching* (Baltimore, 1963), p. 75.

9. Burton Watson, tr., *The Complete Works of Chuang-tzu* (New York, 1968), p. 105.
10. Lau, op. cit., p. 59.
11. Watson, tr., *The Complete Works of Chuang-tzu*, p. 114.
12. English translation adapted from Watson, tr., *Han Fei Tzu: Basic Writings*, p. 107.
13. Ibid., p. 125.
14. Ibid., p. 103.
15. H. G. Creel, *Confucius the Man and the Myth* (New York, 1949), p. 218.
16. This statement by Hu Shih is quoted in Creel, ibid., p. 243.
17. Vitalii Rubin, *Ideologija I Kul'tura Drevnego Kitaja* (Moscow, 1970), p. 42. This is given in *Ideology and Culture in Ancient China* (English translation by Steven I. Levine), p. 29 (New York, 1976). See also Creel, op. cit., pp. 242–44.
18. For Chang T'ai-yen and his later evolution—to a position of appreciation of Confucius and the Classics—see Shen P'u's article, "Ts'ung fan-Ju tsun-Fa tao tsun-K'ung tu-ching," *Hsüeh-hsi yü p'i-p'an*, No. 3 (1973), pp. 29–34.
19. Chow Tse-tsung, *The May Fourth Movement* (Cambridge, Mass., 1960), pp. 301–11. See also his article, "The Anti-Confucius Movement in Early Republican China," in A. F. Wright, ed., *The Confucian Persuasion* (Stanford, 1960), pp. 288–312.
20. Chow, *The May Fourth Movement*, p. 311.
21. See the chapter written by Ku himself on the Confucius of the Spring-Autumn Period and the Confucius of the Han Dynasty. It is included in Ku Chieh-kang, ed., *Ku-shih pien* (Peking, 1930–31), vol. 2, p. 262.
22. See Ch'ien's discussions of K'ang Yu-wei's contributions and of the problems of the New Text and Old Text schools, which are included in a new edition of K'ang Yu-wei, *Hsin-hsüeh wei-ching k'ao* (Peking reprint, 1959). See also Liang Ch'i-ch'ao, *Ku-shu chen-wei chi ch'i-nien-tai* (Peking reprint, 1962). This is based on his 1927 lectures.
23. Creel, op. cit., pp. 7–11.
24. For the problems relating to the quest for a historical Jesus, as well as Bultmann's reactions in favor of a "Christ of faith," and subsequent developments, see James M. Robinson, *A New Quest of the Historical Jesus* (Studies in Biblical Theology, First Series, No. 25), (London, 1959). It is of course understood that the word "kerygma" (preaching), when applied to the Confucian teachings, has a different sense from that of the Christian context. Confucius never made the same claims of divine revelation as Jesus Christ did.
25. Maurice Meisner, "Li Ta-chao and the Chinese Communist Treatment of the Materialist Conception of History," in Albert Feuerwerker, ed., *History in Communist China* (Cambridge, Mass., 1968), pp. 280–82, 296.
26. Kuo Mo-jo, *Shih p'i-p'an shu* (Shanghai reprint, 1950), pp. 90–102.
27. A. A. Zhdanov, *On Music, Literature and Philosophy* (London, 1950), pp. 78–80, 106–12. See also J. M. Bochenski, *Soviet Russian Dialectical Materialism* (Dordrecht, 1963), pp. 37–48, 97–103.
28. See Brunhild Staiger, *Das Konfuzius-Bild im kommunistischen China* (Wiesbaden, 1969), pp. 57–91. See also the many of the published contributions to the Symposium on the History of Chinese Philosophy, organized by the Philosophy Department of the University of Peking, 2–26 January 1957. They are

contained in *Chung-kuo che-hsüeh-shih wen-t'i t'ao-lun chuan-chi* (Peking, 1957). See especially the papers by Chu Po-k'un (pp. 29–36), Chang Heng-shou (pp. 146–56), and Ho Lin (pp. 186–95, 196–202).

29.   For this opinion, see Ts'ai Shang-ssu, *Chung-kuo ch'uan-t'ung ssu-hsiang chung p'i-p'an* (Shanghai, 1951), p. 113.

30.   Ibid.

31.   Hou Wai-lu *et al.*, ed., *Chung-kuo ssu-hsiang t'ung-shih* (Peking, 1956–57), vol. 4, pt. 2, pp. 595–691, 875–911, 958–1002, *passim.*

32.   Ibid., vol. 1, pp. 144–60.

33.   Legge, tr., *The Chinese Classics*, vol. 1, p. 250.

34.   On the Shantung meeting, see a report in *Che-hsüeh yen-chiu*, No. 1 (1963), pp. 54–57. For Fung Yu-lan, see his articles on *jen* included in *K'ung-tzu che-hsüeh t'ao-lun chi*, compiled by *Che-hsüeh yen-chiu* (Peking, 1963), pp. 285–302, 470–73.

35.   Chao Chi-pin, "Jen-li chieh-ku," in *K'ung-tzu che-hsüeh t'ao-lun chi*, p. 413.

36.   See Chao's study on the Analects, *Lun-yü hsin-t'an* (Peking, 1962), pp 7–28.

37.   See Yang's contribution to the Shantung meeting, "Lun K'ung-tzu ssu-hsiang," in *K'ung-tzu che-hsüeh t'ao-lun chi*, 373–400.

38.   See his book on the history of Chinese thought, *Chien-ming Chung-kuo che-hsüeh shih* (Peking, 1973), pp. 13–14. The passage referred to is in *Chuang-tzu 38.* Ch'iu was Confucius' personal name.

39.   Ibid., pp. 28–29.

40.   Ibid., pp. 372–89.

41.   See Julia Ching, "Confucius and His Modern Critics, 1916 to Present," in *Papers on Far Eastern History* X (1974), pp. 136–39. For Liu Shao-ch'i's book, see English translation, *How To Be a Good Communist* (Peking, 1964).

42.   Ching, op. cit., pp. 138–39.

43.   See Kuo's article, "Chung-kuo ku-tai shih te fen-ch'i wen-t'i," *Hung-ch'i* No. 7 (1972), pp. 56–62.

44.   Chao's treatise was first published in 1969, and revised for publication in 1973, in Peking and Shanghai. It has gone through many printings, and reached a wide circulation.

45.   See the critical articles written by Yang Jung-kuo and others, and collected in the brochure, *K'ung-tzu: Wan-ku ti wei-hu nu-li chih te ssu-hsiang chia* (Peking, 1973).

46.   This self-criticism appeared first in the Peking University journal, *Peching ta-hsüeh hsüeh-pao* No. 4 (1973), and is given in *P'i -Lin p'i-K'ung wen-chang hui-pien*, a brochure of collections of criticisms against Lin Piao and Confucius, (Peking, 1974), vol. 1, pp. 65–79. See English translation in *Hsinhua Weekly* (Hongkong, 18 March 1974), pp. 12–14.

47.   Ibid.

48.   Donald W. Treadgold, *The West in Russia and China: Religious and Secular Thought in Modern Times*, vol. 2: *China, 1582–1949* (Cambridge, 1973), pp. 32–33; Joseph Needham, *Science and Civilization in China* (Cambridge, 1956), vol. 2, p. 501.

49.   G. W. Leibniz *Zwei Briefe über das binare Zahlensystem und die chines. Philosophie* (Belser-Presse, 1968); Virgile Pinot, *La Chine et la Formation de l'Esprit Philosophique en France 1640–1740*, (Geneva reprint, 1971), pp. 333–40. Father

du Halde speaks also of Confucianism in his *Description geographique, historique chronologique, politique et physique de l'Empire de la Chine* (Paris, 1735).

50. *Entretien d'un Philosophe Chretien et d'un Philosophe Chinois* (1936 ed).
51. Lewis A. Maverick, *China A Model for Europe* (San Antonio, 1946), pp. 26–35, 112.
52. See Maverick's English translation of Quesnay, given in *China A Model for Europe*, pp. 239–48.
53. See *The Philosophy of History*, tr., by J. Sibree (New York, 1956), pp. 111–38.
54. Treadgold, op. cit., pp. 35–36. See also Reginald F. Johnston, *Confucianism and Modern China* (New York, 1935), pp. 134–38.
55. See L. Wieger, *A History of the Religious Beliefs and Philosophical Opinions in China* (Hsien-hsien, 1923), p. 195.
56. S. LeGall, *Chu Hsi: sa Doctrine, son Influence* (Shanghai, 1923), p. 1.
57. This is quoted in Treadgold, op. cit., p. 43.
58. Ibid., pp. 42–44.
59. Bertrand Russell, *The Problem of China* (London, 1922), pp. 40–42.
60. John Dewey, *Lectures in China* (Harvard, 1973), p. 50.
61. Claude Riviére, *En Chine avec Teilhard, 1938–44* (Paris, 1968), p. 133.
62. Joseph R. Levenson, *Confucian China and Its Modern Fate*, vol. 1: *The Problem of Intellectual Continuity* (Berkeley, 1968), pp. 40–43.
63. Important attempts have been made to shed light upon Confucianism as a *modernizing* influence in Tokugawa Japan. See the work of Marius B. Jansen, ed., *Changing Japanese Attitudes Toward Modernization* (Princeton, 1965). Some of the problems raised in that book were discussed at a conference held recently (June 1974) at Honolulu on the subject of Real or Practical Learning in China and Japan. It was sponsored by the American Council of Learned Societies and organized by Prof. W. T. de Bary of Columbia University.

Chapter Three

THE PROBLEM OF MAN

What is humanism? Has Christianity a humanism? Such questions come to the mind of an Asian with some knowledge of Christianity, but without having followed the evolution of Christian theology of the last few decades. It is generally agreed that humanism refers to an attitude, be that embodied in a systematic philosophy, as that of Plato and Aristotle, or in a way of "wisdom" as that of Confucius and Mencius, that man's primary concern is himself, that human nature is perfectible, and that the human mind can attain truth and wisdom. The usual impression is that Christianity concerns itself with Christ and with God—with things divine—and, if it also concerns itself with man, that is with man as God's creature, with man as sinner in need of grace and salvation. And then, in so far as God is said to have come to earth, to have become Man to save man, then only is man important. But usually, for the educated and thoughtful Asian, it would seem rather his own tradition—especially the Confucian tradition—that gives a central importance to man and to being human.[1] For such an Asian, if there is humanism to be found in Western civilization, it is present more in the Greek culture than the Christian, and more in the Neo-Greek Renaissance culture in fifteenth century Italy than in the religious movement of Reformation that followed in its wake, that stirred up such violent emotions in the name of God, and led to the religious wars which ravaged Europe. And today, it would seem to him, Western humanism has mainly two forms: a secular, liberal humanism born in those societies where political democracy and free enterprise make up the so-called formula for modern life, and a secular, Marxist

68

humanism, proclaiming a militant atheism in the name of the new Man of socialist collectivity. Both of these forms trace their origins to the anti-clericalist eighteenth-century Enlightenment; both have flourished with growing secularizing trends. Each has become, in one way or another, a new "religion" for its own adherents: a public, civil religion, emphasizing individualist or collectivist goals for human life.[2]

For the East Asian who is an observer of humanist trends in world society, Christianity would seem to be God-centered where Confucianism is man-centered. In the Christian Scriptures, the chief actor seems to be God, Creator and Redeemer. It is with God and His attributes that Thomas Aquinas begins his theology, before moving on to Creation and man. In our time, the theology of Karl Barth, in its early stages, celebrated God's greatness and man's misery, although in his later life, he asserted more and more the "humanity of God."[3] But, already by then, many others were moving toward man, Dietrich Bonhoeffer, prisoner of the Nazis, spoke of Jesus Christ as "the man for others" and preached a religionless Christianity. Rudolf Bultmann proclaimed that man cannot speak meaningfully *about* God, whose reality transcends human understanding, except by speaking existentially *of* himself.[4] Paul Tillich started his *Systematic Theology* with an examination of human reason, and through an analysis of its cognitive functions, justified the theological quest to probe into the meaning of Revelation. The Second Vatican Council also contributed to this "human" orientation in theology, proclaiming the highest destiny of man and the "godlike seed" which has been sown in him.[5] The transcendental theology of Karl Rahner, a Catholic, and the process theology of S. M. Ogden, a Protestant, are equally committed to an "anthropologically theological" orientation, beginning with man and human self-understanding.[6] Hans Küng's latest book, *Christsein* (1974) does the same, posing a direct question: "Why be a Christian? Why not just be a human being? What does Christian-ity add to human-ity?"—a question to which his whole book ventures an answer. Christian theology has now become a "self-reflective and thematic expression of faith,"[7] finding its original and proper *locus* in man's own mode of existence and in his self-understanding concerning this existence. Revelation and God have not been put aside. But Revelation belongs to the realm of human experience, an experience by man of God's presence, not only in history, but also in his own being, and through his own interaction with the world. Self-knowledge and the knowledge of God have become inseparable.

In this sense, Christianity today can also be called a humanism—proposing a *radical* vision of man, the Christian who is in the world but not *only* of the world, the Christian whose faith in God must be expressed through his love and service of the world, for God, the Christian whose self-understanding is also an understanding of God.

It is my assertion that such contemporary trends in Christian theology point to a movement toward dialogue with the Confucian life view and world-view. Confucianism is deeply rooted in man and in his openness to the transcendent. In speaking of man and his world, it makes certain statements about his ultimate concern, about God or the Transcendent, present in man and in the subjective universe of man's experiences, as these interrelate with the experiences of others.

In this study, it is my aim to do the same: to begin with man, and go on to the problem of his self-transcendence. This is the method of contemporary Christian theology. It has always been the method of Confucian philosophy. And so, after many centuries of separate development, the two have converged in the same direction and with the same affirmation: that the Way of Man and the Way of Heaven meet—in Man.

THE CONFUCIAN MAN

What is man, and wherein lies his worth? This question has been asked probably as long as man has existed—and by himself. For man has always been fascinated with himself, with his limitations as well as his potentiality for greatness. And man has also been fascinated with this question about himself—because it can never be fully answered.

Both the Old and New Testaments represent Man first and foremost as a creature and child of God. His worth lies in his re-

lationship to God, from whom he has received everything. Man
is, because God *is*. And Man can become God-like: *Eritis sicut Deus*,
(Gen. 3:5)—but in the good sense of the words also, since he has
always borne in himself the image and likeness of God (Gen. 1:27,
5:1, 1 John 3:1–3).

Besides, the human being is usually considered by the Scriptures as a "whole person." His "heart" is the seat of understanding, volition, and emotions. He does not "have" a soul and a body;
he *is* soul and body, related to God as Lord of history and partner
of a sacred Covenant, and committed also to other men in family,
tribal and other relationships. Such words as *soma* (Greek, body)
and *pneuma* (Greek, spirit) are employed, even in St. Paul, usually
as signifying each a "part" of man which stands for the *whole*
person (Rom. 12:1, 1 Cor. 6:20, 1 Cor. 2:11, 13:3, 7:4, 7:34),
who, in turn, is a living "I," and not a metaphysical principle.

But there are also dualistic overtones in the concept of man,
especially in certain passages of St. Paul, where the notion of sin
introduces a note of tension in the human being (Rom. 7:15–25,
8:10–13).[8] These passages point to some important differences
between the Christian concept of man and the Confucian. For
whereas man's propensity for evil as well as for good has never
been denied in Confucianism, the dualism that such implies has
also been minimized in a tradition preoccupied with man's natural perfectibility.

The Confucian Classics do not deny Man's creatureship or
sonship in relation to God. On the contrary, there are several
explicit references.[9] But the Confucian Classics make this affirmation, not by appeal to creation myths, but by emphasizing the
common human nature which all have received from Heaven.
This is inherent in the very term for "human nature," the Chinese
word *hsing* (性), a compound including the term for mind or heart
(*hsin*; 心), and life or offspring (*sheng*; 生). Philological scholarship
demonstrates the association between its etymology and early religious worship. Man is he—or she—who has received the gift of life
and all the innate endowments of human nature from Heaven.[10]

Man acquires self-knowledge by differentiating himself from
other animals, and by identifying himself with other humans.
Like all animals, it is "the nature of Man that when he is hungry

he will desire satisfaction, when he is cold he will desire warmth, and when he is weary he will desire rest."[11] These are the words of Hsün-tzu (fl. 298–238 B.C.), who adds that man is born *evil*, but is able to act *against* his natural inclinations. For, unlike other animals, Man has a unique ability for social and moral behavior: "Fire and water possess energy but are without life. Grass and trees have life but no intelligence. Birds and beasts have intelligence but no sense of duty. Therefore [Man] is the noblest being on earth."[12] To be "human," after all, is to be able to acquire the perfect virtue of benevolence, of "humanness" (*jen*). As the Doctrine of the Mean puts it, "The meaning of *jen* (virtue) is humanness."[13]

The Confucian focus on a common human nature has led to another emphasis: the *natural equality* of all men. For Christians, this doctrine would flow more directly from mankind's common origin as creatures and children of God. For Confucians, the importance is placed in a common, moral nature, and an ability to discern good from evil, which is rooted in a common mind or heart. Indeed, this natural equality exists in spite of social hierarchy, and even in spite of any distinction between the "civilized" —the Chinese—and the "barbarians."[14] Confucius has said: "Within the Four Seas all men are brothers" (Analects 12:5). And Mencius (371–289 B.C.?) has added, that every human being can become a sage-king (6B:2). If certain Chinese terms for "barbarians" often possess "dog" or "reptile" radicals, suggesting a human contempt for the "subhuman," there never was any doubt that the "barbarian" could become fully human by acculturation. After all, even certain sage-kings are considered to have had "barbarian" origins.[15]

In this chapter, I wish to bring out two problems for special discussion. The first is the problem of evil, and the second, that of sagehood. They are, indeed, inherently related. Man's ability to do evil seems to run counter to his ability to transcend himself and become a sage. And the very preoccupation with human nature and human destiny reveals the dimension of transcendence which has always been present in Confucianism, and which throws light upon its similarities and differences with Christianity.

The Problem of Evil[16]

The problem of evil offers good occasion for dialogue between Christianity and Confucianism. Traditional Confucian thought, going back to Mencius, usually upheld the basic goodness of human nature, explaining evil as a deflection from the good, a perversion of the natural. This was accepted by Matteo Ricci, who declared in his famous Catechism that human nature is essentially good although it is capable of both good and evil, the latter arising on account of the presence of concupiscence.[17] But later catechisms emphasized the evil inclinations of man stemming from original sin in such a way that the impression arose that while Mencius taught the essential goodness of man, Christiantity asserts the contrary. It is with this in mind that I shall discuss the problem of evil.

Let it be said first that "evil," as discussed here, refers less to ontological imperfections in the universe—"inequality" in things—or even to the evils connected with human suffering, which come in the train of sickness, old age and death, than to the problem of evil in the human heart: moral perversion in its individual or collective manifestations, which bring about so much suffering and havoc, usually to the innocent. In this reference, the Christian term for evil is sin (Greek: *amartia*), interpreted since the time of Augustine (A.D. 354–430) as referring to both original sin—human solidarity in fallibility—and to personal sin—that for which each person is individually responsible, a doctrine that presumed the presence of human freedom. The Confucian case is more ambiguous. The Chinese word *tsui* (罪) has also a double significance—but of *crime* as well as of sin. The resultant ambiguity has led some people to the incorrect assertion that the Chinese had no guilt-oriented morality, with its internalization of the consciousness of moral evil, but only a shame-oriented one, which is external and superficial, being based on mere human respect.[18]

In his famous book—The Cultures and Philosophies of East and West—Liang Su-ming differentiates between European culture, with its early predominance of religion, later supplanted by the rise of rationalism and science, both now holding sway; the

Indian culture, which has always been and still is preoccupied with religion or other-worldliness; and the contrasting example of Chinese culture, with its central interest in man and in the harmonious relation between man and nature, to the near exclusion of God-talk.[19] This characteristic Chinese attitude is also reflected in its theory of good and evil. Instead of ascribing evil to a super-human principle, or of relegating it to a basically unreal phenomenal world, the Chinese Confucian theory of evil is inseparable from its theory of human nature. Evil exists; it is either inherent in human nature, or the product of contact between an originally good nature and its wicked environment. We know these to be the teachings of Hsün-tzu and of Mencius, respectively. They began the Great Debate in Chinese philosophy, on a topic where East meets West, since the subject contains metaphysical as well as ethical and psychological implications.

According to Christian teachings, the chief characteristic of sin is the *revolt* it entails—a revolt against God and his commandments, as well as a transgression of one's own conscience.[20] This brings to light the *doubly personal* nature of sin, as alienation from God as well as self. Man, as it were, declares war on God by sin— mythically, in the persons of Adam and Eve, and existentially, by every conscious and deliberate offense he has personally committed. Sin denotes a state of opposition, of Man against God, and of Man against his own conscience. And this is possible because of the fundamental dualism present in Man, attracted at the same time to good and evil: "For I do not do the good I want, but the evil I do not want is what I do" (Rom. 7:20).

Has there been a similar sense of revolt in the Confucian consciousness? Yes. The Confucian Classics provide references of sage-kings praying to God for forgiveness of their personal offenses, frequently attributing to themselves the sins of the people under their government. King T'ang, the founder of the Shang dynasty (1766 B.C.?), allegedly said: "If, in my person, I commit offenses, they are not to be attributed to you, (the people) of the myriad regions. If you in the myriad regions commit offenses, these must rest on my person." (Analects 20:3) The Book of Documents is even more explicit about the king's mind:

The good in you (the people), I will not dare to conceal; and for the evil in me, I will not dare to forgive myself; I will examine these things in harmony with the mind of the Lord-on-High. When guilt is found anywhere in you who occupy the myriad regions, it must rest on me. When guilt is found in me, *the one man*, it will not attach to you who occupy the myriad regions.[21]

According to other texts, King T'ang cut his hair and fingers in a sacrifice of propitiation to the Lord-on-High, begging for forgiveness of his sins, and for relief of a drought which he attributed to his sins.[22]

However, Confucian philosophy is to develop, not a theory of sin as offense against God, but a theory of moral evil and its relationship to human nature. This arose after the age of the sage-kings, after the time of Confucius himself. It is to offer some occasion for comparison with Christian teachings on man's inclinations to sin and evil. Of course, in both East and West, the debate was not over human nature as such, but its several "states"—hypothetical or experienced. Take, for example, the myth of the Fall of Man and the theology of sin which has arisen from it. They imply that human nature has had "three moments:" "integral" nature, as it was in Adam before the Fall, "fallen" nature, the result of Adam's unhappy legacy, and "redeemed" nature, as renewed by grace in Christ. For both Mencius and Hsün-tzu, these consituted "original" human nature: man as he is born; and its "existential" state: man as he finds himself in society and culture. Here, according to Mencius, man is by nature good, and evil comes with the formation of bad habits (2A: 6, 6A:1–7), but, according to Hsün-tzu, man is by nature evil, and it is only by dint of going against his original nature, as well as through the influence of education, that man becomes good.[23]

In Confucian China, Mencius' theory was to win the upper hand, although the victory came late—some time after the ninth century with the rise of Neo-Confucianism. Here, it may be said that East and West concur in accepting an "originally good" human nature, with the difference that Mencius saw this in the infant yet untouched by social culture while Christians attribute it to Adam before the Fall. Today, in Communist China, Mencius' theory has again been challenged by writers who favor the ideas of Hsün-tzu. They emphasize the importance of correct education and of the restraining influence of laws on human nature. In some ways, this would place more focus on an inherent sense of *dualism* in man—a characteristic more of Western thought than of Eastern.

In discussing "the theological concept of *concupiscentia*" Karl Rahner points out the essentially "natural" character of *concupiscentia* as something immediately given with human nature, even in its "pure" state. Speaking in existentialist terms of the human person as "man in so far as he freely disposes of himself by his decision," and of human nature as "all that in man which must be given prior to this disposal," he describes "theological" *concupiscentia* as a tension or dualism between "person" and "nature:"

> There is much in man which always remains in concrete fact somehow impersonal, impenetrable and unilluminated for his existential decision; merely endured and not freely acted out. It is this *dualism* between person and nature ... that we call concupiscence in the theological sense. While it does ... find its concrete experiential expression in a dualism of spirituality and sensibility, it is not identical with the latter.[24]

This *concupiscentia* cannot be qualified as "morally evil," since it precedes the free decision. Rahner, however, is aware that, in Rom. 6–8, "concupiscence" has been termed "sin." He reasons, therefore, that it can be called "evil" in one sense: in so far as it is only present in man in its concrete form, in virtue of "the Fall of the first Man," as an *experienced* contradiction in man himself, admittedly so according to Paul, Augustine, the great Scholastics, the Reformers and Pascal. In this case, it is the "concupiscence" not of "pure nature" but of "fallen nature." He also makes a distinction between the "integrity" of Adam in Paradise, and the recovered "innocence" of the perfect Christian:

> In Adam the person's freedom . . . made it possible for him

exhaustively to engage his nature both in a good and in an evil direction. The freedom of . . . the (Christian) saint is the freedom of a man who has succeeded in surrendering his whole being . . . to God totally.[25]

As is well known, after the time of Mencius and Hsün-tzu, Confucian scholars tried to harmonize their teachings, by saying that while human nature possesses the beginnings of virtue, it is not really completely good, and awaits the transforming influence of education. One attempt was to correlate the *yin-yang* theory with Confucian ethics, paralleling human nature with *yang*, the active cosmic principle, and emotions with *yin*, the passive cosmic principle, and making nature the source of goodness and emotions the occasion for evil.[26] This categorization seems arbitrary. But moralists have seldom been sympathetic to emotions as such. Thomas Aquinas, who describes the passions as amoral, tends also to regard them with disfavor.[27]

A philosophical theory of man and of the problem of moral evil came to fore especially with the rise of Neo-Confucianism. This later development in Confucianism forged partly-Buddhist weapons to fight Buddhist predominance and Buddhist neglect of man's social duties. It was mainly in ethics that the claim of a return to Confucius and Mencius was justified. And the new explanation of evil was strongly colored by the new concern with metaphysics.

In this new metaphysics, man represents the summit of the universe, participating in the excellence of the Great Ultimate (*T'ai-chi;* 太極), source and principle of all things, and possessing the nature which comes to him through the interactions of *yin* and *yang* and the Five Elements. Human nature is originally good, or "sincere." Contact with external things provides the occasion for evil, as a deflection from the good rather than a positive presence. This is so because of the two sides of human nature: the heavenly, "essential" nature which is good, and the physical "existential" nature which may be good or bad, depending upon the quality of the *ch'i* (気; vital force, material principle?) with which it is endowed.[28] Just exactly where "essential" nature comes in, and what is precisely meant by the word *ch'i*—the gathering of which gives rise to all things, including man—remains debatable. But the

distinction between "essential" and "existential" nature marks
an important step forward in Chinese philosophical anthropology. It also renders obsolete the earlier, unreal distinction between
human nature as it is at birth and as it is later, since it is impossible to judge of the goodness or evil of an infant's nature. The
oft quoted parable of a man's spontaneous reaction at the sight of
a child's falling into a well—given in the Book of Mencius—can
only be an example of the natural reaction of a *cultured* human
being, and not of raw human nature. In this respect, Paul Tillich's interpretation of the primordial Fall comes closest to the as-
sumptions of this Confucian distinction between "basic" or essential nature and the existential state in which it is found. Tillich
rejects the literal interpretation of the Paradise story and describes
"actualized" creation" and "estranged existence" as identical.
The state of sin represents the transition from "essence" to "existence:"

> . . . everything [God] created participates in the transition
> from essence to existence. He creates the newborn child;
> but, if created, it falls into the state of existential estrange-
> ment . . . [and], upon growing into maturity, affirms the
> state of estrangement in acts of freedom which imply respon-
> sibility and guilt. Creation is good in its essential character.
> If actualized, it falls into universal estrangement through free-
> dom and destiny.[29]

But the neo-Confucian philosophers did not attempt to explain
why one man may receive a pure endowment, and another, a
turbid one. This is just taken for granted. The distinction, after
all, is an ontological, not a moral one. Morality enters the picture
only when human nature moves from stillness to activity, when
emotions have been aroused or stirred: in philosophical language,
when free volitional acts have been posited. Granted this understanding, a contemporary explanation of dualism in man as the
occasion for evil is perfectly consonant with the Confucian views:

> To say that man is fallible is to say that the limitation peculiar
> to a being who does not coincide with himself is the primordial
> weakness from which evil arises.[30]

It is interesting to note here that the Jewish philosopher and theologian, Martin Buber, has commented upon the Chinese "nostalgia" for the "original man," which he considers to be a notion alien to Western mentality. According to him:

> This [Chinese] trust in the primal being is missing in the Western man and cannot be acquired by him. Even Christianity was not able to alter this situation, although it did, in fact, transmit to the West the Oriental teaching of the paradisiacal primal state of mankind. Of the biblical story of the first man, only the Fall is present in a living way in the reality of the personal life of the Western Christian man, not the life before the Fall.[31]

Buber regards the Chinese beliefs as somehow excessively supernatural (!) as compared to the Western consciousness which is aware only of the fallen state, a state of dualism and division.

The Problem of Self-transcendence: Sagehood

The problem of evil is all the more important on account of the problem of self-transcendence. Recognition of moral evil and human fallibility is prerequisite to any desire and resolution to transcend oneself. Human nature is both the *given* and the *yet to become*—that which we can shape, within the limitations of our historical situation.

For the Christian, self-transcendence means essentially becoming God-like, or "holy" (*hagios*)—a Greek word with cultic as well as ethical significance. The "holy," of course, refers especially to God. In the Old Testament, he is the Holy One of Israel, in his transcendent Otherness, revealing himself to the prophet Isaias in the liturgical setting of the Temple (Isa. 10:20). In the New Testament, Jesus Christ appears as the Holy Servant of God (Rev. 4:27–30), who sanctifies himself in order that his own followers may also be sanctified (John 17:19). The Christian regards Jesus Christ especially as a model, for personal imitation. Christian life has always referred to the following of Christ.[32]

The Chinese equivalent to the English word holiness is *sheng*, sage-liness. It does not contain a cultic meaning as does the Greek. It occurs in the Book of Documents,[33] in a description of the legendary Shun, an ancient sage-king, wise minister, ruler, and filial son. There, the quality ascribed to him is especially that of the natural (*tzu-jan;* 自然). Shun is especially he, whose virtue proceeds from "the natural." Another and more frequent attribute is that of "penetration" (*t'ung*). According especially to the Han dictionary, *Shuo-wen chieh-tzu* (ca. A.D. 100),[34] a sage is a man who possesses a penetrating intelligence regarding all affairs. This is echoed in the other Han work, *Po-hu-t'ung* (ca. A.D. 80) which describes him as "possessing a Way which penetrates everywhere, a brilliance which radiates everywhere," and as one who "is in union with Heaven and Earth in his virtue, with the sun and moon in his brilliance, with the four seasons in his regularity, and with ghosts and spirits in his [gift] of divining fortunes and misfortunes."[35] The ritual texts confirm this concept of "penetration." Tai the Elder defines the sage as a man "whose wisdom penetrates the great Way, who responds to [endless] changes without becoming exhausted and who perceives the inner essences of the myriad things."[36] To this, the canonical Book of Rites adds the idea of giving life. The sage is thus presented as he "who gives birth to the myriad things."[37]

And what about the great sages themselves? What did Confucius say about sagehood? What did Mencius say after him?

In the Confucian Analects, we find little talk of the attributes of sagehood. We find, indeed, a certain reluctance to discuss this question. Confucius did not consider himself worthy to be called a sage. He was content in being a transmitter of the sagely Way. And this Way belonged to three kinds of sages: kings, ministers or hermits—that is, men who chose retirement for noble reasons, *not* for escape from social responsibilities. And Confucius referred to himself as their admirer and follower. He was a "student," a man who desired sagehood, and made efforts to achieve it.[38]

Confucius' high regard for sagehood is expressed more by his silence than by his words. His modesty is partly motivated by his high esteem of this state. As he put it, "I do not expect ever to see a sage, and shall be content with seeing a gentleman (*chün-tzu*). I do not expect ever to see a good man (*shan-jen;* 善人), and shall be content with seeing a persevering man."³⁹ He therefore leaves the floor open for future debates regarding whether sagehood is a state into which one is born, or whether it is attainable by human effort and learning.

The word *sheng* (聖) occurs more frequently in the Book of Mencius. Here, sages appear as men who manifest perfectly the virtues which govern human relationships, and Mencius gives, like Confucius before him, such examples as those of the former kings Yao and Shun, the ancient ministers, the Duke of Chou and others, and the hermits, Po-yi and Liu-hsia Hui, who exemplified political loyalty even in retirement.⁴⁰ For Mencius, the sage is a teacher, if not by word, then certainly by example. But where an ordinary man exerts his influence through education over a limited circle of persons, the sage is a "teacher of a hundred generations."⁴¹ He adds to this a polemical orientation: the sage is a man who combats false teachings, like those of Yang Chu and Mo Ti. In this respect, he also declares his own determination: " I also desire to rectify men's hearts, stop perverse teachings, oppose one-sided actions and banish licentious actions."⁴² And then, in a passage describing directly the meaning of *sagehood* itself, Mencius proposes it as the common object of men's hearts. For just as "men's mouths accord in enjoying the same delicacies, men's ears accord in taking pleasure in the same sounds, and men's eyes accord in delighting in the same beauty," so too, their hearts find rest in a common object, that which they all approve of: the moral principles of human nature, "which the sages, before us, also apprehended."⁴³

Where Confucius declined to call himself a sage, later generations did not share the same scruple. They were particularly quick in recognizing *him* as a sage, and even as *the* sage par excellence. This is hinted at in the Doctrine of the Mean, which describes him as a man who traces himself back to Yao and Shun as his "[spiritual] ancestors," and who models his life upon those of the Kings Wen and Wu:

He harmonizes above with the heavenly seasons, and below with [the elements of] water and land. He may be compared

to Heaven and Earth which contain and support . . . all
things, to the four seasons in their cyclical progress, and to
the sun and moon in their alternating task of giving light.[44]

It is the same metaphysical language of the *Po-hu-t'ung* and of the
Great Appendix to the Book of Changes.

The Confucian doctrine of sagehood, and the agreement of
Mencius and Hsün-tzu regarding man's ability to transcend himself—whether through an innate gift or through the malleable influence of education—did not thereby make sages more abundant.
Later thinkers also purported to see passages in the Classics sus-
ceptible to a different interpretation. Are sages born, or made? If
they are born, are they not *superhuman*? Would they have "emotions?"[45] If they are made—*self-made*—why are they so few? Why
did they only exist in the remote or historical antiquity? These
questions preoccupied many thinkers, some of whom preferred to
exalt the concept of sagehood into a Neo-Taoist impersonal ideal,
inaccessible to human realization. Such discussions ran parallel
to Buddhist debates regarding the universal presence and ac-
cessibility of Buddhahood.[46] Theories of "human predestination"
generally prevailed in the more aristocratic ages, in a hierarchically organized society, as during the Wei-Chin periods (A.D.
220–420), when a "grade theory" of human nature corresponded
with the practice of civil recruitment through a "nine-grade rank-
ing system" which gave preferment to scions of important families.[47] The Buddhist reaction came especially in the assertions of
Tao-sheng (d. 434) of the presence of Buddhahood in all sentient
beings, and the possibility of acquiring "Sudden Enlightenment."[48] The Neo-Confucian movement, associated first with Han
Yü (768–824) and then with Ch'eng Yi (1033–1108) and Chu Hsi
(1130–1200), also announced itself in favor of the universal possibility of sagehood—in the name of a return to Confucius and
Mencius.

However, to affirm that man possesses naturally a desire to transcend himself, and that this desire is possible of fulfilment, is not
enough. One still has to show the *way* by which such fulfilment is
to be realized. For without *praxis*, there is no assurance that theory
can be tested, and without testing, theory remains empty—a pow-

erless wish, or rather, a wish capable of destroying the person, through frustration, but incapable of its own fulfilment.

Of course, the best proof of the possibility of such self-transcendence is the example of those who have succeeded in its *praxis*. Buddhism could point to its Buddhas and *bodhisattvas*, Confucianism to its legendary and historical sages, and Christianity to its saints and holy men and women. Now the Christian *holy* man par excellence is Jesus Christ, while the Confucian sage par excellence is Confucius—according to the judgment of generations of disciples and admirers. Each was a historical figure. Each served as a kind of model for immediate followers and later admirers—Jesus Christ more consciously so than Confucius.

I will now discuss this question of models—and of personal emulation of models, whether by the following of Christ or the imitation of sages. After this I will examine the more specifically ethical questions of the Confucian conscience and the Confucian community, especially by presenting a picture of the two models— of Jesus Christ and Confucius.

A Question of Models

I am the Way, the Truth, and the Life. (John 14: 6)
At fifteen, I set my mind on learning.
At thirty, I stood firm.
At forty, I had no doubts.
At fifty, I knew the decrees of Heaven.
At sixty, my ears responded with docility [to the truth].
At seventy, I could follow the desires of my heart, without transgressing what is right. (Analects 2:4)

Jesus Christ and Confucius. Each has served as model for centuries, one in the West and the other in the East. Have they both been conscious of the *normative* character of their lives? What did each require specifically of his followers; and what has become of their instructions, during the time that followed their deaths? What lessons can one still draw today?

Jesus Christ is spoken of today especially as a Man "for others."[49] For he lived, taught and suffered for the salvation of others—as its "Efficient Cause." Besides, his life, teachings and sufferings serve also as a model for imitation—an "Exemplary Cause" of both salvation and sanctification. As the Gospels tell us, Jesus Christ drew to himself a band of followers (Matt. 4:19, Mark 2:14, Luke 5:11, John 1:43). Already, their attachment to him required sacrifices—in the case of the first apostles, of their ships and possessions, and their former calling as fishermen. Jesus also declared to the rich young man, who expressed a desire to follow him, to go and sell all he had, give to the poor, and then return to follow him (Matt. 19:21). To another man, also a would-be follower, he even forebade going home to say farewell or bury his father (Luke 9:59–62), such was the urgency of the following of him! He also demanded self-denial and the carrying of the Cross of his followers (Matt. 10:38, 16:24). In the Gospel of St. John (10:4–5), the following of Christ is described in terms of sheep following the Good Shepherd. And the Book of Revelation (14:4) presents the vision of "virgins" following the Lamb wherever he goes.

Jesus has not given anywhere in the Gospels a systematic exposition of what he requires of his followers. In the Sermon on the Mount (compare Matt. 5–7 and Luke 6:20–49), he presents a generalized picture of the meaning of discipleship. Beginning with the Beatitudes, and promising the Kingdom to the poor and the suffering, he exhorts perfection to his followers: "Be perfect as your heavenly Father is perfect" (Matt. 5:48).[50]

And what is the meaning of this perfection? While Jesus practised moderation, enjoying the good things of this world, he would conclude his life on the Cross: "Greater love no man has than this, that a man lay down his life for his friends" (John 15:13).

Confucius preferred virtue to riches and honors, refusing to sacrifice his principles for the sake of personal advancement, and seeking personal advancement only for the sake of realizing his principles in social and political life. Conscious of a religious mission coming to him from Heaven to save the moral and social order, he led a life which pointed to the beyond in the practice of *jen*, the universal virtue, and in imitation of ancient sages. He was a good teacher, preaching for the healing of the *whole* man. His life and teachings had religious effects. But he did not consider himself a religious savior as did Jesus. He did not lay down his life for the sake of reconciling his brethren with God.

Confucius was capable of certain excesses. The elegant music of Ch'i so delighted him, that he forgot the taste of meat during three months.[51] But he was usually a man of moderation. Like Jesus, he enjoyed the good things of this world, eating well-prepared dishes and drinking good wines. Like Jesus too, he preached reciprocity in human relationships—and reciprocity is based on balance, on a sense of proportions, especially when stated in negative terms: "What you do not wish others to do unto you, do not do unto them" (Analects 15:23).

Confucius made no radical demands of himself or his disciples, as did Jesus. He did not regard as condition for discipleship the renunciation of family life and worldly goods, or the "carrying of the Cross"—even if those few who followed him in his preregrinations had scant time left for their wives and families.

True, Confucius expressed approval of the man of "mad ardor"—of the person who "advances to seek the truth," driven as though by a restless energy, without considering the consequences. He preferred such to the "cautious" man, to him who merely "desists from doing wrong."[52] But he did not regard madness or eccentricity as perfection. His ideal remained a person who acts according to the Mean.

And so, between Jesus and Confucius, there are differences as well as similarities. Jesus declared himself the Way, the Truth and the Life. Confucius never made such claims. The words of the Analects, quoted above, offer his self-revelation—a disclosure of his personal evolution, with its rhythm of gradual growth, as well as of certain moments of sudden self-discovery. Confucius was a humble man. While he proposed ideals of high moral perfection to his disciples—as did Jesus Christ—he never set himself up as a conscious model for their imitation. He pointed rather to the ancient sage kings and ministers—his own exemplars—and to Heaven, whose silent ways are revelatory lessons for those with pure hearts and sincere intentions. "How dare I rank myself with sages and men of perfect virtue?" Said he of himself. "I prefer to say of myself, that I strive without cease [for perfection], and teach others without weariness" (Analects 7:33).

But then, what is sagehood, if not this perseverent striving—as his disciples recognized at once? For them, as for later generations, the Master *was* a model. And so the reply came just as quickly: "This [striving] is just what we, your disciples, have been unable to learn from you" (Analects 7:33).

The Doctrine of Martyrdom

Understandably, Jesus' teachings have given cause for seeing the following of Christ in terms of a total commitment of one's life, which could demand suffering and death as it did of the martyrs, the earliest witnesses to Christ. But this is not a necessary conclusion from reading the Gospels. Strictly speaking, the word "martyrdom" (Greek: μαρτνς, giving testimony)—refers in the New Testament to the witness of words by preaching rather than to that of being killed for the faith. It came to acquire a special meaning of suffering and dying for the faith somewhat later, since such a free gift of one's life offers a strong witness to the person's belief in the reality of Jesus' promises, while also reflecting his sacrificial death. Early Christian expectations of a prompt Second Coming of Christ have also encouraged certain aspirations to martyrdom, by negating the importance of this life. An early martyr, Ignatius of Antioch, expresses these sentiments while preparing for his turn:

> It is better for me to die for Christ Jesus than to reign over the extremities of this earth. Him I search, who has died for us; him I want, who is risen for us. It is my birth which is approaching . . . Let me receive the pure light. When I am there, I shall be a man.[53]

As the age of persecutions passed, martyrdom became a rarer occurrence. The doctrine of martyrdom yielded place to that of eremitical and monastic life, which received by extension the character of martyrdom. It was especially in monastic life that "asceticism," or a teaching of spiritual perfection, developed. The word "ascesis" (Greek: *askeo*) itself suggests the need of exercise, of making efforts, exerting oneself and struggling against one's own evil tendencies. The Christian striving for perfection is somehow at war with himself. There is an implicit dualism: he must conquer himself in order to win himself over to God.[54]

A good illustration of this inner struggle of self against self is given in Dietrich Bonhoeffer's poem "Who am I?" A political prisoner, he knew that he appeared calm and composed to others, a giant before men, so to speak, but also that he was but a child before God, aware of a conflict going on within himself. As he expressed it:

> Who am I? This or the Other?
> Am I one person today and tomorrow another?
> Am I both at once? A hypocrite before others,
> and before myself a contemptible woe-begone weakling?
> Or is something within me still like a beaten army fleeing in
> disorder from victory already achieved?
> Who am I? They mock me, these lonely questions of mine,
> Whoever I am, Thou knowest, O God, I am thine![55]

Has Confucianism a doctrine of martyrdom? Yes. In Analects 15:8, Confucius is quoted as saying: "The determined scholar and the man of virtue will not seek to live at the expense of injuring their *jen* (仁; virtue). They will even sacrifice their lives to preserve their *jen* complete." And Mencius has said: "I like life, and I also like righteousness. If I cannot keep the two together, I will let life go and choose righteousness."[56] Chinese history has witnessed many persons who preferred death to going against their conscience. The patriot Wen T'ien-hsiang, who died at the hands of the Mongol invaders (1282), carried on him the lines that said: "Confucius spoke of preserving *jen*; Mencius spoke of choosing *yi* (義). From now (death) on, I may be without shame."[57]

Confucian teachings encourage the pursuit of virtue and the imitation of the sages—many of whom had suffered privations and death as a result of their moral convictions. But Confucian teachings do not promote a *desire* for martyrdom as such, because they do not have a developed eschatology. Both Confucius and his disciples participated in ancestral cults and in other religious rituals, showing an implicit belief in an afterlife. They did not share in the early Christians' anticipation for the *parousia*. Confucians preferred to pursue sagehood in this life, without preoccupying themselves with the next, and without withdrawing from social activities and responsibilities. For this reason, Confucianism never developed a monastic life, and fought *against* Buddhist monasticism as a negation of human values, and a manifestation of selfishness. According to Confucian teachings, self-cultivation is not so much an end in itself, as it is a basis for service of others—in the family, the country and the world. The Confucian is a man *for others*, even in his pursuit of sagehood.

Without a monastic life, did Confucianism develop an ascetic and mystical tradition, with a doctrine of self-conquest, of prayer and penance? The answer is once more, Yes. In response to his favorite disciple, Yen Yüan's question about *jen*, Confucius had replied, "To subdue one's self and return to propriety is perfect virtue (*jen*)" and then went on to enumerate the "steps" involved in this ascesis: "Look not at what is contrary to propriety; listen not to what is contrary to propriety; speak not what is contrary to propriety; make no movement which is contrary to propriety" (Analects 12:1).

This answer hardly gives what can be called "steps"—a systematic introduction to self-conquest and self-perfection. But it is an explicit statement of the need of exercise and struggle in the pursuit of perfect virtue or sageliness. It is a doctrine which later Confucians, especially in the Sung dynasty, took seriously—sometimes too seriously, as Confucianism came to acquire a mistaken reputation of being merely a practical morality of prescriptions and proscriptions.

Do Confucians, like Christians, have a strong sense of the dualism of man, of a self-alienation which needs to be overcome?

No, the Confucian position is less "dualistic" than the Christian one. Although Hsün-tzu taught the doctrine of human nature being originally evil, he affirmed its perfectibility through education—as did also his later followers. With the gradual ascendancy and dominance of Mencius' ideas of man being originally good, the Confucian school developed increasingly a view of man and the universe which was one of harmony rather than conflict. On the one side, self-exertion (*kung-fu;* 工夫) is recommended; on the other, it is assumed that the goal of sagehood is situated at the end of a process of self-cultivation, and not a prize to be won at the cost of intense struggle against self. The great Confucians, especially Wang Yang-ming, taught that man possesses the seed of sagehood within his own nature, and need only awaken to its reality to become a sage.[58]

Of course, Confucians had experienced inner conflicts. Throughout the centuries, in some ways perhaps more today than ever before, people have been torn asunder by a conflict of duties and responsibilities. Can one always be at the same time a filial child and a patriotic citizen? Must one neglect one's parents in the service of the country? Should one report one's parents misdeeds and crimes to state authority?[59] And, is a wife's obligations to her parents or country stronger than those to her husband and spouse? These are some of the many problems which have beset the Confucian conscience.

And what is the meaning of the Confucian conscience? Is it a faculty which discerns good from evil, or is it also something more? Is it concerned more with knowing than with willing? Is evil more the result of ignorance rather than of moral weakness? These are some of the questions which now await examination.

THE CONFUCIAN CONSCIENCE

The word "conscience" (Latin: *conscientia*; Greek: *syneidesis*) refers, according to the Stoics, to knowledge about the good and one's relationship to the good. Ovid calls it "deus in nobis" and Seneca, the indwelling holy spirit, observer of our good and bad deeds. In the Book of Wisdom (17:10 ff), *syneidesis* is given a pejorative meaning, as the "bad" conscience, while the good conscience is the spirit, the soul, the heart, which admonishes man within himself, crying out to God, who alone searches the heart and the reins. In the New Testament, the word receives once more a positive meaning, especially when it is ennobled by faith in Christ. It is spoken of as a spiritual disposition, a power to act as well as the act itself.[60]

Confucian teaching has always acknowledged man's possession of an inner faculty of moral discernment—his conscience.[61] Mencius says that the sense of right and wrong is common to all men (2A:6). It is, indeed, that which distinguishes the human being from the beast, that which assures a natural equality to all human beings. Mencius also speaks of a knowledge of the good (*liang-chih；* 良知) and an ability to do good (*liang-neng；* 良能) that man has without need of learning (7A:15). The philosopher, Wang Yang-ming (1472–

1529) made of this the basis of his entire philosophy—metaphysics as well as ethics. Yang-ming speaks of *liang-chih* as an ability to discern between good and evil—as well as the application of such discernment to particular situations, in view of practical behavior. It refers, however, not merely to man's moral sense and intuition, but also to the *ground* of the moral faculty itself, and of human existence.[62]

The difference between the Confucian teaching of conscience and the Christian lies especially in the Christian's emphasis on God, the giver of moral law and the judge of human conscience. Confucian teaching implies that conscience is a gift. It is that which comes with life. But Confucian philosophy does not dwell on God's role as supreme lawgiver and judge. It prefers to analyze the meanings of conscience itself.

It is interesting to note here the greater resemblance between Confucian teaching and the traditional Catholic doctrine of a *natural moral law*—that which is based on human nature itself, the law written in men's hearts.[63] Usually specialists of comparative law have a negative opinion.[64] They point to the Confucian *disparagement* of positive law (*fa;* 法) as evidence that it has only a penal character. Certainly, the Confucian tradition places much more emphasis upon the moral personality of the ruler than upon the laws governing the country. But this does not mean Confucian philosophy would not agree to the self-evident principle—attributed to natural law—that man knows as though by moral instinct to do good and avoid evil, even if this same instinct does not enlighten him as to *what* is good and *what* evil. However, the Confucian tradition has not given the name of "law" to this basic human ability of discernment—the very ground indeed of man's possibility of self-transcendence. In the Confucian consciousness, law is always something *imposed* from outside—whereas man's ability to do good—according to the school of Mencius—is considered as an innate endowment, even if in need of education and development. Thus, the Confucian theory of conscience emphasizes the immanence of such a moral law, without denying its openness to transcendence. To make use of the soteriological terms of Japanese Buddhism, one may say, in this regard, that the Catholic teaching joins the Confucian theory here in showing more sense of self-

reliance (*jiriki;* 自力), where Protestant theology, with its preference for Scriptural law, insists upon faith alone and exclusive
dependence on God's power (*tariki;* 他力).

"The Heart of Man"

If conscience is man's moral faculty, it is also more than that. The
word can refer also to a deeper reality—to the *seat* of the moral
faculty itself, the innermost center of the soul, its apex, the *locus*
for man's meeting with God, the source and principle of human
freedom and human responsibility.

Already in the Old Testament, we find the constant reiteration
that God looks less at our exterior actions, than at our "heart."
"I will give them a [new] heart, and . . . a new spirit . . . ."
(Ezech. 11:19). In the Sermon on the Mount, Jesus also lays emphasis on the importance of having the right inner dispositions:
"Blessed are the pure of heart" (Matt. 5:8). St. Paul speaks of the
"circumcised heart" (Rom. 2:5, 29). "Have this *mind* in you
which was also in Christ Jesus" (Phil 2:5). To repent, and turn
to God is to have a change of heart, *metanoia.*[65]

The Chinese word for mind-and-heart, *hsin* (心), derived originally from an image of fire. It referred to intentions, feelings, as
well as the activity of knowing and judging. The mind-and-heart
is that which discerns between right and wrong, as well as that
which commands conformance with its judgments.[66] The Neo-
Confucian philosophers speak of *hsin* as that which controls both
nature (*hsing;* 性) and emotions (*ch'ing;* 情). It is also the *locus* of
man's meeting with Heaven. "He who gives full realization to his
heart (*hsin*) understands his own nature, and he who understands
his own nature knows Heaven" (Mencius 7A:1). And Wang Yang-
ming has said:

> The heart (*hsin*) is the Way (Tao), and the Way is Heaven.
> If one knows [his own] heart, he would also know the Way
> and Heaven.[67]

The heart comes to us from Heaven (Mencius 6A:15). It also
leads us back to Heaven. It represents both the symbol and reality
of man's oneness with Heaven. Even more than Christianity, Confucianism has made explicit the continuum between the various

levels of conscience, between conscience as moral faculty and as the *ground* of such faculty, as mind-and-heart.

The heart is also the reason for man's oneness with himself. The Confucian man is not a dualist, a man at war with himself. The Confucian man knows himself to be one, in his heart. He seeks to keep to his heart, to be true to his heart. "Seek, and you will get it; let go and you will lose it. If this is the case, then seeking is of use to getting and what is sought is within yourself" (Mencius 7A:3).

The Confucian honors Heaven as the giver of life and humanity, from whom he has received everything, sense organs as well as a human heart. The Confucian treasures Heaven's gifts, and seeks to develop them to the full. The Confucian, however, speculates little over such questions as spiritual immortality, a preoccupation which is also more Greek than Semitic.

Much less important than the word *hsin* are the words "spiritual soul" (*hun;* 魂) and "sentient soul" (*p'o;* 魄). They are not to be found in any of the Four Books. In the *Annals of Tso*—a Confucian Classic—the word *hun* refers to all conscious activity, the word *p'o* to bodily form. The common element of the two ideograms orginally depicted a person wearing a mask: the "impersonator" at the ceremony wore the mask, and the dead man's spirit took up residence in it. The words, therefore, were early associated with ritual practices of honoring the dead. In popular belief, the higher soul, *hun*, ascends to heaven, and the lower soul, *p'o*, joins the earth. With the development of a Confucian metaphysics, *hun* became related to vital force (*ch'i*) and *p'o* to bodily form itself. In the Book of Rites, it is said that "the spiritual soul (*hun*) and the vital force (*ch'i*) return to Heaven [after death]; the body and the sentient soul (*p'o*) return to earth."[68]

It seems usually assumed that the sentient soul becomes eventually a part of the earth itself. But how about the spiritual soul? Its final fate is left unclear. We read in Wang Ch'ung's *Lun-heng* arguments *against* believing in dead persons surviving as spiritual beings or ghosts, which shows that disagreement on this question— a question Confucius refused to answer—existed. But the question only became prominent with the coming of Buddhism into China, and the ensuing debate between Taoists and Buddhists. Interestingly, the Taoists claimed especially that the *Confucian* sages, including the Master himself, became immortals, while the Buddhists denied the possibility of personal immortality.

The Confucian position may be summed up this way: the age-old custom of venerating the dead, the passages in the Classics about sage-kings enjoying an intimacy with the Lord-on-High or Heaven, point to an early belief in some form of personal immortality. But Confucius himself kept silence on this question, while participating actively in the rituals honoring the dead (Analects 11:11, 3:12). The passage in the *Annals of Tso* relating the discussion of survival after death is interesting, but continues to emphasize the immortality of virtue, personal accomplishments and words.[69]

The Universal Virtue

The Confucian man is one—in his life and in his heart. The Confucian man need practice only one virtue: that which makes him fully and perfectly human, that which embraces all other virtues. It is the universal virtue, *jen* (仁).

The Confucian *jen* offers certain parallels to the Christian virtue of love or charity (*agape*). It has been translated as human-heartedness, benevolence, love. The Christian teaching of charity has its *raison-d'être* in God's love for man, which is revealed in Jesus Christ.[70] The Confucian teaching of *jen*, on the other hand, does not offer explicitly Heaven's love for man as a reason and model for imitation. According to the Classics, Heaven is the source of life, the protector of man and the provider of his needs. But the virtue of *jen* is rather based on human nature itself. Man is able to practice *jen*. He is not truly human unless he does so.

Charity is a universal virtue. It is the "bond of perfection" (Col. 3:14), the inner principle of dynamism which imparts to the whole life of virtue its warmth, value and firmness. It embraces and animates all other virtues. This is true also of *jen*. Before the time of Confucius, *jen* was regarded as an aristocratic virtue, as the kindness shown by a superior to an inferior. But the teachings of Confucius transformed it into a universal virtue, that which can be practiced by all.[71]

And what is the meaning of *jen*? Confucius has been asked many times. Each time, he has given a somewhat different answer. To the disciple Fan Ch'ih, he says it means to "love men" (Analects 12:21). To Yen Hui, he speaks of *jen* in terms of subduing oneself and returning to propriety (Analects 12:1). To still another, he offers the famous Golden Rule: "What you do not wish others to do unto you, do not do unto them" (Analects 12:2, 15:23).

Jen is perfect virtue; he who has *jen* is already perfect, a sage. For this reason, Confucius shows a certain caution in speaking of *jen*. He says:

> I have never seen one who really loved *jen*, nor hated what was not *jen*. He who loved *jen* would esteem nothing above it; and he who hated what was not *jen* would practice *jen* and would allow nothing that was not *jen* to affect him. Is there anyone who for a single day is able to employ all his strength for *jen*? I have never seen one with insufficient strength. There may be such a person, but I have not seen him (4:6).[72]

According to Confucius, *jen* should come before any other consideration (4:6). The gentleman never abandons it even for a moment (4:5). It comes only after one has done what is difficult (6:20). One may have to give one's life for *jen* (15:8). And yet, *jen* is not a distant, far-off entity. "I desire *jen*, and *jen* is close at hand" (7:29).

In its etymology as well as in the interpretation given it by Confucius, *jen* is always concerned with the relationship between man and man. It is associated with both loyalty (*chung;* 忠)—loyalty to one's own heart and conscience—and reciprocity (*shu;* 恕)—respect of, and consideration for others (Analects 4:15). *Jen* is also related to *li* (禮; propriety, ritual). The latter refers more to ritual and social behavior, the former, to the inner orientation of the person.[73]

Jen is rooted in human sentiment as well as in a fundamental orientation of life. *Jen* means affection and love. "The man of *jen* loves others" (Mencius 4B:28). Indeed, he loves *all* and *everyone* (7A:46). He "extends his love from those he loves to those he does not love" (Mencius 7B:1). Hsün-tzu concurs with this definition of *jen* as love. The Book of Rites describes *jen* also as love. The Han Confucian Tung Chung-shu (176–104 B.C.) defines *jen* as the love of mankind, while Yang Hsiung (53 B.C.–A.D. 18) calls it "universal love." The early lexicon *Shuo-wen* (c. A.D. 100.) equates love with affection (*ch'in;* 親).[74]

The Confucian interpretation of *jen* as universal love, however, differs from that of some other early schools of thought, especially the Mohist, that founded by Mo-tzu. Mo-tzu advocated a love of all without distinction. The followers of Confucius emphasized the need of discernment, even of distinction. "Charity begins at home." So too does *jen*. The roots of *jen* are filial piety and brotherly respect (Analects 1:20). The Confucian man reserves for his parents and kin a special love (Doctrine of the Mean 20). And Mencius has said:

> The gentleman is careful [and sparing] with things, but shows them no *jen*. He shows *jen* to the people, but is not [sentimentally] attached to them. He is [affectionately] attached to his parents while showing *jen* to the people. He has *jen* for the people and is considerate of things. (7A:45).[75]

The Confucian interpretation of *jen* is sometimes called a "graded love." But it is not a calculating kind of love. It is rooted in human feeling, and in a sense of responsibility. It is sentiment, virtue, and commitment. It is the noblest quality a human being can possess.

The understanding of *jen* as a universal virtue—transcending the particular virtues—continued after the death of Confucius. With the emergence of the Sung philosophers, it also assumed an added meaning: that of creativity, of life and consciousness, and also of ultimate reality.[76] According to Ch'eng Hao, the man of *jen* forms "one body" with all things, and the virtue of righteousness, propriety, wisdom and truthfulness are all expressions of *jen*. He recommends the student to understand *jen-t'i* (仁體; *jen*-in-itself) and to strive to make it part of himself, and then to "nourish" it with the practice of virtues. Chu Hsi teaches the life-giving power of *jen*. It is that through which Heaven and Earth give life to men and things. Chang Tsai speaks of *jen* as the work of the sage, the man who is

> . . . to give heart to Heaven and Earth, to establish the Way for living peoples, to continue the interrupted teachings of

the former sages, and to open a new era of peace for coming generations.[77]

Except for the absence of an explicit mention of God, this expression of a mystical love of men and the cosmos should recall to mind the words of John and Paul, of Henry Suso, and closer to our days, of Teilhard de Chardin. The life-giving movement it describes as flowing down from Heaven and Earth to Man and then back to Heaven and Earth is a good analogy for an understanding of charity as the life-giving grace in Christian theology.

It is with this understanding of *jen* and of the Man of *jen* that we may be led to an understanding of "the oneness of Heaven and Man" (*T'ien-jen ho-yi;* 天人合一). For if the ideal of sagehood implies the unity between Man and Heaven, then the heart (or the mind), which is at the center of Man's being, is the *locus* for this communion. This concept of the Man who communes with the Absolute in his inner being is very close to the ideal of Christian mysticism—defined, theologically, as the flowering of charity.

THE CONFUCIAN COMMUNITY

The Confucian man is no dualist. He is not divided against himself, and his love of others is not strained. He loves most those who, by Heaven's ordinance, are most closely related to himself. And he extends this love to others—to friends first, and then to all in society and the world. He has a deep sense of community, of responsibility toward others.

The Five Relationships

The Confucian regards human society in terms of personal relationships and ethical responsibilities resulting from such relationships. The well-known "Five Relationships" include the ruler-subject, father-son, husband-wife, elder and younger brother, and friend and friend. Three of these are family relationships, while the other two are usually conceived in terms of the family models.[78] For example, the ruler-subject relationship resembles the father-son, while friendship resembles brotherliness. For this reason, the Confucian society regards itself as a large family: "Within the four seas all men are brothers" (Analects 12:5).

The responsibilities ensuing from these relationships are mutual and reciprocal. A subject owes loyalty to his sovereign, and a child filial affection to his parent. But the sovereign is also expected to care for his subjects, and the parent for his child. Indeed, Mencius so interpreted the Confucian doctrine of "Rectification of Names" —that a sovereign be a [good] sovereign, a subject a [good] subject, a father a [good] father, and a son a [good] son—as to infer that a wicked ruler might forfeit the rights of his position, becoming a mere "tyrant" whom his subjects could depose (1B:8). But he never extended this inference to cover the *natural* relationships of human kin. Sons, for example, are encouraged to protect their parents' good name, in spite of the knowledge of their wrongdoings.

The system of Five Relationships, all the same, emphasize a basic sense of hierarchy. The only truly horizontal relationship is that between friends, and even here, seniority of age demands a certain respect, as also with brothers. The husband-wife relationship bears more natural resemblance to that between elder and younger brothers, but is more usually compared to the ruler-subject relationship. And the duty of filial piety, the need of procuring progeny for the sake of assuring the continuance of the ancestral cult, has been for centuries the ethical justification for polygamy.

The family has always been the center of Confucian life and ethics, and family life itself has demonstrated the nature of Confucianism itself, not only as a system of ethics, but also as a philosophy of religion. In many Chinese houses in Hongkong, Taiwan and Southeast Asia—as well as in Korea and Japan—the ancestral altar is still maintained. Here, a number of tablets is kept, each representing a dead ancestor. They are traditionally made of wood, although a sociologist has noticed how paper tablets have replaced wooden ones in certain Hongkong families today,[79] those who have left behind their older tablets on the mainland. In front of these tablets burns a dim lamp, near which are placed incense and candles. All this is evidence of the religious significance of the Confucian family, a community of the living and the dead.

Filial piety is the first of all Confucian virtues, that which comes before loyalty to the sovereign, conjugal affection, and everything else. The ancestral cult has continued throughout the centuries, from time immemorial, to strengthen these sentiments of filial piety and familial loyalty. It has always exercised an integrating and stabilizing influence, pulling together, not merely the large, patriarchal family, but also the whole clan, all the descendants of the same ancestors, and the entire Chinese kinship system. Births and marriages are related to the ancestral cult and the duty of filial piety, since every birth increases the number of descendants, and since marriage is intended as a means for continuing the family lineage and the ancestral cult itself. Filial piety has usually assured for aged parents, the support of their mature children, while the strong sentiment of family and kin has promoted mutual help among family relatives, and even beyond the family circles, among persons coming from the same ancestral town, albeit not related by blood or marriage, as well as among persons bearing the same surnames, and so, allegedly or possibly, of the same ancestors.[80]

Familial relations provide a model for social behavior. Respect your own elders, as well as others' elders; be kind to your own juniors and children, as well as others' juniors and children. These are the words of Mencius (1A:7). They have provided inspiration for generations of Confucians. They have been the reason for the strong sense of solidarity not only in the Chinese family, but also in Confucian social organizations, and even among overseas Chinese communities today. If Confucianism remains alive today, if Confucianism is to remain alive for many generations to come, the credit belongs to this strong sense of human solidarity, based fundamentally on familial sentiments but implying a belief in a universal brotherhood.

The hierarchical orientation in Confucianism has been strengthened in later developments, with its establishment as state philosophy in the Han dynasty, the incorporation of *yin-yang* metaphysics and of Legalist notions of authority and obedience into this state orthodoxy. In the words of the Han thinker, Tung Chung-shu:

> In all things there must be correlates. Thus if there is the
> upper, there must be the lower. . . . The *yin* is the correlate

of the *yang*, the wife of the husband, the subject of the sovereign. . . .[81]

From the five relationships, Tung selects the three: ruler-subject, husband-wife and father-son. He calls them the "Three Bonds." According to his reinterpretation, the sovereign is the *master* of the subject, the husband of the wife, and the father of the son. The relationships continue to require reciprocal duties and responsibilities. But the superior partners have more rights, and the inferior more duties.[82]

The incorporation of *yin-yang* metaphysics into Confucian social ethics has, however, underlined another dimension of Confucian humanism: its openness to the divine, the transcendent. Tung Chung-shu has especially articulated the doctrine of the oneness of Heaven and Man, in terms of the "triad:" Heaven, Earth and Man. According to him, man is a replica of Heaven, the microcosm of the macrocosm, both in spirit and in body. He is far superior to all other creatures. Heaven, Earth and Man are at the origins of all things: "Heaven gives them birth, Earth gives them nourishment, and Man gives them perfection."

> These three are related to each other like the hands and feet; united they give the finished physical form, so that no one of them may be dispensed with.[83]

Tung Chung-shu has especially exalted the notion of kingship. The ideal king is the perfect man, the human paradigm, the co-equal of Heaven, the mediator between the ways of Heaven and Earth, and the ways of human society.

> Heaven's will is constantly to love and benefit, its business to nourish and bring to age. . . . The will of the king likewise is to love and benefit the world, and his business to bring peace and joy to his time. . . . If the ruler of men exercises his love and hate, his joy and anger, in accordance with righteousness, then the age will be well governed; but if unrighteously, then the age will be in confusion. . . . So we see that the principles of mankind correspond to the way of Heaven.[84]

Of course, not every man is a king. But Confucian philosophy has always emphasized every man's duty to participate in government, to assist the king in assuring good government. Every official, for example, is exhorted to become the father-and-mother of his people. And Confucian sage-models include not only sage-kings, but also sage-ministers. Indeed, a Confucian is expected to serve the state unless other responsibilities, such as toward his parents, prevent him from doing so, or unless the times are such that service would compromise his principles.

Besides, Confucian philosophy has always spoken in universal terms. Just as there is Heaven above, so too there is the world below: all under Heaven. Confucius was no particularist, no nationalist. He travelled from state to state, seeking a ruler who would use his services, for the good of the whole world. He envisages good government always in terms of the world. So too his later followers, throughout the centuries when China remained the center of a known world, a known universe. The Confucian community is a world community, a human community.

The Confucian man must, of course, prepare himself for this task. And he is exhorted to do so, by remaining faithful to this integrated view of man and of life, a view which transcends the differences between subject and object, self and world. The Confucian book, the Great Learning, offers a good illustration of this organic unity between self-perfection and the ordering of family, country and world. Differentiations between various levels are overcome by an all-comprehensive, circular process:

Things have roots and branches, and affairs have beginnings and ends. To know the order of priority is to be near the Way (Tao). The ancients who wished to make manifest the principle of virtue in the world, first made sure that their own states were well governed. To assure the good government of their states, they first cultivated their persons. To assure this personal cultivation, they first made sure that their minds and hearts were upright. To assure that their minds and hearts were upright, they first made sure that their intentions were sincere.

It is not possible to neglect the roots and order well the branches. It is not possible to neglect the essential, and order well the details.[85]

A Community of Culture

The Christian Community, the Church (*Ecclesia*), considers itself an assembly called forth by God, a community of believers.[86] It is, of course, an assembly of communities, of local churches. But it remains an assembly, a community in itself, because of the common bond of faith uniting all its members, in spite of differences of time, place and culture, in spite, also, of differences of political ideology and social organization. And it is a community because the bond of faith, which joins man to God, and believer to believer, is much more important than its own social organization or juridical statutes. Faith is the very life of the Christian community.

The Confucian society also has its rulers, laws and statutes. But it is more than a society. It is also a community of personal relationships. It is joined together, not by religious belief—although such is also present—but by the acceptance of a common culture, a culture which esteems the person above the law, and human relationships above the state. Culture is the life of the Confucian community. In traditional China, when the Confucian state allegedly embraced the then known world, Confucian culture was also regarded as *human* culture—that which distinguished the civilized from the barbarian.

Confucian culture was at the same time religious and secular. It did not distinguish between these two realms. Its basic faith— the oneness of Heaven and Man—inspired a great optimism in human nature and its perfectibility, a faith which impelled the quest for a universal way of life and a universal order on earth. The Confucian Man regarded Heaven as the source of his life and being, and looked to it for protection and the satisfaction of his needs. He considered Earth as his dwelling place, in life and death, a storehouse of resources as well as a living garden, nourished, like himself, by gifts from Heaven. He regarded himself as participating in the life and being of both Heaven and Earth, and related to other men through this common participation, and a common origin from Heaven.

Confucianism has never known an organized, ecclesiastical priesthood. The emperor was the mediator between Heaven and the people, by virtue of his position as political ruler. He was assisted by his ministers—an educated bureaucracy of men versed in rituals and ethics. Together, they represented a kind of lay priesthood, although their dignity and mission flowed more from their education and merit than from any personal *charisma*.[87] They constituted a special class in society, representing a commitment to service of state and society, in the name of the common good.[88] They were sometimes called "gentlemen" (*chün-tzu*).[89] Time and again, from among these ranks, a "prophet" would emerge who raised his voice of protest against misrule, directing his complaints to the "kings" as did his Hebrew counterparts. Such a man would be a true follower of Confucius and Mencius. Such a man would speak in the name of the Classics, the sages, and of Heaven.

It is interesting to note here that the Confucian Man has always been regarded as "king"—real or potential, with the duty to govern or to assist in government. The teaching of the Great Learning is addressed to all: to manifest the principle of virtue (by personal cultivation), *to love the people* (ordering well family and state), and to rest in the highest good (including giving peace to the entire world). "From the Son of Heaven down to the commoners, it is the same: all must regard personal cultivation as the root [and foundation]" (Chapter one).

In a later chapter—on Political Relevance—I shall discuss in greater detail the Confucian ideals of king and minister: how the dynastic institution of kingship, with priority placed on hereditary succession rather than personal charisma and merit, increased the distance between real and ideal, giving a greater importance to the minister, a man chosen more for merit than birth. I suggest that this contributed to a kind of "power balance," with the minister serving always as *critical* advisor as well as executive officer. The Confucian doctrine of political loyalty never demanded passive obedience. Even at its worst, the faithful minister was ready to give up his life for admonishing his ruler.

Conclusion

In the course of this study, we seem to have discovered more similarities than differences between Confucian and Christian notions of man. But we must not overlook the differences, especially where these lie in varying emphases of the two traditions. For example, Confucian teachings have focused more upon human perfectibility where Christianity has tended to stress human fallibility. Thus, Confucianism projects the image of a man in harmony with society and the universe, where Christianity appears to support the idea of a man at war with himself and his sinful nature, struggling to overcome a world estranged from God. This difference has also been formulated in terms of complacency and dynamism. The harmony-loving Confucian has been depicted as resistant to change, where the militant Christian is allegedly changing the face of the earth. But there is yet another side to the picture. Estrangement and alienation have also been responsible for outrageous violence against man and nature.

And so, what about the strengths and weaknesses of the two humanisms?

The admirers of Confucianism have emphasized that Confucianism *is* humanism, that the heart of its teachings is man's self-realization and self-fulfilment, described in terms of acquiring wisdom and sageliness. The critics, however, have pointed out *de-humanizing* tendencies, in particular, its hierarchical orientations which have so evolved as to grant only obligations and no rights, to the inferior partner of each of the "Five Relationships." The admirers of Christianity likewise indicate how divine revelation has made known the real possibilities of human greatness, while its critics regard it as the enemy of humanism, on account of its preoccupation with the next life and with God.

It appears that Confucian and Christian humanisms must each preserve a delicate balance of inner tensions, in order to remain authentic expressions of human aspirations. Confucianism has need of a more articulate theory of human fallibility, and even more, of human suffering and its meaning in the order of values. Christianity, on the other hand, has need of a more profound inquiry into the question of human goodness, even outside the framework of a doctrine of redeeming grace. Here, I believe that it can yet learn from the Confucian *pedagogy*, in so far as the varying emphases on human fallibility or perfectibility can themselves *promote* the consciousness of guilt and frustration, or that of strength and commitment. It is, for example, quite impossible for the Confucian tradition to produce a novel of human wickedness as Anthony Burgess' *A Clockwork Orange*[90] which represents another step in the increasing fascination of fiction and society with the analysis of sin—and perhaps without adequate acceptance of freedom and responsibility.

The history of the unfolding of Confucian culture has witnessed many vicissitudes, of human greatness as well as of foibles, of institutional fossilization as well as rebirth. When judging Confucianism against its records of ups and downs, one must have the caution of asking: is it Confucianism that failed, or is it something else? Did not Confucianism become subjugate to state authority, as a system of state orthodoxy? Has it not led to the intrusion of Legalist ideas of authority and obedience, which, in turn, gave rigidity to the ethics of human relationships? But then, with all that, are there yet certain ideals and values which remain vital and inspiring, throughout the passage of time?

Certainly, contemporary man, whether in a socialist or open society, sees many practices associated with the Five Relationships as worthless, even inhuman. Why should youth always yield to age, and woman to man? Why should the past be exalted rather than the present—or the future? Has not the backward-looking tendency of Confucian culture itself been responsible for the tragedies of China's recent past, as she found herself helpless in front of the youthful and dynamic "barbarians" of the West, who assaulted her with weapons and technology—all that was formerly despised by the Confucian gentleman and his culture of leisure?

There is much that is true of the criticisms levelled against the Confucian culture. The debacles it has suffered are themselves telling witnesses of the need for rejuvenation, in a culture so ancient. But they are not reasons for imagining that Confucian culture is already dead, and can have no future.

Human cultures have their cycles of life and death. Confucian culture has witnessed many such cycles, with the burning of books (213 B.C.), and with the later predominance of Buddhism and Taoism, as well as with the recent challenges of Western secularism and Marxism. So far, every time, Confucian culture has been able to resurrect itself, frequently after having learned certain lessons, whether for good or ill.

Any creative dialogue between two traditions must rest upon their points of convergences, rather than their differences. For the dialogue between Christianity and Confucianism, an understanding of faith in man as openness to the transcendent remains the most promising starting point.[91] It is this faith which has given Confucianism its dynamism, which has also counteracted the abuses of Legalism—and so many crimes attributed to Confucianism have emerged from the infiltration of Legalist concepts into the Confucian system. It is this faith which provides a starting point for contemporary theology itself, and which also, for the Christian, takes priority over law and precepts, being itself the only *rationale* for any authentic legal order. And lastly, it is this faith, in each case, which makes possible that creative exercise of freedom which brings man nearer to his transcendent goal, the achievement of a *radical* human-ity.

NOTES

1. On the subject of humanism, Christian and Confucian, see a Chinese work, T'ang Chun-i, *Chung-kuo jen-wen ching-shen chih fa-chan* (The Development of the Chinese Humanist Spirit) (Hongkong, 1958), in which the author, understandably, traces the origin of Western humanism to Greek and Roman philosophy. He mentions, however, the gradual fusion of Christian religious notions and the secular philosophical notions in the development of this humanism (see especially pp. 69–76), and concludes the book with a discussion of the value of religious belief and the problem of the future of Chinese culture (pp. 337–99), taking into consideration all the traditional forms of Chinese religion as well as Christianity. For Christian humanism itself, see also Roger L. Shinn, *Man: the New Humanism* (Philadelphia, 1968): E. Schillebeeckx, *God and Man*. Translated by E. Fitzgerald (New York, 1969).

2. For ideas of civil religion, see Jürgen Moltmann *et al.*, *Religion and Political Society* (New York, 1974), for its development in America, see Russell E. Richey and Donald G. Jones, ed., *American Civil Religion* (New York, 1974). It should be

noted that a chief expositor of civil religion in America is Robert N. Bellah, a specialist of Japanese Confucianism and author of *Tokugawa Religion* (Glencoe, 1957). See his article in Richey *et al.*, pp. 21–44.

For the ideas on secularization, see Harvey Cox, *The Secular City* (New York, 1965), and D. Callahan, ed., *The Secular City Debate* (New York, 1966).

For the secular, Marxist humanism, see Henri de Lubac, *The Drama of Atheistic Humanism.* Translated by E. M. Riley (New York, 1951). See also the discussions on man which took place during "Christian-Marxist dialogues," and published in such books as Roger Garaudy and Karl Rahner, *From Anathema to Dialogue*, tr. by L. O'Neill (New York, 1966).

This whole problem has also been summed up succinctly in Hans Küng, *Christsein* (München, 1974), pp. 17–22.

3. Bengt Hagglund, *History of Theology*, tr. by Gene J. Lund (St. Louis, 1968), pp. 397–404.

4. Bonhoeffer, *Letters and Papers from Prison* (London, 1964), pp. 278–80; Bultmann, *Faith and Understanding* (London, 1969), pp. 53–60.

5. "Pastoral Constitution on the Church in the Modern World," in *The Documents of Vatican II*, ed. by Walter M. Abbott, S.J. (New York, 1966), pp. 209–22.

6. See especially the article by John C. Robertson, Jr., "Rahner and Ogden: Man's Knowledge of God," *Harvard Theological Review* 63 (1970), pp. 377–407. See also Peter L. Berger, *A Rumor of Angels: Modern Society and the Rediscovery of the Supernatural* (New York, 1969), pp. 61–123.

7. Robertson, op. cit., p. 377.

8. For the notion of man in the Christian scriptures, see W. Eichrodt, *Man in the Old Testament*, tr. by K. and R, Gregor Smith (Chicago, 1951), H. Conzelmann, *An Outline of the Theology of the New Testanent*, tr. by J. Bowden (New York, 1969), pp. 173–80. See also Jürgen Moltmann, *Mensch: Christliche Anthropologie in den Konflikten der Gegenwart* (Stuttgart, 1971), English translation by John Stundy: *Man: Christian Anthropology in the Conflicts of the Present* (Philadelphia, 1974), ch. 1; *Neues Glaubensbuch: Der gemeinsame christliche Glaube*, ed. by J. Feiner and L. Vischer (Freiburg im B., 1973), English translation in *The Common Catechism: A Book of Christian Faith* (New York, 1975) pt. 3. *Evangelischer Erwachsenen Katechismus*, ed. by W. Jentsch *et al.*, (1975), Part 5. See also Reinhold Niebuhr, *The Nature and Destiny of Man* (New York, 1941), vol. 1.

9. Book of Documents, Part 4, Book 2, in James Legge, tr., *The Chinese Classics* (Oxford, 1893), vol. 3, pp. 177–78; Book of Odes, Part 3, Book 3, in Legge, ibid., vol. 4, p. 64.

10. See Donald J. Munro, *The Concept of Man in Early China* (Stanford, 1969), pp. 65–67. See also his lengthy notes (n. 45–46) on pp. 214–15.

11. *Hsün-tzu: Basic Writings*, tr. by Burton Watson (New York, 1963), p. 159.

12. Ibid., p. 45.

13. Doctrine of the Mean 20.

14. Munro, op. cit., ch. 1.

15. Mencius 4B:1.

16. See Julia Ching, "The Problem of Evil and a Possible Dialogue between Christianity and Neo-Confucianism," *Contemporary Religions in Japan* 9(1968), pp. 161–93.

17. See Ricci's Catechism, *T'ien-chu shih-yi* (The True Idea of God), Part 7.

There is a translation in vernacular Chinese (from the classical) by Liu Shun-te. (Taichung, 1966); see pp. 170–98.

18. In *Guilt and Sin in Traditional China*, Wolfram Eberhard offers much historical and sociological evidence to refute assertions that China has known no guilt-mentality (Los Angeles, 1967).

19. Liang Su-ming, *Tung-hsi wen-hua yü ch'i che-hsüeh* (1922). This book is available only in Chinese. By lack of God-talk, Liang is speaking especially of the more philosophical writings. Both the Books of Documents and Odes are full of references to the Lord-on-High and Heaven.

20. See the articles on Sin by Piet Schoonenberg and Karl Rahner in *Sacramentum Mundi: An Encyclopaedia of Theology*, English translation by C. Ernst *et al.*, (New York, 1970), vol. 6, pp. 87–94. See also *Evangelischer Erwachsenen Catechismus*, pp. 256–78.

21. Book of Documents, Book 3, Ch. 2, in Legge, *The Chinese Classics*, vol. 3, pp. 189–190.

22. References are found in *Lü-shih ch'un-ch'iu*, ch. 9, sect. 2, as well as in *Lunheng*, ch. 5, sect. 19. See also the chapter on universal love in *Mo-tzu: Basic Writings*, translated by Burton Watson (New York, 1963), p. 44. This account of T'ang's sacrifice, together with the prayer of the Duke of Chou related in the Book of Documents (chapter on the Metal-bound Coffer), Part 5, Book 6, in Legge, *The Chinese Classics*, pp. 352–61, remain the only two known instances of *propitiatory* prayer in early China.

23. *Hsün-tzu*, sect. 23, in Watson, op. cit., pp. 157–71. For an exaltation of Hsün-tzu's theory over Mencius', see for example Yang Jung-kuo's History of Chinese Philosophy (*Chien-ming Chung-kuo che-hsüeh shih*) (Peking, 1973), p. 68.

24. Karl Rahner, "The Theological Concept of Concupiscentia," *Theological Investigations*, tr. by C. Ernst (Baltimore, 1960), vol. 1, p. 369.

25. Ibid., p. 374. Although there is no "primordial Fall" in orthodox Confucian teachings, there has been, in popular Buddhism, a tendency to regard human beings as having been originally good, and having later become evil in the course of history. This is associated with the notion of *kalpa* (world era). In Confucian thought, such an idea is sometimes implicit in the assertion of the many former sages, and the alleged moral degeneration of later ages.

26. See Ching, "The Problem of Evil," op. cit., 168.

27. Aquinas treats of the passions in *Summa Theologica* 1–11, Q. 22–48. He considers them as sense appetites, belonging to the irrational part of the soul, in a human person whose chief characteristic is reason.

28. See Chang Tsai's *Hsi-ming* (Western Inscription) and *Cheng-meng* (Corrections of Youthful Ignorance), from which this is taken. English translation is found in Wing-tsit Chan, *A Source Book of Chinese Philosophy* (Princeton, 1963), pp. 497–517. Let it be noted that the words "essential" and "existential" do not represent a literal translation, but are used for the sake of greater clarity of the concepts.

29. Paul Tillich, *Systematic Theology* (London, 1957), vol. 2, pp. 40–42.

30. Paul Ricoeur, *Human Fallibility* (Chicago, 1965), p. 224. For a survey of contemporary works on the subject of evil and on related themes, see Hermann Häring, "Satan, das Böse und die Theologen—Ein Literaturbericht," in *Bibel und Kirche*, vol. 1 (1975), pp. 27–30, 66–68.

108   THE PROBLEM OF MAN

31.   See Martin Buber, "China and Us," (1928), in *A Believing Humanism* (New York, 1967), p. 189.
32.   For the hermeneutic of the "holy", see Hans Küng, *Rechtfertigung*: *die Lehre Karl Barths und eine katholische Besinnung* (Einsiedeln, 1957), Exkurs II, pp. 302–10.
33.   Book of Documents "Counsels of Great Yü" and the "Great Plan," English translation in Legge, *The Chinese Classics*, vol. 5, pp. 54, 327.
34.   Hsü Heng, *Shuo-wen chieh-tzu* (Lexicon, with explanations by Tuan Yu-ta'ai), (Taipei, 1955), p. 598.
35.   Pan Ku, *Po-hu-t'ung-yi* (Taipei, 1968), pp. 276–81.
36.   *Ta-Tai Li-chi* (Book of Rites by the Elder Tai). "Duke Ai's Questions on Five Meanings." See Benedict Grynpas, tr., *Un Legs Confucéen: Fragments du Ta Tai Li Ki* (Brussels, n. d.), p. 50.
37.   I refer here especially to the Doctrine of the Mean, which is also ch. 28 of the Book of Rites.
38.   Analects 7:33.
39.   Analects 7:25.
40.   Book of Mencius 4A:2.
41.   Book of Mencius 7B:15.
42.   Book of Mencius 3B:9.
43.   Book of Mencius 6A:7.
44.   Doctrine of the Mean, ch. 30, in Legge, tr., *The Chinese Classics*, vol. 1, pp. 427–28.
45.   For such discussions, see Fung Yu-lan, *A History of Chinese Philosophy*, tr. by Derk Bodde (Princeton, 1953), vol. 2, pp. 187–89.
46.   Ibid., pp. 274–84.
47.   See Ching, "The Problem of Evil," p. 169.
48.   Fung Yu-lan, vol. 2, pp. 274–84.
49.   See especially Dietrich Bonhoeffer, *The Cost of Discipleship*, tr. by R. H. Fuller (London, 1948), ch. 1.
50.   Ibid., ch. 2, on the Sermon on the Mount. See also Hans Küng, *Christsein*, pp. 235–38. Küng emphasizes the following of Christ as a person, not as an abstract principle (see pp. 535–36).
51.   Analects 7:13. For a portrait of Confucius, see D. Howard Smith, *Confucius* (New York, 1973), p. 76ff.
52.   Analects 13:21, 5:21, I have explained this teaching of Confucius in my book, *To Acquire Wisdom: the Way of Wang Yang-ming* (New York, 1976), ch. 1.
53.   On the subject of martyrdom, see Louis Bouyer, *La Spiritualité du Nouveau Testament et des Pères (Histoire de la Spiritualité chrétienne*, vol. 1), (Paris, 1946), ch. 8. The quotation from Ignatius of Antioch is taken from his letter to the Romans. The English translation is my own, made from the French given by Bouyer on p. 247.
54.   For the note of renunciation and that of struggle in ascesis, see Karl Rahner, *Theological Investigations* (vol. 3: The Theology of the Spiritual Life), pp. 60–68, and Bonhoeffer, *The Cost of Discipleship* (Foreword).
55.   Bonhoeffer's poem, "Who am I?" is quoted on pp. 15–16 of the "Memoir" by G. Leibholz, given in *The Cost of Discipleship*.
56.   Book of Mencius 6A:10.
57.   This is taken from the literary testament left behind by Wen T'ien-hsiang.

See his Collected Writings (*Wen-shan hsien-sheng ch'üan-chi*, 1936 ed.), ch. 19, p. 685.
58. See Ching, *To Acquire Wisdom*, ch. 2.
59. Analects 8:18. For the shifts of emphasis from filial piety to patriotism and party discipline in the People's Republic of China, see C. K. Yang, *The Chinese Family in the Communist Revolution* (Cambridge, 1959), pp. 176–78.
60. On conscience, see Bernard Häring, *Das Gesetz Christi*, English translation by Edwin G. Kaiser, *The Law of Christ* (Paramus 1961), vol. 1, pp. 135–43, *Neues Glaubensbuch*, pp. 473–76.
61. See Cheng Chung-ying, "Conscience, Mind and Individual in Chinese Philosophy," *Journal of Chinese Philosophy* 2 (1974), pp. 6–25.
62. See Ching, *To Acquire Wisdom*, ch. 4–5; see also Cheng's article, pp. 24–25.
63. On the subject of natural law, see Bernard Häring, *The Law of Christ*, vol. 1, pp. 238–50. See also N. H. Söe, "Natural Law and Social Ethics," in John Bennett, ed., *Christian Social Ethics in a Changing World* (New York, 1966), pp. 289–91, for his critique of natural law.
64. Among others, John C. H. Wu, himself a jurist, has discussed *positively* the presence of "natural law" in Chinese philosophy. See "Chinese Legal and Political Philosophy," *The Chinese Mind*, ed. by Charles A. Moore (Honolulu, 1967), pp. 217–76. See also p. 235, n. 18, where Wu also gives a summary of Hu Shih's views on this subject, taken from Hu's article, "The Natural Law in the Chinese Tradition," *Natural Law Institute Proceedings* 5 1(951).
65. Bernard Häring, *The Law of Christ*, vol. 1, pp. 206–09.
66. Munro, op. cit., pp. 50–51.
67. This is quoted in Ching, *To Acquire Wisdom*, ch. 5.
68. *Li-chi* (Book of Rites), ch. 26 (On Sacrificial Victims), see also ch. 47 (Meaning of Sacrifices); Donald Munro, op. cit., p. 50 and p. 209, n. 4.
69. Wang Ch'ung, *Lun-heng*, ch. 62 (On Death), English translation in W. T. Chan, *A Source Book of Chinese Philosophy* (Princeton, 1963), p. 300. On this whole question of immortality and its debates, see also these monographs: Hu Shih, "The Concept of Immortality in Chinese Thought," *Harvard Divinity School Bulletin* (1946), pp, 26–43: Walter Liebenthal, "The Immortality of the Soul in Chinese Thought," *Monumenta Nipponica* 8 (1952), pp. 327–97. The passage in the Annals of Tso referred to is taken from the seventh year of Duke Chao, see J. Legge, *The Chinese Classics* v. 5, p. 613. In Matteo Ricci's Catechism (*T'ien-chu shih-yi*, 1603 ed., ch. 3), the Chinese scholar in the dialogue expresses the belief that the spiritual soul eventually disintegrates, while the Western scholar (Ricci's *alter ego*) seeks to prove, by the help of Scholastic philosophy, that it is immortal.
70. On the subject of Christian charity, see R. Schnackenburg, *The Moral Teaching of the New Testament*, tr. by J. Holland Smith and W. J. O'Hara (Freiburg, 1965), ch. 3.
71. See Wing-tsit Chan, "Chinese and Western Interpretations of *Jen* (Humanity)," in *Journal of Chinese Philosophy* 2 (1975), pp. 107–09.
72. English translation adapted from James Legge, *The Chinese Classics*, v. 1, p. 167
73. Herbert Fingarette, *Confucius—the Secular as Sacred* (New York, 1972), pp. 37–38; Munro, op. cit., pp. 28–29, 208–09, 219.
74. The references are to *Hsün-tzu*, ch. 27, Book of Rites, ch. 19, Tung Chung-shu, *Ch'un-ch'iu fan-lu*, pp. 29–30.

75. English translation adapted from D.C. Lau, *Mencius* (Baltimore, 1970), p. 192.

76. Wing-tsit Chan, "Chinese and Western Interpretations of *Jen*," pp. 115–16.

77. Chang Tsai, quoted in Chu Hsi's *Chin-ssu lu* 2; English translation is my own.

78. Fung Yu-lan, *A Short History of Chinese Philosophy*, ed., by Derk Bodde (New York, 1948), p. 21.

79. That the ancestral cult is still alive is attested to by Arthur P. Wolf, in his study on "Gods, Ghosts and Ancestors," in *Religion and Ritual in Chinese Society*, ed. Arthur D. Wolf (Stanford, 1974), pp. 146, 155–62. He treats especially of Taiwan but refers also to the Chinese mainland and elsewhere.

80. C. K. Yang, *Religion in Chinese Society* (Berkeley, 1961), pp. 29–53.

81. Tung Chung-shu, *Ch'un-ch'iu fan-lu*, 53, quoted in Fung Yu-lan, *A Short History*, p. 196.

82. Fung Yu-lan, ibid., p. 197.

83. Tung Chung-shu, 19, quoted in Fung Yu-lan, ibid., pp. 194–95.

84. Tung Chung-shu, 43, quoted and translated in W. T. de Bary, ed., *Sources of Chinese Tradition* (New York, 1960), p. 163.

85. Great Learning, taken from the text attributed to Confucius. English translation adapted from James Legge, *The Chinese Classics*, I,356. This passage is referred to by Bernard Häring, in *Christian Renewal in a Changing World*, tr. by Sr. M. Lucidia Häring (New York, 1968) , p. 95. Häring comments on the closeness of the spirit of this text with that of the Gospels.

86. Hans Küng, *Die Kirche*, (Freiburg 1967), pp. 99–107.

87. I have in mind especially Max Weber's *The Religion of China*, English translation by Hans H. Gerth (New York, 1964). Weber sees the Confucian *literati* as performing a sort of priestly role, but denies that China has ever had any experience of "ethical prophecy of a supramundane God who raised ethical demands." See pp. 229–30.

88. The "universalist" orientation of Confucian life and education has certainly caused a neglect of specialization, particularly in science and technology. And yet, such an orientation is the very life of a humanism true to the whole man, even if it may inspire curiosity and an urge to discover and dominate the world around us. The problem with Confucianism was the positive prohibition against technological specialization, deemed to be below the ethical attention of the gentleman.

89. For the meaning of *chün-tzu* in Confucian ethics, see Antonio S. Cua, "The Concept of the Paradigmatic Individual in the Ethics of Confucius," *Inquiry* 14 (1971), pp. 41–55.

90. This was published in London in 1962. Of his own religious views, the novelist, whose full name is John Anthony Burgess Wilson, says: "I was brought up a Catholic, became an agnostic, flirted with Islam, and now hold a position which may be termed Manichee—I believe the wrong god is temporarily ruling the world and that the true god has gone under." (This is quoted in A. A. DeVitis, *Anthony Burgess*, New York, 1972).

91. See "A Manifesto for a Reappraisal of Sinology and Reconstruction of Chinese Culture," (1958), signed by Carsun Chang, T'ang Chün-i, Mou Tsung-san and Hsü Fu-kuan, and given in English in Carsun Chang, *The De-*

velopment of Neo-Confucian Thought (New York, 1962), vol, 1, pp. 462–64. See also Robert P. Kramers, "Some Aspects of Confucianism in its Adaptation to the Modern World," *Proceedings of the IXth International Congress for the History of Religions* (Tokyo and Kyoto), 1958 (Tokyo, 1960), pp. 332–33. (T'ang Chun-i's ideas can be further pursued in *Chung-kuo wen-hua chih ching-shen chia-chih*—The Spiritual Values of Chinese Culture—Taipei, 1960, pp. 326–44.)

Chapter Four

THE PROBLEM OF GOD

INTRODUCTION

As has been said, there can be no religion without faith, and no
faith without a dimension of transcendence: the God-dimension.[1]
This does not mean that God is always recognized as God. The
word God belongs more to the language of philosophical theology
than to that of religious consciousness. In the history of European
thought, it was, for a long time, associated with the need of giving
proof for God's existence. And yet, neither the Old nor the New
Testament set out to prove this. They rather assume that God
exists—that He is what *is*.

The dominant tradition in Confucianism resembles the Jewish
tradition and the Christian Gospels in refraining from proving
God's existence, while acknowledging it explicitly. But whereas
God is the chief actor in the Christian Bible, and occupies the central place in Christian theology, he appears only in occasional
references in the Confucian Classics and their commentaries. Besides, the *affirmation* of God in the dominant Confucian school—I
refer here to the Classics themselves and to Confucius and many
of his followers—has also been accompanied by the *negation* of God
by some other followers of Confucius. It is therefore possible for
Confucianism itself to be characterized either as theist or atheist—
or rather agnostic. It is, however, more accurate to say that Confucianism appears more theistic than atheistic. Such is also the
judgment of the present-day critics of Confucianism.

The Problem of God in Confucianism is all the more interesting
because of the evolution in the understanding of God. I refer to a
gradual transition from the earlier theistic belief to the later
philosophical interpretation of the Absolute. Here, I wish to refer

112

to Friedrich Heiler's book *Prayer*, which speaks of Prophetical Religions—with their belief in a personal God—and Mysticism—where the emphasis is more upon the oneness of self and the universe, with so-called pantheistic tendencies.[2] It seems to me that Confucianism offers an example of a transition from the earlier personal deity of the Classics to the later God-Absolute of the philosophers. It also seems to me that this assertion can find support in the evolution of prayer and meditation and mysticism. I shall not elaborate upon this here, except to say that the later evolution in philosophical understanding did not preclude the survival of an earlier belief in a personal God. This is attested to by the long history of the Confucian cult of Heaven. It is also attested to by the survival of such a belief in the popular consciousness of the Chinese people today—a reason for the careful efforts of today's critics of religion in the People's Republic to continue to criticize Confucianism and its religious dimensions.

And what relevance can such a study of the problem of God in Confucianism bring to our contemporary understanding of God? Surprisingly perhaps, one can find much relevance, not only in the discovery of the God of the Classics—a personal God—but also in the Neo-Confucian focus upon a God of process and becoming, a God of mind and subjectivity, as offered by the later philosophical tradition. Even where the problem of God is concerned, the Confucian tradition has always kept a predilection for starting its reflections with man—with his understanding of the universe and of himself, in each of which he discovers something greater, that which also explains the oneness between self and the universe. Now this path—the path of man leading to the knowledge of God—is also that of contemporary philosophy and theology.

THE PERSONAL GOD

The Christian concept of God has its root in the Jewish Old Testament, which presents a divine revelation throughout its pages, from the story of creation, to the history of a chosen people and their patriarchs, kings and prophets. The story in Exodus 3:1–15 relating the theophany to Moses is especially significant on account of the revelation of the name *Yahweh*. The various levels of meaning present in this word are themselves revelatory. Yahweh means: "I am who am". Yahweh *is*, in his own words, the God of the Jewish patriarchs, of Abraham, Isaac and Jacob. Yahweh also means: "I make to be, whatever comes to be"—when the verb is understood causatively. He is the Creator and Maker of all things, the Lord of all. Yahweh can also be interpreted in the context of his promise to Moses: "I will be *with you*"—to take verb "be" here in a relational sense. Yahweh is not only *Sein*, but also *Dasein*, to use the vocabulary of German existentialism, This threefold meaning of the word itself, so it has been asserted, contains a threefold revelation: God's immanence *in* history—the revelation being regarded as a historical event, God's transcendence *above* history, as well as his "transparent" presence through history—through his saving actions. He is the Lord of nature as well as of history. And he is the *unique* God, a God with personal attributes, who alone can claim the title El-Elohim.[3]

In the New Testament, God is *Theos*—a Greek word suggestive of Hellenic polytheism and its religious universe presided over by the divine Zeus, father of the gods. By the time this word entered the New Testament vocabulary,[4] the Greek concept of God had already undergone a real philosophical evolution, with the works of Plato and Aristotle, both of whom discerned a transcendent and metaphysical One, over and above the Many. Not that this metaphysical knowledge of God is ever discussed at length in the Gospels or other writings. Rather, there is present an unquestioning assurance of God's self-evident reality, based on the fact of the historical revelation not only to Moses, but especially in Jesus Christ. The men of the New Testament are witnesses to Christ—in whom they have encountered God. They are preoccupied, not with a philosophical construction of the concept God, but with his personal revelation.

The God of Jesus' revelation is the God of Israel and the Fathers, the God of Abraham, Isaac and Jacob (Matt. 15:31, 22:32, Mark 12:26, Luke 1:68, 20:37, Acts 13:17, 22:14, 2 Cor. 6:16, Heb. 11:16). He is also especially the God and Father of Jesus Christ (Rom. 15:6, 2 Cor. 1:3, 11:31, Eph. 1:3). He has clearly personal attributes. He is creator of the universe and lord of time, acting freely in historical dialogue with men. He is the law-giver and also the Thou of prayer. He is above all, the God of Love (1 John 4:16); his love having already shown itself in the Old Testament shows itself even more in the New, through the Person of Jesus Christ.[5]

It is with this notion of the personal God in mind that we shall now examine the Confucian tradition. Has it, or has it not, a similar belief? We shall do so without going into controversial questions regarding God—in either Christianity or Confucianism. We shall not, for example, compare the notion of God in the Old and the New Testaments, or discuss the problem of an awe-inspiring and arbitrary deity *versus* a God of mercy and compassion. We begin by assuming that God is both awe-inspiring and loving, at least in Christianity.[6] And we shall then discuss the portrait of personal God in the Confucian Classics, as Creator and Lord of history. Here we shall bring out such problems as the relationship—or identity—between the Lord-on-High and Heaven, and the Heaven-Earth duality. And we shall do so especially by showing how there is evidence in the Confucian tradition of both affirmation and negation of God—of the personal God. For most of Chinese history, the affirmation has triumphed, as expressed in the survival until the early twentieth century of the cult of Heaven. At present, however, the negation has become even more vigorous, with the dominance in China of a Marxist ideology.

The Affirmation of God

Confucianism is a tradition associated with books. Confucian Classics hold the place of the Christian Scriptures for its followers. These Classics include works of various genres: poetry, historical documents, recorded conversations and others. Certain of these Classics—in particular the Books of Odes and of Documents—affirm a belief in a personal God, Creator of all life and Lord of nature and history. They introduce their readers to a world of moral values, human action, and reliance upon a superior power. Strictly speaking, they are not regarded as forming a deposit of divine revelation. Yet they speak of history as a dialogue between man and God—with the *one* man being usually the political ruler, who is also a kind of religious mediator. Faith vibrates through the lines of these texts: faith in God, from whom all things come, and who continues to govern the universe, rewarding the good and punishing the evil. Myth is not absent from these texts, although it occupies a discreet place. Moral teaching predominates, but it is not without theological meaning. Allusions to God are frequent, more in relation to man and history than to nature.[7]

The concept of God to be found in the Confucian Classics has been the object of study for missionaries, philologists, textual exegetes, and even archaeologists. But much work remains to be done when compared to the amount of exegesis spent on the parallel notion found in the Jewish and Christian scriptures. Where China and Confucianism are concerned, we have yet certain unresolved problems, related, for example, to the origins of the Chinese religions in which the idea of a supreme deity arose. For our purposes here, I shall discuss only what appears to be the general consensus of available scholarship. I shall begin with the Books of Odes and of Documents, two of the Five Classics, and then move on to other texts, including the Analects of Confucius and the Book of Mencius. I am speaking here of the notion of a *personal* God, the Creator, and Lord of history. I refer more to *affirmation* than to revelation. The question is of a religious belief which is taken for granted, rather than an exposition of such a belief.

There are many terms in the Confucian Classics which may refer to the notion of God; this fact alone has been the source of many difficulties and misapprehensions. The two most important terms are *Shang-ti* (Lord-on-High) and *T'ien* (Heaven). Speaking etymologically, the word *Ti* (帝; Lord), present in the earliest writings—on the so-called "oracle bones"—had a cultic meaning, being associated with sacrifices. *Ti* was especially the God of the earliest Chinese dynasty in history: the Shang, traditionally dated as having begun around 1766 B.C.—although archaeological evidence only goes back to about 1300 B.C. *Ti* belonged to a religion in which ancestral cults held a predominant place; according to some, it represented a divinization of the ancestral spirit of the ruling family.[8]

The word *T'ien*, (天) on the other hand, suggests a more naturalistic association, or at least, a sky-hierophany. However, it is allegedly derived from the picture of a man with a big head—also of anthropomorphic origin. In China's first lexicon (first century A.D.) this ideogram is explained in terms of its two apparent components: "one" (一) and "great" (大), namely, the "one Great".[9]

The word *T'ien* is present also in the "oracle bone" writings, where it does not refer to any God. This happens only with the literature of a later period: that of the Chou period (1111–249 B.C.), or the Confucian Classics. *T'ien* appears to have been the God of the Chou people, who were culturally and ethnically related to the Shang, but who came later to the central political stage. The fusion of the *Ti* and *T'ien* traditions evidently occurred during Chou times, as the Lord-on-High, also called Heaven, became recognized by all as a supreme deity, lord of other gods, spirits and deified ancestors called upon in prayer, for blessings and approvals. The character of divine transcendence came into sharper focus. The *personal* character of God was safeguarded, however, in the frequent accounts of prayers addressed to God—either as Lord-on-High or Heaven, or sometimes as both. The *ethical* implications of the belief in God were especially emphasized. God is the source and principle of the moral order, the judge of good and evil. To this Lord, the royal ancestors of the Chou house were clearly subordinate.[10]

A problem introduced by the term Heaven is the presence of its opposite: Earth. In the Books of Odes and Documents, the term Heaven frequently appears by itself, while that of Earth usually appears in association with Heaven. In the Book of Changes—also one of the Five Confucian Classics—the *idea* of Heaven-and-Earth, and of Heaven *versus* Earth, becomes prominent with the use of two different terms: *Ch'ien* (乾; Heaven) and *K'un* (坤; Earth,) incorporating respectively the principles of *yang* (陽; active, masculine) and of *yin* (陰; passive, feminine).

It has been suggested that *Ti* (Lord) as deity was also related to the cult of the Earth goddess, whic his a reason for the independent Sacrifice offered to Earth as distinct from that offered to Heaven, not only in Chou times, but also long afterwards. However, in the language of prayer—including the liturgical language of the Sacrifice to Heaven—the terms *Ti* (Lord) or *Shang-ti* (Lord-on-High) and *T'ien* (Heaven) were used interchangeably as expression of the belief in one supreme deity. Possibly the terms Heaven and Earth refer sometimes to distinct hierophanies, and sometimes to the *power behind both*; Heaven, however, was definitely exalted above Earth, not only in the Book of Changes, but also in other classical texts. This was also clear from the importance assigned to the cult of Heaven itself. And Heaven, of course, was exalted above the gods of the grain, of mountains and rivers, as well as of the ancestral spirits of kings and commoners.[11]

The Creator

Confucianism has not developed any doctrine of creation. But the Confucian Classics clearly enunciate a belief in God as the source and principle of all things, the giver of life and the protector of the human race. In the Book of Documents, the "Great Declaration"—a speech attributed to King Wu, the founder of the Chou dynasty—declares:

> Heaven-and-Earth is the Father-and-Mother of the myriad creatures, and Man is the most highly endowed of these myriad creatures.[12]

In the Book of Odes, certain stanzas coming also apparently from Chou times confirm this belief, referring to God sometimes as Lord-on-High, and sometimes as Heaven:

> How vast is the *Lord-on-High*,
> The ruler of men below:
> How arrayed in terrors is the *Lord-on-High*:
> His ordinances are full of irregularities.
> *Heaven* gave birth to the multitudes of the people,
> . . .[13]

and again:

> Heaven, in giving birth to the multitudes of the people,
> To every creature annexed its law.
> The people possessing their constant nature,
> They have a love of virtue.[14]

Just as Heaven is called the giver of life, the first parent of mankind, so too the love of earthly parents becomes an image of the divine favor:

> O my father, who begat me:
> O my mother, who nourished me:
>
> . . .
>
> If I would return your kindness,
> It is like great Heaven, illimitable.[15]

In time of distress, and in words of anguish and complaint, prayer is addressed to Heaven as the Father and Mother of man:

> O vast and distant Heaven,
> [You] who are called Father and Mother,
> [I am] without crime or offense,
> [And yet I] suffer great distress![16]

It appears that Heaven, as supreme deity, was regarded as sole creator of the human race and the universe, at least during the Chou dynasty. Later on, Earth became associated with Heaven in the work of creation, through the influence of the *Yin-yang* school of thought. The Appendices to the Book of Changes show the intrusion of *yin-yang* concepts into Confucianism itself. Here, *"Ch'ien* is Heaven and hence is called Father: *K'un* is Earth and hence is called Mother."* The universe is regarded, at least metaphorically, as the fruit of the union between Heaven and Earth.[17] This development was not definitive to the Confucian understanding of the Creator. But it certainly contributed to a certain confusion regarding the God-Creator: whether this be singular or dual, or whether "creation" is a spontaneous, self-determining process.

The *Yin-yang* school also placed emphasis on the role of the Five Agents—Water, Fire, Wood, Metal and Earth—in the correspondence between the heavenly order and the human one. This led to the emergence of Five Gods—or Lords-on-High. Although this development had little lasting influence upon later Confucianism, it shows the increasing deviation from an earlier belief, a belief more in conformity to the ancestral religion as well as the revelation of the sky hierophany. It helps also to explain the *negation* of God in Confucianism itself, as those scholars who took cognizance of superstitious beliefs and practices associated with the notion of a supreme deity or even of a plurality of deities, became more and more critical, and voiced their disapproval of religion itself.

The Lord of History

Even more than as Creator, God is recognized as the Lord of human history, the source of all power and authority. God has not created man in order to neglect him. God is always with man— especially with the good ruler, who is repeatedly told to "have no doubt nor anxiety, because the Lord-on-High is with you."[18] Indeed, rulership itself is derived from a special Mandate of Heaven:

> Heaven, to protect the inferior people, made for them rulers, made for them teachers, that they may be able to assist the Lord-on-High, to secure the peace of the four quarters [of the Earth].[19]

Through the rulers, the kings, Heaven continues to govern the world. From Heaven come victories and prosperity:

> The Lord surveyed the hills,
> Where the oaks and the *yih* trees were thinned,
> And paths made through the firs and cypresses.
> The Lord, who had raised up the state, raised up a proper ruler for it.
>
> . . .
>
> When [it] came to King Wen,
> His virtue left nothing to be desired:
> He received the Lord's blessing,
> And it was extended to his descendants.[20]

God, indeed, guided King Wen personally, giving him instructions as follows:

> The Lord said to King Wen:
> "Be not like those who reject this and cling to that;
> Be not like those who are ruled by their likings and desires;"[21]

and once more; to King Wen, as Yahweh has done to King David and King Solomon:

The Lord said to King Wen,
"I am pleased with your intelligent virtue,
You do not proclaim it aloud nor portray it,
You show no consciousness of effort,
You act in accordance to the Lord's laws."[22]

If, on the one hand, God has a special relationship with the ruler, on the other hand, God's powers of seeing and hearing are described in terms of those of the people under the ruler's government:

Heaven hears and sees as our people hear and see:
Heaven approves and manifests its awesomeness as our people approve and manifest their awesomeness.
The above and the below reach each other:
How reverent must the masters of the earth be![23]

As the Lord of history, God has chosen one man to be ruler and guide, for his people. Exalted in dignity, the ruler deserves to govern only when he understands his place as the people's servant. From these lines and others like them in the Classics, Confucius' follower, Mencius, would learn to emphasize the importance of the people above the ruler: he exists for them, not they for him.[24] These lines and others like them, continue to offer some clue to the tendency in today's China, the People's Republic, to refer to the people as almighty. And these lines and others like them assure us of Heaven's active role in the dialogue between Man and God.

The Will of God

When we come to the recorded sayings of Confucius—the Analects—and of Mencius, we find that the term Lord-on-High seldom occurs, and usually only in the context of references and allusions to the other Classics. The term Heaven does come up, although not frequently in passages of prayer, as with the Odes and Documents. In the Analects, Confucius is presented as invoking Heaven in his moments of distress and crisis, such as at the death of his favorite disciple (11:8), as a source and principle of his own virtue and mission (9:5), and witness to the integrity of his life and actions (7:22) and as a mysterious Power which controls life and destiny. In one instance, he allegedly said: "He who offends against Heaven has none to whom he can pray" (17:19). It is a statement of support to the idea that Heaven represents for him a personal God, transcending all other spirits—as the absolute Thou of human prayer.[25]

An important term which is found in the Analects is that of *T'ien-ming* (天命). This occurs also in the Odes, the Documents, the Spring-Autumn Classics and other texts. It refers to the Will or Decree of Heaven, and has often the particular meaning of "Mandate of Heaven", the divine origin of rulership. It can also refer to Destiny or Fate. Where Confucius is concerned, the term connotes apparently the meaning of "God's Will"—the will of a personal God. Confucius speaks of it with reverence. Unless one knows this Will (*ming*), he says, one cannot be a gentleman, that is, a person of high moral character (20:3). And yet, he also says of himself that he did not know the "Will of Heaven" (*T'ien-ming*) until the age of fifty (2:4).

Is it possible that Confucius conceived of Heaven's Will as predestined Fate? This has sometimes been alleged, and most strongly by the critics of Confucius in the People's Republic of China.[26] The references they rely upon (Analects 9:1, 16:8), however, are not conclusive. The former reference speaks of a necessary and salutary "fear" of Heaven's Will, and the latter of the "silence" of Heaven which is observed in the ways of Nature. There exists also, of course, a chapter in the book *Mo-tzu* attributed to the fifth century B.C. author, entitled "Against Fatalism," and obviously written as a polemic against the Confucians of those days. Motzu believed evidently in a personal deity and revered his Will. But the polemic itself was directed at the latter-day disciples of Confucius, and not at the man himself.

The word Fate may refer either to a blind force or Destiny, or to the iron law of a merciless deity. Interestingly, the critics of Confucius in the People's Republic prefer to assert his belief in a personal deity with an unchangeable Will, and criticize him severely for this kind of religiosity. Perhaps, this points to a mistaken notion of "personal Godhood" itself.

When we come to the Book of Mencius, we find a clear change

in the meaning of the term Heaven. According to Mencius, Heaven is present within man's heart, so that he who knows his own heart and nature, knows Heaven. It represents, therefore, a greater immanence. It also refers more and more to the source and principle of ethical laws and values. Mencius speaks of Heaven's Will (*T'ien-ming*), but usually with reference to the technical meaning of Heaven's Mandate of rulership. Where Confucius makes infrequent mention of the personal deity, Mencius speaks much more of Heaven—but not always as personal deity.

The mystical dimension of Confucianism is also attested to by the Doctrine of the Mean where the term "Way of Heaven" (*T'ien-tao;* 道) takes over. This Way is eternal and unceasing, transcending time, space, substance and motion. It is characterized by the universal harmony found in nature as well as in Man. It is a fuller expression of the "Unity of Heaven and Man": an integration of the cosmic-moral and human-social levels of thinking (Ch.22).

Nevertheless, the Doctrine of the Mean—as also the Book of Mencius—continues to approve of sacrifices offered to God as Lord-on-High as well as to ancestors. According to Mencius: "Though a man may be wicked, if he adjusts his thoughts, fasts and bathes, he may sacrifice to the Lord-on-High" (4B:25). And the Doctrine of the Mean states: "The ceremonies of the sacrifices to Heaven and Earth are meant for the service of the Lord-on-High and the ceremonies performed in the ancestral temple are meant for the service of the ancestors" (Ch. 19).

And so, while philosophical development expressed a mystical inclination, the philosophers themselves and their writings attest to the continued approval of a cult which represents a belief in a personal deity. This was to continue throughout the history of China, until the early twentieth century, when the establishment of a Republic put an end to the state cult to Heaven. The cult was itself an exclusive one, performed by the emperor—son of Heaven—alone, with the assistance of his Confucian ministers. Nevertheless, in the popular consciousness, as distinct from the philosophical writings, the notion of a supreme and personal deity has remained all through the centuries.

The Negation of God

Already, Confucius' Analects disclose a greater preoccupation with human affairs without so much reference to God as in the Books of Odes and Documents. They express a continued reverence for things divine, and deference for the sage-kings of old. But they do not offer such examples of poignant prayer to the Almighty as found in the pages of Odes and Documents. The Analects speak of a humanism open to the divine, but not excessively preoccupied with the divine. Where Odes and Documents refer to direct instructions given by God to the sage kings, the Analects and the Book of Mencius make mention rather of the "silence of God": that Heaven speaks, not in words, but by deeds and actions, by the operations of nature. Such a divine silence received emphasis at a time of social and political transition and even turbulence. It did not represent agnosticism or scepticism in either Confucius or Mencius. But its expression in both prepares us for the growing "secularizing" tendency in early Confucianism, a tendency which reached the negation of God within the Confucian tradition itself, especially with the writings of Hsün-tzu (fl. 238 B.C) and of Wang Ch'ung (A.D. 27–100?)[27]

Hsün-tzu gives expression to the separation of the two orders: the cosmic-divine, and the human-moral. Writing in a logical and systematic fashion, he seeks to demonstrate the futility of such religious practices as praying for rain, for cure from bodily illness, and of physiognomy or the art of foretelling a person's future by his physical configuration. In doing so, Hsün-tzu demythologizes the notion of Heaven as a personal deity, listening with favor to man's prayer. For him, Heaven is nothing more than physical nature:

> Heaven's ways are constant. It does not prevail because of a sage like Yao; it does not cease to prevail because of a tyrant like Chieh. Respond to it with good government, and good fortune will result: respond to it with disorder, and misfortune will result. If you encourage agriculture and are frugal in expenditures, then Heaven cannot make you poor . . . . If you practice the Way and are not of two minds, then Heaven cannot bring you misfortune.[28]

Obviously, the religious sceptic remains a political and moral teacher. Hsün-tzu appears anxious to assert the independent importance of the human and social realm of action. According to him, one who understands the distinctive functions of Heaven and Man may be called a perfect man.

> You pray for rain and it rains. Why? For no particular reason, I say. It is just as though you had not prayed for rain and it rained anyway.[29]

Hsün-tzu denies the existence of a supreme deity, in control of the cosmic and human universe. He also specifically denies the existence of baleful ghosts and demons. While he uses occasionally the word *shen* (神), which for other writers denotes the spirits of the ancestors and of the powers of nature, he defines it as "that which is completely good and fully ordered" (sec. 8), making it a quality of moral excellence. He is the most thoroughly rationalistic of the early Confucian writers. But he does not discourage certain practices, as the art of divination by use of tortoise shells and milfoil stalks, or the performance of mourning and sacrificial rites. Indeed, he gives positive encouragement to ritual practices, while interpreting them as purely human inventions designed to ornament man's social life and guide him in the proper expression of his emotions. According to him, Heaven, Earth and Man become one in harmony through ritual performance.[30]

Hsün-tzu did not remain alone in his demythologization of Heaven, and in his denial of the existence of spiritual beings. He was joined in this by the later Wang Ch'ung, also a Confucian moralist. Both show a certain influence of naturalism coming from philosophical Taoism. But Wang Ch'ung was even more deeply influenced by the *Yin-yang* school and its naturalistic interpretation of the cosmic order in terms of the interaction of the two basic principles, the active and the passive. Wang Ch'ung was an early materialist who explains the universe in this way:

> When the material forces (*ch'i*; 気) of Heaven and Earth come together, all things are spontaneously produced, just as when the vital forces (*ch'i*) of husband and wife unite, children are naturally born . . . . How do we [know] that Heaven is spontaneous? Because it has neither mouth nor eyes . . . .

> How do we know that Heaven has neither mouth nor eyes? We know it from Earth. The body of Earth is made up of dirt, and dirt of course has neither mouth nor eyes. Heaven and Earth are like husband and wife. Since the body of the Earth has neither mouth nor eyes, we know that Heaven also has neither mouth nor eyes.
>
> The Way of Heaven is to take no action. In spring it does not act to start life, in summer it does not act to help growth . . . . [31]

As also with Hsün-tzu, the negation of God brings with it the negation of spiritual beings, including that of man's spiritual immortality. Wang Ch'ung says quite categorically:

> Man can live because of his vital forces. At death his vital forces are extinct. What makes the vital forces possible is the blood. When a person dies, his blood becomes exhausted. With this his vital forces are extinct, and his body decays and becomes ashes and dust. What is there to become a spiritual being?[32]

The Confucian tradition offers both affirmation and negation of God—but no effort to seek to *prove* God's existence, which represents the great effort of Christian tradition. The Confucian tradition may be described as possessing at the same time theistic and agnostic or even atheistic tendencies, with the former dominating generally over the latter. The Confucian tradition possesses also a *mystical* tendency, present already in Mencius and developed especially by the great representatives of Neo-Confucian philosophy. With these later figures, we come to another dimension of the problem of God as it is found in Confucianism; that of the relationship between God and the Absolute.

THE ABSOLUTE

The Confucian Classics offer us adequate evidence in support of a belief in God as a personal deity. But they offer very little philosophical interpretation concerning the nature and attributes of God. They are more concerned with God's *action*—in creation and in history. And they emphasize the importance of knowing God's Will, so that one might *act* in accordance with it.

The later development in Confucianism, especially during the Han dynasty, shows the result of eclecticism, especially the absorption of ideas coming from the *Yin-yang* school. Han Confucianism focuses upon a mystic correspondence theory of Heaven, Earth and Man—of the natural and cosmic order and the moral and social order. The increasing reference to Heaven-and-Earth points to a stronger emphasis upon immanence rather than transcendence, while the belief in a personal deity became more and more obscured.

But it was Buddhist religious philosophy—much more than Han Confucianism—that stimulated the rise of Neo-Confucianism and its metaphysical concerns. Many of the principal Neo-Confucian philosophers had been earnest students of Buddhism before reaching their own philosophical positions. They continued usually to make meditation—"quiet-sitting"—even after their decision to affirm and strengthen the Confucian interpretation of life and the universe. They borrowed from Buddhist terminology and Buddhist metaphysical ideas in their combat against a Buddhistic inclination toward cosmic pessimism and negation of man's social responsibility.

The Absolute of Neo-Confucian philosophy represents therefore a convergence of Confucianism and Buddhism—through the mediation, sometimes, of religious Taoism. But it is to remain related to all that is "not absolute". It is discovered in becoming rather than being, in the self—and the universe as related to the self—rather than in "the other." It is not removed from life and activity.

This does not mean that the Neo-Confucian Absolute is radically different from any Christian understanding of God, expressed in philosophical language. On the contrary, as we shall see, there are strong resemblances between the Neo-Confucian Absolute and the *mystical* notion of God expressed by the medieval Eckhart and the modern Teilhard de Chardin. There is much affinity also to those philosophical expressions as voiced by such great thinkers as Schelling, Hegel, and A.N. Whitehead. The Neo-Confucian Absolute is not a representation of a dead God. It has become very contemporary.

I propose to discuss the problem of the Absolute in Neo-Confucian philosophy by taking up, in turn, the question of the Absolute as Becoming—found in Chou Tun-yi (1017–73) and Chu Hsi (1130–1200), both of the Sung dynasty—and of the Absolute as Mind—expressed especially by Wang Yang-ming, of the fifteenth century. These two interpretations represent generally two different starting points: the world and the self. I make mention of this while reminding the reader that the Chinese tradition never knew of a rigid separation between the world and the self, as it never developed a rigorous theory of knowledge based on such a separation. I maintain also that while the Confucian thinkers discussed belong to a bygone age, the philosophies they represent are far from dead. Once again, I wish to recall the vehemence of the recent anti-Confucius campaign (1973/74) as evidence supporting the continued survival or vitality of certain Confucian ideas, which have therefore warranted such massive attacks.

The Absolute as Becoming

The Chinese language has no proper verb *to be*. The various substitute forms in usage suggest broad relationship rather than strict identity or non-contradiction. Frequently also, what is suggested is more *becoming* than *being*.

It is important to keep this in mind when examining the Neo-Confucian notion of the Absolute, at once the source of all being and goodness, that which holds the universe together, that which explains its inner and ultimate meaning, and that to which, somehow, all things return.

The Neo-Confucian philosophers have given many names to this Absolute. They have referred to it as the Great Ultimate (*T'ai-chi*). They have referred to it as Heavenly Principle (*T'ien-li;* 天理) or simply Principle (*Li*). They have also referred to it as *Jen* (Humanity, Benevolence, or Love), the ethical virtue which they transformed into a cosmic life-force.

The great Neo-Confucian who has achieved a philosophical synthesis of the speculative thought which blossomed forth during the tenth and eleventh centuries is Chu Hsi. He rendered definite the elevation of the Four Books as the principal *corpus* of speculative Confucian wisdom, and wrote commentaries to them. He vigorously criticized Buddhist religious metaphysics, with its tendency toward cosmic pessimism and ethical indifference. Yet he did not hesitate to borrow selectively from Buddhist ideas and vocabulary, in his reinterpretation of Confucian teachings, bringing to light a transformed view of the world and of man. In doing so, he has also focused attention on the metaphysical First Principle, the Absolute. It is given a place of central importance in the organismic philosophy of Neo-Confucianism.

As synthesizer, Chu Hsi has both inherited and transformed the philosophical legacy which came down to him from his predecessors, Chou Tun-yi, Chang Tsai (1020–27), Ch'eng Hao (1032–85) and Ch'eng Yi (1033–1107). He has done a work comparable to that of Thomas Aquinas, who synthesized the philosophies of the great Scholastics, his predecessors, with the help of the newly discovered Aristotle.

From Chou Tun-yi, Chu Hsi acquired his understanding of the First Principle, source of all being and becoming. The term used in Chinese is that of *T'ai-chi*, that is, the Great and Ultimate—a term derived from the Appendix to the Book of Changes, a Confucian Classic. It is also described as the *Wu-chi* (無極), which can be rendered either as "Non-Ultimate" or "Limitless" owing to the manifold meaning of the word *chi* (ultimate, limit, etc.) as well as the ambiguous character of the Chinese negative (*Wu*). The passage from Chou Tun-yi, quoted by Chu Hsi, is essentially an explanation accompanying the famous "Diagram of the Great Ultimate", a work allegedly of Taoist origin. It illustrates the process of change and becoming through circular representations—of the *T'ai-chi*, which is also *Wu-chi*, of the generation from this First Principle, of two modes of change: *yin* and *yang*, through spontaneous alternation of motion and rest:

> The Non-Ultimate and also the Ultimate: The Ultimate generates *yang* through motion. When this motion reaches its ultimate (limit), it becomes rest. Through rest the Ultimate generates *yin* . . . . Motion and rest alternate and become the root, each of the other. . . .[33]

As this stands, the passage already offers many difficulties of interpretation. The first concerns the Non-Ultimate which is also the Ultimate. The difficulty would diminish if one could fix the translation of *Wu-chi* as Limitless, a negative way of connoting plenitude of perfection. But the Chinese term keeps open the alternative translation of "Non-Ultimate." It becomes an example of paradoxical identity, so often discovered in Chinese philosophy. It has been interpreted as referring to a power informing the entire universe—which is itself a single organism—and present everywhere within it rather than at any one cardinal point. One is at once reminded of Pascal's remark concerning the universe, how the center is everywhere and the circumference is nowhere.

Chou Tun-yi does not clearly say whether the Great Ultimate is only the source of all becoming, or whether it too undergoes change. He merely proceeds to say that the alternation of *yin* and *yang* gives rise to the Five Elements—themselves agents of change rather than material substances—of Water, Fire, Wood, Metal and Earth. A further transformative union of these Five with *yin* and *yang* brings forth the masculine (*ch'ien*) and feminine (*k'un*) forces, which, in turn, engender the "myriad things" of the universe, of which man is the most perfect. Chou Tun-yi does not even say why there must be an Ultimate, or clearly postulate that this *is* the Absolute. He merely repeats that the Great Ultimate is also the "Non-Ultimate".

It is Chu Hsi himself who has clarified for us some of these problems. Making use of the method of negation so characteristic of Chinese metaphysics, Chu Hsi interprets Chou Tun-yi's propositions by saying that:

> The Ultimate has neither spatial restriction nor physical form. There is no location in which it may be placed. When it is considered in the state prior to motion, there is nothing but rest. . . . Motion is the motion of the Ultimate and rest is its rest, although motion and rest themselves are not the Ultimate. That is why Chou speaks of it [also] as Non-Ultimate (or Limitless).[34]

In other words, the Great Ultimate is said to be above all limitations of space and form, and, in a sense, even of motion and rest. And yet, paradoxically, it is also said to be both the source and principle of all change and becoming—as well as of rest and passivity. It is the Absolute—not as detached from relativity and change, but as found itself in relativity and change.[35] For being and becoming somehow penetrate each other, each the source of the other. Thus, Chu's efforts are directed toward the construction of a world view which explains the countless phenomena of existence as having come from one original source, pure and undifferentiated, the totality of reality. And so, where *T'ai-chi*, the Great and Ultimate, fullness of all perfection, represents the way of supereminence in the human predication of the divine, *Wu-chi*, at once Non-Ultimate and Limitless, represents the way of negation in such predication. Together, we find a dipolar description of the Absolute, at once transcending all change and yet immanent in change.

According to both Chou Tun-yi and Chu Hsi, the source and principle of being and becoming is also the source and principle of all moral goodness. According to Chu Hsi specifically, this principle is immanent as well as transcendent: present in the wholeness of the universe, and present also in each and every creature:

> The Ultimate is simply the principle of the highest good. Each and every human being has in himself the Ultimate: each and every thing has in itself the Ultimate. What Master Chou calls the Ultimate is a name which represents all the virtues and the highest good in Heaven and Earth, in man and in things.[36]

Although present and immanent within all things, the Ultimate is not "cut up into [many] pieces." It remains the one principle, the one reality, like "the moon reflecting itself in ten thousand streams." With such words, Chu Hsi gives witness to the philosophical influences coming to him from Hua-yen and T'ien-t'ai Buddhism, with their teaching of "one in all and all in one," of the "Storehouse of the Absolute" in its totality, which has within itself the natures pertaining to all other things. He also offers an echo of Nicolas of Cusa, and his presentation of God through the "coincidentia oppositorum". Nicolas speaks of a God who is at once the greatest and the smallest, present in all things, as all things also are present in him. For Nicolas, God is the source of all wisdom and goodness, the supreme, universal, creative unity of the possibility of things—like Chu Hsi's Great Ultimate. For Nicolas also, the world can have no center and no circumference, unless God be described as both—as Chu Hsi's Non-Ultimate, the Limitless. For both Chu Hsi and Nicolas, the universe is a reflection of the Ultimate or invisible God, from whom it proceeds and on whom it is entirely dependent.[37]

Even more than Nicolas of Cusa, A.N. Whitehead, the modern philosopher, has offered a description of the interrelationship between God and the World which presents a closer proximation of Chu Hsi's philosophy. To use Whitehead's own words:

> It is as true to say that God is permanent and the World fluent, as that the World is permanent and God is fluent.
>
> It is as true to say that, in comparison with the World, God is one and the World many, as that the World is one and God many.
>
> It is as true to say that, in comparison with the World, God is actual eminently, as that, in comparison with God, the World is actual eminently.
>
> It is as true to say that the World is immanent in God, as that God is immanent in the World.
>
> It is as true to say that God transcends the World, as that the World transcends God.
>
> It is as true to say that God creates the world, as that the World creates God.
>
> . . .
>
> The theme of Cosmology, which is the basis of all religions, is the story of the dynamic effort of the World passing into everlasting unity, and of the static majesty of God's vision, accomplishing its purpose of completion by absorption of the World's multiplicity of effort.[38]

The theme of cosmology, dominant in Chou Tun-yi and Chu Hsi, has been continued by the twentieth century Confucian philosopher, Fung Yu-lan, at least in the days before the anti-Confucius Campaign. For Fung, the Absolute is called *Tao* or Heaven—that in which one is all and all is one, the transcending Principle (*Li*), the fullness of which is Great Ultimate (*T'ai-chi*), as well as Vital Force (*Ch'i*).

Fung Yu-lan also uses another word: *jen* (humanity, benevolence).[39] He describes the life of the sage, the perfect man, in terms of *jen*. He also speaks of *jen* as that which makes possible man's oneness with the Universe. The man of *jen* becomes a citizen of Heaven, through the presence in him of that which unites subject with object, self with the Absolute. Fung insists upon the *philosophical*, that is, non-religious, nature of his ideas, while acknowledging their affinity to mysticism—a mysticism proper to philosophical thinking, which he inherited from Mencius, from Chu Hsi and the other great Neo-Confucians.

Also in our own times, the conception of God expressed by Teilhard de Chardin, a paleontologist and mystic who lived many years in China without learning the Chinese language or philosophy, offers strong echoes of both Nicolas of Cusa and Chu Hsi, while maintaining always a historical dimension which comes with the Christian theology of redemption:

> God reveals himself everywhere . . . as a "universal milieu," only because he is the "ultimate point" upon which all realities converge.
>
> However vast the divine milieu may be, it is in reality a "center."
>
> The Creator, and especially the Redeemer, have steeped themselves in all things and penetrated all things.[40]

But how about the notion of a personal God, so evident in earlier Confucianism? Has Chu Hsi rejected it, or lost sight of it?

Some of the Jesuit missionaries who worked in China obviously thought so. They praised early Confucianism for its affirmation of the personal God, while criticizing later Confucianism for an allegedly "materialist" philosophy.

And yet, if we read Chu Hsi himself, we cannot but discover otherwise. In answer to a question posed to him concerning the interpretation of the term "Heaven" as it is found in the Classics, Chu Hsi says that the word should be understood according to its varying contexts. In some passages, it refers to the Azure Sky, the Emporyean, in others, to the Supreme Ruler or Master (*Chu-tsai;* 主宰), and in still others to Principle (*Li;* 理).[41]

Elsewhere, Chu has also referred to the Azure Sky as that

which—in a pre-Copernican universe—rotates in endless revolution. He has also commented upon the more anthropomorphic presentations in the Classics regarding the Lord-on-High (*Shang-ti*) by explaining that while it is not correct to say that there is "a man in the Heavens" who is Lord and Ruler of the world, it is equally wrong to say that "there is no [such] Ruler." Thus he appears to consider the Empyrean to be the *locus* of some divine power, and makes use of the same word to refer to the supreme Ruler, Lord-on-High:

> The Odes and Documents speak as though there is a human being there above, commanding things to come to pass, as in [passages] where they mention the Lord (*Ti*) as being filled with wrath, etc.
> But even here what they refer to is [the action of] Principle. There is nothing more eminent under Heaven (i.e., in the universe) than Principle. Hence, it is called Ruler. "The august Lord-on-High has conferred even upon the inferior people a moral sense." [The word] "conferred" conveys the idea of a Ruler.[42]

Thus, as far as Chu Hsi is concerned, the two words "Heaven" and "Lord-on-High" both refer to some "Ruler-on-High"—God. But Chu has endeavored to remove the anthropomorphic overtones of these words, while affirming the presence of some divine power ruling over the world. He has also identified this Ruler's action with that of Principle—that which, in his own words, both flows from and is one with *T'ai-chi*, the Ultimate, source and principle of all things. And so, the belief in a supreme deity has subsisted, although Chu prefers to emphasize the deity as metaphysical Absolute more than as personal Absolute.

The Absolute as Mind

Where Chou Tun-yi, Chu Hsi and even Fung Yu-lan prefer to discover the Absolute in the World, and perceive a mutual penetration of the Absolute and the World, other Chinese philosophers have preferred to find the Absolute in an experience of the Self. This does not mean to say that the Chinese make a clear distinction

between Self and the World.[43] On the contrary, the Chinese philosophical tradition lacks such a clear distinction. Confucian philosophy
especially has not evolved any strong theory of knowledge based on
the logical separation of subject and object. But Confucian philosophers did possess a general awareness of a certain dualism between Man and Nature. The very emphasis upon the "Oneness of
Heaven and Man" presupposes such a dualism which is harmoniz-
ed and overcome by a form of philosophical transcendence over
the subject/object dichotomy. This is true of both the schools
of Chu Hsi and of his rivals. But if Chu Hsi begins with the
World, and then speaks of the Ultimate as present in both the
World and in Self, Lu Chiu-yüan (1139–93) and others begin with
the Self, to speak of ultimate reality in terms of a subjectivity
which infuses all objectivity. Such a philosophy has been described
as the School of the Mind, in contrast to Chu Hsi's philosophy,
which belongs to the School of the Principle.

The Chinese word Mind (*Hsin;* 心) is derived etymologically from
a flame symbol. As a philosophical term, it is especially found in
the Book of Mencius and also in the later translations of Buddhist
Mahayana sutras, where it refers to ultimate reality. In Buddhist
usage, this is sometimes represented in terms of negation—as No-
Mind (*Wu-hsin;* 無心), or in terms of a basic substance—as Original
Mind (*Pen-hsin;* 本心).

The Neo-Confucian philosophers restored to this word its pristine meaning—as man's psychic principle—while retaining the
Buddhist metaphysical connotation. Lu Chiu-yüan, for example,
identifies Mind with Chu Hsi's Principle (*Li*). He refers to it also
as the Mind of the sages, who participated in the *Tao* (Absolute)
and in the Mind of *Tao*:

> Sages appeared tens of thousands of generations ago. They
> shared this Mind; they shared this Principle. Sages will ap-
> pear tens of thousands of generations to come. They will
> share this Mind; they will share this Principle. Sages appear
> over the Four Seas. They share this Mind; they share this
> Principle.[44]

Lu's philosophical heir, Wang Yang-ming, continued to interi-
orize the metaphysical Principle. He too speaks of Mind as that

which explains the meaning both of the universe and of man, identifying it not only with Principle (*Li*), but also with Nature (*Hsing*—ie., human nature and the nature of things). But Wang Yang-ming also takes a further step, going deeper into the Mind, and discovering therein, levels of profundity of both meaning and presence. He identifies Mind with Original Substance(*Pen-t'i*; 本體), speaking thereby of the Mind's Original Substance, which, in turn, is identified with both Heavenly Principle (*T'ien-li*) and with ultimate reality (*Tao*).

> The Original Substance of the Mind is nothing other than the Heavenly Principle. It is orginally never out of accord with Principle. This is your True Self. This True Self is the Master of [your] physical body. With it, one lives; without it, one dies.[45]

And so, for the good of the physical body itself, one should take good care of the True Self, keeping always intact its Original Substance. And then, as he shreds off the superstructures which his "false self"—his ego—has erected as barricades behind which he has formerly attempted to hide himself and limit his activity, as he clears away the selfishness which hinders his inner vision, he will discover this innermost core of his own being. He will then become transformed, completely true to himself and to the universe in which he lives, following its natural courses of operation which will lead him to the realization of perfect goodness, which is the ultimate revelation of the Absolute in himself.

In this way also, Wang Yang-ming offers his understanding of the Absolute as present in the Relative and Subjective—in the Mind of Man. With mystic fervor, he speaks of a process of spiritual cultivation possibly culminating in an experience of enlightenment, which is essentially the discovery of the True Self. The language itself is reminiscent of Christian mystics, especially of Meister Eckhart, for whom "the spark of the soul is the light of God's reflection, which is always looking back to God."[46]

Eckhart's distinction between God and the Godhead probably offers the best analogy for an understanding of the Neo-Confucian subjective Absolute, described in terms of increasing immanence in relation to both the world and man. Words like Original Mind

(*Pen-hsin*), Original Substance (*Pen-t'i*) and even *Jen* all refer, according to such analogy, to the Confucian "Godhead" as distinct from the Confucian "God." The former is reality, hidden at the heart of things, and especially in the heart of man, where the latter is its manifestation of human consciousness.

Between Eckhart and Wang Yang-ming, one finds the same emphasis on the oneness of all things. For Eckhart, this is the oneness of God and Man; for Wang, it is that of "Heaven and Earth and all things;" for both, it is experienced and reflected in man's heart and mind, the *locus* itself of this unity. Eckhart speaks of man's "blood kinship with God." Yang-ming refers to the Mind as that "drop of blood" which proves our relationship to the ancient sages, themselves the best imitators of the ways of Heaven.[47]

In a powerful language, Eckhart has described the soul's union with God in terms of the divinization of man. He speaks of the soul stealing out of itself and entering into Pure Being:

> The "I" is there reduced to utter nought and nothing is left there but God. Yet, even God she [the soul] outshines here as the sun outshines the moon, and with God's all penetrativeness she streams into the eternal Godhead where in an eternal stream God is flowing into God.[48]

Wang Yang-ming's philosophy also offers resonances of German idealist philosophy, especially that of Schelling and Hegel, whose thought systems offer a metaphysical expression of medieval mystical doctrine. For Schelling, God is the Absolute Self, that which is above all reality, and yet comprehensive of all reality. For Hegel, God is the Absolute. He is also infinite Life, Truth, Idea and Spirit. He regards these notions in terms of the dialectical process, which integrates the finite in the world of experience into the infinite.

Wang Yang-ming's philosophy of the Absolute Mind is also reflected in his own philosophical heir, Hsiung Shih-li (1885–), who identifies ultimate reality (*Pen-t'i* or Original Substance) to the Original Mind (*Pen-hsin*), as well as to the metaphysical *jen*, the ethical virtue of Love and Benevolence which has acquired ontological status. *Jen* is universal virtue; it is also reality, creativity and absolute becoming.

Jen is the Original Mind. It is the original reality that we share with Heaven and Earth and all things. Mencius speaks of the Four Beginnings [of virtue] separately, and from the point of view of the manifestation of the Original Mind. . . . *Jen*-in-itself is the source of all transformations and the foundation of all things.[49]

Jen, of course, is represented by a written character in Chinese (仁) composed of the words "man" (人) and "two" (二). It is an expression of relation, of intersubjectivity. And it has become absolutized without losing certain qualities of relativity. And here, Hsiung Shih-li joins Chu Hsi's twentieth century heir, Fung Yu-lan, who begins his philosophy with the World only to transcend the distinction between the object and the subject, finding also the absolute *Jen* in both World and Self.

The Absolute as Relation

Of the many words used by the Confucians to represent the Absolute, this word *jen* deserves closer attention. Originally designating the virtue of kindness on the part of superiors for inferiors, the word took on the meaning of a universal virtue with Confucius and his followers, and has been variously rendered as Humanity, Benevolence, and Love. In the subsequent development of Neo-Confucian metaphysics, it acquired a vitalist dimension, referring to life and creativity, but without losing its essential meaning as a universal virtue which governs the relationship between human beings. In the systems of Chu Hsi and Wang Yang-ming, as well as in those of Fung Yu-lan and Hsiung Shih-li, *jen* occupies a central position, representing the integration of the various ethical, metaphysical and cosmological levels of reality.[50] *Jen* refers to the bond of altruistic love between men. *Jen* also refers to the bond between man and the universe. And *jen* refers, besides, to the life of the universe itself, even to the totality of reality which makes the universe what it is. *Jen* is Principle(*Li*) and Great Ultimate (*T'ai-chi*). *Jen* is also Mind and True Self. And *jen* remains always the virtue which defines the essence of the true man.

The obvious parallel in the Christian tradition is that of *agape*, charity or Love. But the starting point of the evolution of meaning is different with the Christian virtue of charity. It begins with the revelation contained in the Scripture: that God is Love (1 John 4:39). Christian charity is conceived in terms of an imitation by Man of God's Love. But it has also evolved, extending in meaning to include that of grace and of life, of man's participation in God's life of love. All the same, it includes the same two notions as the Confucian *jen*: of love as virtue and as life. And, in the thought of Teilhard de Chardin, even Christian charity appears to become transformed with the doctrine of the Cosmic Christ, center of the Universe. Love becomes the hidden energy and dynamic meaning of all reality. Speaking of the distinction between the "Within" and "Without" of things—a very Eastern perception—Teilhard's words suggest a strong evolutionary thrust:

> Driven by the forces of love, the fragments of the world seek each other so that the world may come to being. This is no metaphor; and it is much more than poetry. . . . To perceive cosmic energy "at the fount" we must, if there is a *within* of things, go down into the internal or radial zone of spiritual attractions.
>
> Love in all its subtleties is nothing more, and nothing less, than the more or less direct trace marked on the heart of the element by the physical convergence of the universe upon itself.[51]

Life and hominisation. Love and its Energy. The personal and personalizing Universe. Is not this language reminiscent of that of the Neo-Confucians, and especially of Hsiung Shih-li's characterizations of the Confucian *jen*, a notion representative of that which is at once rational and yet affective, immanent and yet transcendent, constant and yet dynamic? Indeed, has not this Chinese word, with its rich philosophical connotations—developed during the centuries—of love, benevolence, life and creativity, great potential for help and insight in understanding further the Christian God of Love? *Jen* began, as mentioned earlier, as a virtue of horizontal relationships. It gained in breadth and in depth, acquiring a dimension of verticality, and serving as a *raison-d'être* for the oneness of Heaven and Man.

And so, it is in human relationship that the Confucian philosopher-sage has discovered the meaning of virtue and morality, and especially of love. And then, going from the microcosm to the macrocosm, he has discovered the same force of love existing in the universe itself, the reason for the creativity of the universe, a love which is life, in both Man and the World. Thus, he is led to the discovery of the Absolute, of that to which he also gives the name of Heaven. But then, he has not forgotten his starting point, the realm of human relationship. Over and over again, he returns to this relationship in order to rediscover Love, Life and the Absolute.

Jen is the word which sums up the meaning and greatness of Man. It points out the presence in Man of what is greater than himself, of what is also in the universe and yet greater than the universe. *Jen* refers to the meeting of Heaven and of Man—in human relationship.

THE SITUATION TODAY

Our discussions of the problem of God in Confucianism would be of merely historical interest should the situation today be vastly different from that of the Classics and the Philosophers. Before going further, we must therefore answer this question: how much relevance do Confucian beliefs in God retain in contemporary Asia? Has the earlier belief in a personal deity been entirely superceded by the later philosophical notion of the Absolute? And has the philosophical Absolute itself yielded place to modern secularism—whether in a Marxist ideology or not?

This problem of the relevance of our discussion is of course inextricably interwoven with the problem of the viability of Confucianism itself. Here, it is important to remind ourselves of the geopolitical aspect of the religious situation in East Asia today. The former Confucian world of China, Korea, Japan and Vietnam is now governed by very different political systems, Marxist and non-Marxist. An anti-Confucius Campaign had especially swept over the People's Republic of China during the year 1973/74. On the other hand, the governments in power in both South Korea and Taiwan give official support to Confucian values, and continue to maintain a cult of Confucius himself. Whether the critiques in China had really demolished Confucian influence itself, and whether official encouragement in South Korea and Taiwan had actually promoted such influence, are however open questions.

The problem of viability is all the more difficult on account of the nature of Confucianism itself as a *diffused* religion—should one call it that—rather than an organized one. This explains its elusiveness in face of attack and its continued strength after the loss of status as state ideology. This explains in part also the persistence of earlier notions into later periods. Where an organized religion requires the support, among other things, of an institutionalized priesthood for its own survival, a diffused religion has never known or needed such support. And, as diffused religion, Confucianism has become virtually inseparable from a traditional moral order which has undergone great changes, but which continues to manifest a remarkable resilience.

It appears that the notion of a personal deity has survived up to the twentieth century, on the one hand, through an official cult offered to Heaven, and on the other, through the popular belief in a Heavenly Ruler, sometimes called *T'ien-lao-yeh* (天老爺; Heavenly Master). It also appears that the Absolute of the philosophers continues to occupy the attention of those Chinese scholars who consider it their task to reinterpret the Confucian tradition. Indeed, where the Chinese scholars of an earlier generation, including Hu Shih, had tended to emphasize the secular dimension of Confucian humanism, others who have emerged, with few exceptions, have shown a more positive appreciation of its religiosity. This was specifically the theme of the well-known "Manifesto for a Reappraisal of Sinology and Reconstruction of Chinese Culture."[52] Its signatories point out the identification of the Way of Heaven (*T'ien-tao*; 天道) and the Way of Man (*Jen-tao*; 人道) as the central legacy of Confucianism and exhort greater attention on the part of Western Sinologists to this properly Confucian spirituality. However, these same scholars have generally remained reticent regarding the problem of God. They merely remark that the personality characteristic of the God of early Confucianism yielded place gradually to a transpersonal character which such terms as "Heaven" or the "Heavenly Way" acquired.

On the other hand, Chinese Marxist scholars in the People's Republic have repeatedly pointed out the religiosity of the Confucian tradition. They criticize it for its "metaphysical idealism" (*wei-hsin*; 唯心). They see some difference between what they call Chu Hsi's "objective idealism" and Wang Yang-ming's "subjective idealism," but assert that the two share as common goal the elaboration and development of the inner, mystical dimension which has been present in Confucianism since the time of Mencius. They also denounce the religious-ascetic aspects of the Neo-Confucian doctrine of self-cultivation as "clericalism" or "monasticism" (*seng-lü chu-yi*; 僧侶主義), and Neo-Confucian metaphysics and ethics as "scholasticism" (*ching-yüan che-hsüeh*; 經院哲学). They even use the word "theology" (*shen-hsüeh*; 神学) to designate neo-Confucian ideas on Heaven and the Way, which, they say, belong to the realm of religious superstitions.[53] Of Wang Yang-ming they say:

> Wang . . . considers himself a pope. The extension of *Liang-chih* (knowledge of good) is a simple religious doctrine . . . From such fictions of mystical religiosity, we can see how Idealism is ultimately related to theology.[54]

In the writings of Yang-Jung-kuo, an arch critic of Confucianism, such a critique has been extended backward in time, and articulated against the teachings of Confucius himself, who, according to him, taught a concept of *jen* which was but the subjective transformation of an earlier, religious notion of *T'ien-ming* (Will of Heaven). As he expresses it, the entire history of thought during the so-called Spring-Autumn and Warring States periods (722–222 B.C.) was characterized by the struggle between atheism and religious thought—especially as polarized between the schools of Legalism and Confucianism.[55]

Should such interpretations be regarded merely as a result of indiscriminate attack on the Confucian heritage, articulated by Marxists who are too well acquainted with the critiques of religion made by Feuerbach and Marx? Should they not also be regarded as expressive of a certain persuasion among scholars trained more in Western methods of analysis—including the Marxist—and so more prepared to discern ideas of the Absolute, of God, and also of religiosity in an age-old Chinese tradition?

Have We the Same God?

Have we the same God? The assumption so far has been, Yes, Yahweh is the God of Israel, and also the universal God, just as the Lord-on-High represents the God of the Shang house, becoming by extension the God of all. Yahweh is a personal God, full of power and mercy, just as the Lord-on-High is father and mother of the people.

There are, of course, some differences. The word "Yahweh" implies a notion of self-subsistence, but cannot be directly expressed in the Chinese language which lacks the verb to be. While both Yahweh and the Lord-on-High are presented as giver of life and lord of history, the Confucian tradition has never developed a *theory* of creation *ex nihilo*. The later substitution of the word Heaven for that of Lord-on-High also strengthened the direction of immanence and the idea of a spontaneous creation. Besides, the word "Heaven" lacks inherently a notion of personality, and its increasing usage has been accompanied by an evolution in the meaning of the word itself—in a mystical, perhaps "pantheistic" direction. At the same time, the reference of the word to a supreme being, having much the same characteristics as the Lord-on-High, continues to persist, and has remained to this day.

Certainly, Heaven has been regarded by the Classics as intimately involved in both the natural processes of life and reproduction as well as in human history itself. The very teaching of the Mandate of Heaven can be said to resemble, at least in part, that of the Covenant between Yahweh and his people. But where Yahweh became Theos in the New Testament, assuming more and more characteristics of love and compassion, manifested in the historical revelation of Jesus Christ, the Confucian Lord-on-High and Heaven lack any such clear historicity. As recipients of the Mandate of Heaven, the legendary sage-kings as well as the historical emperors represented a kind of divine incarnation, but were never personally deified. None of them ever made any claim to the uniqueness of revelation of the divine, as did Jesus Christ.

Indeed, for the Confucian, the supreme deity is also that which is in process (Book of Changes), the transcendent is also that which is immanent (Odes, Documents, Mencius, Doctrine of the Mean) and the notion of God embraces within itself many paradoxes. In fact, this very paradoxy is the reason for the Classics to give many names to God, while refraining from lengthy discussions about his nature and attributes, speaking only of his presence and power. Certainly, among other things, the continuance of the cult of Heaven, offered by the emperor annually to the deity on high, assured the survival of the notion of Heaven as supreme deity— and not merely as a representation of the ultimate reality hidden in the universe, still less as a physical emporyean. It is interesting to note here that whereas the Gothic cathedrals, with their sky-scraping spires, have become the symbol of the medieval Christian's desire to attain the transcendent God, the Temple of Heaven, which stands today outside Peking, is a vast compound surrounding its own "Holy of Holies"—an outdoor marble altar under the blue sky itself, hierophany of divinity. The Confucian world-view sees a greater continuum between the divine and the human—and the interpenetration of one in the other—where the Christian insists upon a greater difference, the "otherness" of God.

In spite of this, the fact that the Confucian cult of Heaven was the prerogative of the emperor alone meant that the mass of the populace had no direct part in the yearly liturgical celebration to the supreme deity. They had to content themselves with *lesser* cults, especially those offered to local and ancestral spirits. And so, if Heaven was *philosophically* closer to the people, it must have seemed more removed from them *cultically*. Personal prayer to Heaven was of course never forbidden. But it became institutionalized, and we have few examples of such.

The Historicity of God

By the historicity of God I refer to the historical character of God's self-revelation to man as this is understood in Christianity.[56] I contend that this marks an important difference between the Christian and the Confucian notion of God.

One cannot just say that there has been no historical "revelation" in the Confucian tradition. The truth is much more complex. While the knowledge of God as Lord-on-High and Heaven had come to the Chinese people through "natural hierophanies",[57] these in turn appear to have been largely mediated through sage-kings and other charismatic, almost prophetic, individuals. Even the later Neo-Confucian philosophers were fond of pointing back to a passage in the Book of Documents taken out of a chapter allegedly transmitted to posterity in the old, pre-Ch'in script: the "Counsels of GreatYü." The authenticity of the chapter is subject to doubt—as the great philosopher Chu Hsi himself pointed out. But the cryptic formula contained therein has been regarded with deference by a whole line of Confucian thinkers, including Chu Hsi and others, as well as their counterparts in Japan and Korea. I refer here to sixteen Chinese characters, which may be translated as follows:

Man's mind-and-heart (*jen-hsin*; 人心) is prone to error,
While the mind and heart of the Way (*Tao-hsin*; 道心) is subtle.
Remain discerning and single-minded:
Keep steadfastly to the Mean (*Chung;* 中).[58]

As commonly agreed, this "central message"—the secret transmission of the sages—presents a warning and an exhortation, through the statement of a duality between human fallibility and the subtlety and evasiveness of the Way (*Tao*), for the sake of encouraging constant discernment and psychic equilibrium. The implicit vision is that of the union of Heaven and Man—with Heaven understood as that which holds the cosmos together, the fullness of being and goodness.

The historicity of this revelation is of course open to question. That Chu Hsi should doubt the textual authenticity of this passage, and yet make use of it in his own philosophical hermeneutics, points to the priority he placed upon the *idealized* character of the sages' revelation. Not that he or the others consciously doubted the historical existence of the ancient sages. But neither he nor the others regarded the historicity of their allegedly revealed teachings as of primary importance. What is essential is the *meaning* of the teaching itself.

When comparing the Christian tradition to the Confucian, what becomes clear is the primary importance given to the *historical* character of God's revelation to man—first to the Jews on

Mount Sinai, and then to all, in Jesus Christ. The earlier revelation on Sinai may be compared in some ways to the sacred legacy of the Confucian sages. It contains as its core, the teachings concerning God himself—Yahweh—and his relationship to his chosen people. It invites a response in faith and obedience. But the claim of historicity is not easy to substantiate.

In Jesus Christ, however, we confront an authentic historical figure. One may accept or deny his alleged claims. But one cannot but be impressed by the *historicity* of this revelation—as understood by its interpreters. The entire life of Jesus Christ—birth, career, death and resurrection—represents this historical revelation. Can this revelation find any parallel in the Confucian tradition? Is there not in the Confucian teaching of sagehood, a soteriological dimension, by which the sage is conceived of as a person with a conscious mission to save the world from socio-political as well as moral degeneration? And is this not also related to the Buddhist doctrine of the *bodhisattva*, who foregoes his own *nirvana* in order to achieve the salvation of others?

It is true, that the soteriological dimension is present in both Confucianism and Buddhism, although in different manners. But the *uniqueness* of the historical dimension of this salvation is absent.

Such a historical dimension may be discerned more readily in the Pure Land doctrine of the Buddha Amitabha and his Bodhisattva Avalokitesvara—in Chinese, Kuan-yin (観音), the female transformation of the original Indian male personality.[59] But the Buddhist tradition has never made a *unique* historical claim for the particular savior in question. And no such claim has ever been made in the Confucian tradition. Here, as Mencius points out, sages are expected to occur at regular intervals in history.[60] But the fact that they have not done so can be no support to any unique claim to revelation.

The *difference* between the Christian and the Confucian understanding of God lies principally, therefore, in the Person of Jesus Christ himself—and in his significance for mankind. The Confucian tradition speaks of many sages—even if most were legendary ones. The Christian religion has known of many holy men and women, but point to Jesus Christ as the unique revelation of God. Christianity bears the imprint of the historicity of the Christ-event, in a manner which is different from what Confucianism bears of Confucius or any other sage. At the heart of Confucianism, stands the teaching of the oneness of Heaven and Man. At the heart of Christianity, stands Jesus Christ, regarded as the Savior, in Whom God has revealed Himself to Man in a unique way.

NOTES

1. See Paul Tillich, *Systematic Theology* (Chicago, 1963), vol. 3, pp. 130–34, John E. Smith, *Experience and God* (New York, 1968), Introduction and ch. 2, Louis Dupré, *The Other Dimension: A Search for the Meaning of Religious Attitudes* (New York, 1972), p. 8. I have no intention of saying that all religions help mankind with equal efficacy in the task of self-transcendence. There may be important differences, just as there are "surrogate relgions" which make an idol of state, leader, or doctrine.
2. For the English translation of Heiler's book (*Das Gebet*, 1921), see the work translated and edited by Samuel McComb (New York, 1932). Friedrich Heiler was a disciple of Nathan Söderblom, who wrote of the belief in God in different religions. See especially chapter 6 in Heiler's book.
3. For the names of God, see Walther Eichrodt, *Theologie des Alten Testaments* (Stuttgart, 1968), vol. 1, pp. 110, 116–21. See also especially John Courtney Murray, *The Problem of God* (New Haven, 1964), ch. 1.
4. Karl Rahner, "Theos in the New Testament," *Theological Investigations*, tr. by C. Ernst (Baltimore, 1965), vol. 1, pp. 79–148; Gerhard Kittel, ed., *Theological Dictionary of the New Testament*, tr. by G. W. Bromiley (Grand Rapids, 1965), vol, 3, pp. 65–119 (article by E. Stauffer).
5. See Hans Conzelmann, *An Outline of the Theology of the New Testament* (*Grundriss der Theologie des Neuen Testaments*, 1968), English translation by John Bowden. (New York, 1969), pp. 13–15, 99–105. Also see Henri de Lubac, *The Discovery of God*, tr. by A. Dru (London, 1960), pp. 13–17, 119–212, *passim.*, Heinrich Ott, *God*, tr. by I. and U. Nicol (Richmond, 1974), pp. 66–78; E. Schillebeeckx, *God and Man*, tr. by E. Fitzgerald (New York, 1969), pp. 18–40.
6. I refer to such problems as presented by Ernst Bloch in his work *Atheismus im Christentum* (Frankfurt, 1968), where his rejection of a domineering, awe-inspiring God entails the denial of God himself.
7. See especially Antoine Tien Tcheu-kang, *Dieu dans les huit premiers classiques chinois* (Fribourg, 1942) for an examination of the relevant texts, Tu Erh-wei, *Chung-kuo ku-tai tsung-chiao yen-chiu* (Studies about the Religions of Ancient China), (Taipei, 1959), especially pp. 92–100 for an anthropological approach, Werner Eichhorn, *Die Religionen Chinas* (Stuttgart, 1973), pp. 31–35, for the relationship between the ancestral cult and the notion of a supreme deity. See also especially Joseph Shih, "The Notions of God in the Ancient Chinese Re-

ligion," *Numen* 16 (1969), pp. 99–138, "Mediators in Chinese Religion," *Studia Missionalia* 21 (1972), pp. 113–26, and "Non e Confucio un Profeta?" *Studia Missionalia* 22 (1973), pp. 105–21. The last two mentioned articles relate less to the problem of God as such, and more to the idea of early Confucianism as approaching that of Heiler's prototype of "prophetical religion."

8. The question is: did *Ti begin* as a divinized ancestor, or was it rather the transformation of an earth-god, or rain-god—or even moon-god—into a supreme deity, also regarded as a kind of divinized ancestral spirit? There are different opinions on this subject. See Carl Hentze, *Mythes et symboles lunaires* (Antwerp, 1932), Bernhard Karlgren, "Legends and Cults in Ancient China," *Bulletin of the Museum of Far Eastern Antiquities* No. 18 (1946), pp. 199–365; see also the works of archaeologists and paleographers: Cheng Te-k'un, *Archeology in China* (Cambridge, 1960), vol. 2,233, Tsung-tung Chang, *Der Kult der Shang-Dynastie im Spiegel der Orakelinschriften: Eine paläographische Studie zur Religion im archaischen China* (Wiesbaden, 1970), pp. 211–36.

9. See Fu Ssu-nien, *Hsing-ming ku-hsün pien-cheng* (On the Ancient Meanings of Nature and Destiny) (Changsha, 1940), pt. 2, 1a–8a; Bernhard Karlgren, *Grammatica Serica Recensa* (Göteborg, 1964), pp. 104, 233, Chang, op. cit., pp. 236–42; see also Mircea Eliade, *Traité d'Histoire des Religions* (Paris, 1964), for a discussion of the sky-hierophany in different religions.

10. The fusion of *Ti* and *T'ien* in referring to a deity on high appears to be the general consensus of Chinese scholars. See Ku Chieh-kang, ed., *Ku-shih pien* (Arguments on Ancient History) (1926 ed., Hongkong reprint, 1962), vol. 1, pp. 199–200, (1930ed.), vol. 2, pp. 20–32.

11. Joseph Shih, op. cit., pp. 122–25. Shih uses especially Hentze's and Tu Erh-wei's works. See also Bruno Schindler, "The development of Chinese Conceptions of Supreme Beings" *Asia Major*: Introductory Vol. (1922) 298–366.

12. James Legge, tr., *The Chinese Classics* (Oxford: Clarendon Press, 1865), Vol. 3, 283.

13. Legge, *The Chinese Classics*, vol. 4, p. 541.

14. Legge, *The Chinese Classics*, vol 4, p. 505.

15. Ibid., p. 352.

16. Ibid., p. 340.

17. For the word *Ch'ien*, see Karlgren, op. cit., p. 57. For the Book of Changes, see Hellmut Wilhelm, *Change: Eight Lectures on the I-ching*, tr. by C. F. Baynes (Princeton, 1973), p. 39.

18. Legge, *The Chinese Classics*, vol. 4, p. 623.

19. Legge, vol. 3, p. 286.

20. Legge, vol. 4, p. 450.

21. Legge, vol. 4, p. 452.

22. Legge, vol. 4, p. 454.

23. Legge, vol. 3, p. 74.

24. Mencius 1A5, 4A9, 7B14.

25. For Confucius' religious attitudes, see D. Howard Smith, *Chinese Religions*, 35.

26. For critiques of Confucius' alleged belief in Fate, see especially Yang Jung-kuo, *Chung-kuo ku-tai shih-hsiang shih* (The History of Thought in Ancient China) (Peking, 1954), pp. 170–12.

27. See Joseph Shih, "Secularization in Early Chinese Thought," *Gregorianum*

50 (1969), pp. 403–04, and his other article, "The Notions of God," op. cit., pp. 136–38.
28. See Burton Watson, tr., *Hsün Tzu: Basic Writings* (New York, 1963), p. 79.
29. Ibid., p. 85.
30. Ibid., pp. 89–111.
31. See Wing-tsit Chan, *A Source Book in Chinese Philosophy* (Princeton, 1963), p. 296. I have adapted Chan's translations somewhat.
32. Ibid., p. 300.
33. Ibid., p. 463.
34. Ibid., p. 639.
35. The resemblance to process philosophy and theology is obvious, for which reason I also use the word "Absolute" with misgiving, and for lack of a better term. See Charles Hartshorne, *A Natural Theology for Our Time* (LaSalle, 1967), pp. 1–28.
36. Ibid., p. 638.
37. For Nicolas of Cusa, see *Of Learned Ignorance*, Bk 1, ch. 4.
38. See A. N. Whitehead, *Process and Reality: An Essay in Cosmology* (New York, 1969), pp. 410–11.
39. For Fung Yu-lan, see Chan, *A Source Book*, 762. For Fung's later intellectual evolution since 1949, see *Fung Yu-lan te tao-lu* (The Path of Fung), (Hongkong, 1974).
40. For Teilhard de Chardin, see *The Divine Milieu*, tr. by B. Wall (New York, 1960), p. 91.
41. For Chu Hsi's interpretation of Lord-on-High and Heaven, see *Chu-tzu ch'üan-shu* (Complete Works of Chu Hsi), (1714 ed.), ch. 49. See also J. Percy Bruce, *Chu Hsi and His Masters* (London, 1923), p. 282. Bruce is eager to point out theistic dimensions of Chu's philosophy, sometimes seeing more parallels with the Christian notion of a personal deity than is justified.
42. See Chu Hsi, ch. 43; Bruce, op. cit., p. 298. The quotation within the passage is from the Book of Documents (Legge, vol. 3, p. 185).
43. See John E. Smith, "Self and World as Starting Points in Theology," *International Journal for Philosophy of Religion* (1970), pp. 97–111.
44. *Hsiang-shan ch'üan-chi*, (Complete Works of Lu Chiu-yüan), 22, English translation adapted from Wing-tsit Chan, *A Source Book in Chinese Philosophy*, p. 580.
45. *Ch'uan-hsi lu*, part 1. English translation adapted from Wing-tsit Chan, *Instructions for Practical Living* (New York, 1963), pp. 80–81. See also Julia Ching, *To Acquire Wisdom: the Way of Wang Yang-ming* (New York, 1976), ch. 5, 6.
46. See *Meister Eckhart*, ed. by F. Pfeiffer, tr. by C. de Evans (London, 1924–31), Tractate 8, p. 338. The German idealist philosophers as Schelling and Hegel would offer later on a metaphysical elaboration of Eckhart's mysticism. See Wilhelm Weischedel, *Der Gott der Philosophen* (Darmstadt, 1971), vol. 1, ch. 8.
47. See Julia Ching, *To Acquire Wisdom*, ch. 5, n. 107.
48. *Meister Eckhart*, Tractate 11, p. 366.
49. Hsiung Shih-li, *Hsin wei-shih lun* (A New Consciousness-only Doctrine) (1946 ed.), pp. 79–80. For an account in English of his philosophy, see Wing-tsit Chan, *Religious Trends in Modern China* (New York, 1953), pp. 32–43.

50.   Wing-tsit Chan, "The Evolution of the Confucian Concept *Jen*," *Philosophy East and West* 4 (1955), pp. 295–319.

51.   Pierre Teilhard de Chardin, *The Phenomenon of Man*, tr. by Bernard Wall (New York, 1959), p. 291.

52.   The Manifesto was published in Chinese in the journal, *Min-chu p'in-lun* (*Domocratic Critique*) (Taipei, January 1958). For an English translation, see Carsun Chang, *The Development of Neo-Confucian Thought*, (New York, 1962), vol. 2, pp. 455–84. See also Liu Shu-hsien, "The Religious Import of Confucian Philosophy: its Traditional Outlook and Contemporary Significance," *Philosophy East and West* 21 (1971), pp. 157–76.

53.   Hou Wai-lu *et al.*, *Chung-kuo ssu-hsiang t'ung-shih* (A Survey History of Chinese Thought) (Peking, 1960), vol. 4, pt. 2, pp. 905–12.

54.   Ibid., pp. 904–05.

55.   Yang Jung-kuo, *Chien-ming Chung-kuo ssu-hsiang shih* (A Simplified History of Chinese Thought) (Peking, 1973), pp. 25–28.

56.   On the problem of God's historicity, see Hans Küng, *Menschwerdung Gottes* (Freiburg, 1970), pp. 543–50.

57.   See Joseph Shih, "The Ancient Chinese Cosmogony," *Studia Missionalia*, 13 (1969), pp. 129–30. Shih refers here especially to Taoism. But a similar "natural hierophany" forms the foundation of the Confucian religious view. See also his other article, "Revelation in Chinese Religion," *Studia Missionalia*, 20(1971), pp. 237–66.

58.   See Julia Ching, "The Confucian Way (*Tao*) and its Transmission (*Tao-t'ung*)" *Journal of the History of Ideas*, 35 (1974), p. 385. I speak here more of the historical dimension in the Confucian "Revelation", rather than its idea of God.

59.   See Henri de Lubac, *Aspects of Buddhism*. Translated by George Lamb. (New York, 1954), xi, pp. 24–34; Heinrich Dumoulin, *Christianity Meets Buddhism*, (LaSalle, 1974), pp. 103–04; Kenneth Ch'en, *Buddhism in China* (Princeton, 1964), pp. 339–42.

60.   Book of Mencius 7B:37; Legge, *The Chinese Classics*, vol. 2, p. 500.

Chapter Five

THE PROBLEM OF SELF-TRANSCENDENCE

INTRODUCTION

The life of the conscience has many levels of depth. There is the level of ethics, involving moral decisions and the practice of virtue, that which concerns the person himself as well as his relationship to others. There is also a more interior life, that in which the heart or conscience savors its own presence, turns to God in prayer and supplication, or finds pleasure in reflecting upon the words of Sacred Writings. In Christianity, this is usually considered as spiritual theology or the realm of spirituality. It concerns itself with religious experience as such, with the life of the spirit—of the Holy Spirit's action in the soul. It is now being increasingly recognized that this realm provides a common meeting ground for the different religious traditions of both East and West, considered earlier as of interest only to specialists of comparative religion. And so, Christian spiritual theology is being broadened as well as deepened by the consciousness and knowledge it is gaining of other religions, now no longer regarded *a priori* as inferior— as the "natural" *versus* the "supernatural."

It is my intention to present here a general profile of Confucian "spirituality"—not only of such spiritual exercises as prayer and meditation, but also of meditation as leading to mysticism on the one hand, and of prayer in relation to public cult and rituals on the other. Confucianism is usually known as a system of practical morality. Few know of its metaphysics; fewer know of its mystique. I hope to provide better information on this subject and clarify some of the main issues. I think that a better knowledge of the place of prayer in Confucianism will help to cast light upon its understanding of God. I also think that Confucian meditation,

151

with its clear ethical orientation, can be of more help to the Christian than the Buddhist—Ch'an(Zen)—counterpart, which is frequently overpreoccupied with acquiring mystical experience. And I believe that the similarities and differences between the Confucian cult and rituals and the Christian liturgical and sacramental system will help to explain the deeper philosophical and theological similarities as well as the differences effected by the separate and independent evolutions of Confucianism and Christianity.

Friedrich Heiler's monumental work, *Prayer* (*Das Gebet*) offers two clear models for comparative purposes: the prophetical religions and mysticism. By the former he refers to those religions founded on faith in a divine revelation, with a serious regard for God's transcendence and a keen concern for ethical values and precepts, as in Judaism, Christianity and Islam. By the latter he speaks of flight from the world and from self, for the sake of meditating upon the Infinite and the Absolute. This is essentially the *praxis* of Hinduism, Buddhism and Taoism, religions which emphasize self-transcendence in terms of self-forgetfulness, in view of finding the divine in the human.[1]

Heiler has been criticized for polarizing the two prototypes, for generally exalting the prophetical religions above mysticism.[2] But he does not neglect the presence of mystical tendencies in prophetical religions or vice versa. And he usually—though not always—avoids theological presuppositions of the superiority of one type over the other. Besides, the use of these two models helps to bring into sharper focus the distinctive features of the various religious traditions and their manifestations of piety. The best contrast, for example, is provided by Christianity and Ch'an (Zen) Buddhism. Christian spirituality is founded on faith in Christ's revelation; Christian prayer—even mystical prayer—remains always an expression of faith in the transcendent God and his gift of grace. Zen meditation, on the other hand, takes for granted the primary importance of self-exertion (Japanese: *jiriki;* 自力) in the spiritual life. The question of God's existence has only a minor importance. The focus of Zen is rather upon striving for inner enlightenment in mystical experience.

Has the use of these heuristic models anything to offer to an understanding of Confucianism as compared to Christianity? At first sight, one may incline to be doubtful. The obvious questions are: Is Confucianism a religion at all? And, if it is, may it not perhaps be more "prophetical" than "mystical"—with its frequent references to sages, to Confucius and Mencius and earlier sage-kings—with its cult of Heaven and its strong ethical-social emphases? Besides, are not prayer and mysticism only of peripheral interest to Confucianism? Has it produced any authentic mystics?

Is Confucianism a religion at all? This is not the place for a lengthy discussion of this question. I hope that in every chapter of this book, I have provided some clue to the answer to the question. But I think that an examination of the place in Confucianism, of prayer, meditation and mysticism as well as of rituals, will help to clarify the nature of Confucian religiosity itself. Is this religiosity more prophetical than mystical? I do not intend either to supply proofs on one score or the other, except to refer to what I have already said in earlier chapters, concerning, for example, the presence of faith and revelation in Confucianism, as well as the development of the idea of a metaphysical Absolute which almost took the place of the personal deity. Besides, the answer to such a question should also emerge with the examination proposed. As we shall see, where prayer has usually been associated with cultic practices in Confucianism—an evidence of its "prophetic" propensities, meditation and even mystical experience associate it more with the "mystical" religions. And so, even if the mystical *versus* prophetical typology does not entirely suit a comparative study of Confucianism and Christianity, it can still serve to bring to better light the religious dimensions of Confucianism.

Prayer as Conversation with God

There can be no spiritual progress in any of the world's great religious traditions without some form of prayer and meditation. For the Christian, the word "prayer" (Greek: *dialechis*; Latin: *homilia, conversatio*) refers usually to conversing with God, or the lifting of one's heart to God.[3] Implicit in both of these definitions is the presence of duality, of a relationship between Man and God, acknowledged as a relationship between an inferior and a superior. This feature is borne out by evidence in both the Old and the New Testament, with the inferior partner in the dialogue being either an individual person or a group—the people of Israel, or the disciples of Jesus. In the Scriptural context, prayer usually refers to petition, be that for favors or forgiveness (Ps. 74:1ff, 51), but also to disinterested worship and thanksgiving (1 Chron. 29:11f), and sometimes to heart-rending complaint or even accusation, as in the case of Job (16:6–17:16, 23:2–17) or with Jesus on the Cross (Matt. 27:45, Mark 15:34). Besides, for the Christian, the example of Jesus in the New Testament is the best lesson in prayer, as given in the Sermon on the Mount, in the teaching of the Our Father (Matt. 6:9–15, Luke 11:1–4) and at Gethsemane (Matt. 26:39ff, Mark 14:35ff, Luke 22:41ff). Also implicit in this understanding of prayer is the basic attitude of the petitioner or the worshipper: an attitude of confidence in God's goodness, as well as of awe before the Holy One.

Confucianism also possesses a tradition of prayer, associated especially with the days of the sage-kings, as the Classics testify. Theirs was the belief in a supreme and personal deity, called Lord-on-High, Heaven, or both, exalted above a hierarchy of other spirits, of the Earth and Grain, of Mountains and Rivers, as well as of the spirits of deceased ancestors.[4] The Book of Odes remains probably as the richest source of such personal prayer and invocation, originating frequently in liturgical contexts, and comparing very well with many of the Psalms. Whether addressed as Lord-on-High or Heaven, God is always extolled in his greatness and sovereignty, before which man must maintain an attitude of reverence:

Sovereign is the Lord-on-High,
Beholding [the world] below in majesty
. . .[5]

How vast is the Lord-on-High,
The Ruler of men below!
How majestic is the Lord-on-high,

How unfathomable His ordinances!
. . . .[6]

Let me be reverent, let me be reverent.
Heaven's [Ways] are evident,
And its ordinances are not easy.
. . .
It ascends and descends about our doings;
It daily inspects us wherever we are.[7]

God's blessings and protection are invoked, either by the king, for himself and his people, or by the king's subjects, for the king, as in the following prayer:

Heaven protect and establish thee,
With the greatest security.·
And make thee entirely virtuous,
That thou may enjoy happiness.
And grant thee much increase,
That thou may have all in abundance.
Heaven protect and establish thee,
And grant thee all excellence,
That all may be right with thee,
That thou may receive a hundred favors from Heaven.
May [Heaven] send thee enduring happiness,
Which the days are not sufficient to enjoy.
. . .[8]

Although high above, sovereign and transcendent, God is also father and mother of the people. In time of distress, prayer takes on the urgency of passionate plea and complaint, issuing forth as a cry of the heart:

O vast and distant Heaven,
Thou [you] who art called Father and Mother,
[I am] without crime or offence,
[And yet] I suffer great distress!
. . .[9]

Great Heaven, unjust,
Is sending down these exhausting disorders.

Great Heaven, unkind,
Is sending down these great miseries.
. . .
O unpitying, great Heaven!
There is no end to the troubles.
. . .[10]

I look up to the great Heaven—
Why am I plunged in this sorrow?
. . .
I look up to the great Heaven—
When shall I be favored with repose?
. . . [11]

What did Confucius himself contribute to this tradition of prayer? Confucius declared a reluctance to discuss certain religious issues, such as life after death, or the spirits and ghosts (Analects 11:11). But he was no religious rebel.[12] He shared the religious beliefs of his educated contemporaries, and participated carefully in the cultic life, especially in the ancestral cult. His program was directed at a "revival of antiquity" (*fu-ku;* 復古), an effort aimed at making the past and its legacy meaningful and relevant to the present. Tradition says that he personally edited the Classics handed down by the sage-kings. Although we cannot accept this statement literally, there is every reason to assert that he identified himself with these writings, which he revered, and which would come down to us with enhanced value because of him, even if many of them did not assume a final form until long after his death.

We have no record of lengthy prayers coming from Confucius' lips. According to the official cult accepted by the school of Confucius, worship of the supreme deity, Lord-on-High or Heaven, is the exclusive privilege of the rulers of China. Many lengthy prayers are associated with this cult. But few expressions of personal prayer to God have come down to us. All the same, we have evidence that Confucius invoked Heaven in his personal life, especially in times of crisis, such as at the death of his favorite disciple, Yen Yüan. The Analects record Confucius' bitter sorrow, and his expression of despondency: "Alas, Heaven is destroying me! Heaven is destroying me!" (11:8).

Just as for the Christian, the life of faith in God, as shown in the keeping of his commandments, is the best expression of continual prayer. So too for Confucius, the life of the just man is itself a prayer, an expression of faith in God and in the spirits. It is indeed worth much more than specific acts of prayer or propitiation. In this light we may understand Confucius' response to his disciple, Tzu-lu, who asked for leave to pray for the master, during his sickness. Confucius first asked, as though surprised: "May such a thing be done?" The disciple replied, "It may. In the Eulogies it is said: 'Prayer has been made for thee to the spirits of the upper and lower world.' " At which Confucius answered, confidently, "My prayer has been for a long time." (Analects 7:34.)

Of course, this is a response expected of a man who has devoted his life to sagehood and perfection. It is the response of a man who said of himself, that he committed himself to the quest of sagehood at the age of fifteen, stood firm in this quest at thirty, had no more doubts at forty, and *knew the decrees of Heaven* at fifty. Indeed, at sixty, his ears became completely obedient to the call of truth, and at seventy, he was able to follow all the desires of his heart, without transgressing what was right (Analects 2:4). Such was the spiritual life and evolution of Confucius.[13]

Mysticism: Jesus and Confucius

Conversation with God, the lifting of the mind and heart to God, can be done mentally as well as vocally. In this regard, Scriptural reading has always been considered a great help. The New Testament offers us evidence of Jesus' practice of reading the Jewish Scriptures (Luke 4:17ff) and his good knowledge of them. For the Christian, the Scriptures and the sacraments have always been regarded as the principal sources of the spiritual life. Meditation has usually meant reflective reading of, or prayerful reflection on, the Scriptures, a search for the inner meaning of the words and episodes, with the hope of effecting one's own conversion (*metanoia*) and of approaching God in Jesus Christ. In early Christianity, liturgical worship frequently provided the context for such prayerful reflection of carefully selected texts, as synagogue services had done for the Jews. This permitted the gradual development of various methods of mental prayer, especially within the monastic life. The Benedictines, for example, developed their methods of spiritual reading (*lectio divina*), organizing it around the liturgical year.[14]

Prayer tends toward simplification, and mysticism represents this simplifying tendency. The Greek word, *mystikos*, comes from the verb *muw*, meaning "closing", and suggesting the closing of the eyes. It was originally associated with the practices of the mystery cults, and came to assume the connotation of the mysterious and esoteric, of a ritual mystery.[15] The word came into Christian theological usage with the treatise on mystical theology written in the fifth century by the pseudo-Dionysius. It signifies a kind of direct or immediate communion with God, a higher level of mental prayer in which the whole person, not just his intellect, meets God in a special and unusual experience.[16]

According to Heiler, mysticism may be better understood when viewed in opposition to prophetic piety, according to which prayer remains always a dialogue between two unequal partners: Man and God. Mysticism tends to flee from ordinary life in its desire to experience a higher consciousness, while prophetic piety affirms life with joy and resoluteness, on account of its faith in God as giver of life. Mysticism tends toward ethical indifference, preferring asceticism to morality, while prophetic piety regards moral action as fulfilment of God's will. Mysticism tends to be individualistic and nonsocial, where prophetic religion places emphasis on community and the social group. Mysticism consists in the unification and simplification of all psychic activity, achieved by isolation from the world and suppression of the emotions, until barriers between God and Man disappear in the ecstatic experience. Prophetic piety, on the other hand, reveals a continual dualism in its experience of fear and hope, distress and trust, doubt and faith, and in its constant consciousness of the distance between God and Man. Mysticism seeks the silent and self-sufficient God, the *deus absconditus*, where prophetic religion exalts the Creator, the *deus revelatus* who manifests his will in nature and history.[17]

Before going further, it may be useful to ask what the New

Testament has to say about mystical prayer, and whether Jesus himself was a mystic, or has taught others a way of mysticism.

These questions are difficult to answer. The Synoptic Gospels have given us examples of Jesus' prayers, but offer no evidence of their mystical tendency. The Gospel of St. John offers a long passage—the Last Discourse and Jesus' high-priestly prayer (Ch. 13–17)—uttered on the eve of his death. It sends out echoes which may be termed mystical, concerning the oneness between Jesus and the Father. But the historicity of the passage as such is open to doubt; the form under which it now appears may represent a later effort at theologizing which came out of a Hellenistic world.

There are other passages in the New Testament which refer to Jesus' prayer without disclosing its nature or content. Allegedly, he spent forty days and nights in the desert (Matt. 4:1ff, Luke 4:1 ff). He is also reported as frequently praying alone by himself at night (Matt. 14:23, Mark 6:46), or in the company of a few chosen disciples (Luke 9:28). Such texts have given occasion for encouraging Christians to practise private, mental prayer, and to seek for the closest union with God that is possible.[18] But they say nothing more. The usual assertion is that while Christianity has produced many great mystics, it is not essentially a mystical religion. Christianity is based on faith in Jesus and his message, rather than on any subjective experience of the divine, acquired in mystical prayer. Whatever allusions there are to mysticism in the New Testament remain, therefore, secondary to the central teaching of faith. Christianity is a "prophetic religion," having more in common with other such revealed religions as Judaism and Islam than with the mystical religions of the Greeks, of the Buddhists or Taoists.

And now, how about Confucius and Confucianism? Did Confucius himself practice meditation and mental prayer? Has Confucianism a tradition of mysticism?

Confucius was known as an avid student and even transmitter of the Classics. Without doubt, he meditated upon the meaning of the words and texts, attempting to make them relevant not just for himself, but also for his contemporaries and for the society of his time (Analects 2:11, 15, 7:17). For him, however, such reading and study made possible a communion of spirits with the ancient sages, rather than with God-on-High(Analects 7:5, 8:19–21, 9:5). There is little ground for considering Confucius personally as a mystic, even if the Taoist work, *Chuang-tzu*, suggests this, with some irony. The Analects have left us a description of Confucius in a contemplative mood, when he declared:

> "I would prefer to be wordless."
> Tzu-kung said: "If you, Master, do not speak, what shall we, your disciples, have to record?"
> The Master said: "Does Heaven speak? The four seasons pursue their courses and all things are continually being produced, *but* does Heaven say anything?" (17:19).

This is the closest evidence we possess of Confucius' *mystical* inclination. The historicity of this passage, however, is difficult to substantiate.

All the same, the Confucian school does possess its own tradition of deep spirituality and even mysticism. Both the Odes and the Documents represent to us the ancient sage-kings as partners in dialogue with the Lord-on-High or Heaven, receiving from them instructions and commandments, and asking of them blessings and protection. But this appears closer to the tradition of the Jewish kings and prophets than to that of mystics lost in contemplation of the divine. The Confucian mystical tradition can be better discovered in the Book of Mencius and in those chapters in the ritual texts which speak less of the rites as such, and more of interior dispositions of the mind and heart.

THE CONFUCIAN MYSTIQUE

Where Confucius stands as a prophet, Mencius projects also the image of a teacher of mysticism, as well as of moral regeneration and political reform. Mencius alludes to the presence within the heart of that which is greater than itself. According to him, knowledge and fulfilment of one's own mind and heart leads to knowledge and fulfilment of one's nature as well as that of Heaven:

> For a man to give full realization to his heart is for him to understand his own nature, and a man who knows his own nature will know Heaven. By retaining his heart and nurturing his nature he is serving Heaven. Whether he is going to

die young or to live to a ripe old age makes no difference to his steadfastness of purpose. It is through awaiting whatever is to befall him with a perfected character that he stands firm on his proper destiny. (7A:1.)[19]

If the Book of Mencius points to a dimension of interiority and of mysticism, without going into the subject of meditation, the Confucian ritual texts offer also general orientations for meditation itself, but without discussing methods and techniques. They present a picture of Confucian spirituality very different from that depicted earlier through examples taken from the Odes. They are sometimes said to represent the intrusion of Taoist influence into the school of Confucius. But they have been accepted by tradition as an essential part of the Confucian heritage. Certain of these texts, particularly from the Doctrine of the Mean, have also contributed later on to the development of a specific form of Neo-Confucian meditation, which goes by the name of quiet-sitting (ching-tso; 靜坐). We shall discuss this subject after having examined the evidence of the ritual texts.

Emotional Harmony and Quiet-Sitting

Rites and music have always been considered the two cornerstones of the Confucian moral and social order. They serve also as principal support of the person's spiritual being. Although the Classic of Music is no longer extant, the Book of Rites still contains a chapter on music, which extols music as a help to inner tranquility and equilibrium—in itself a reflection of the harmony of elegant music. According to this chapter, "it belongs to man's nature, as from Heaven, to be still at his birth." In the process of growth, he is acted upon by external influences, and responds by showing "likes and dislikes." Unless these are properly regulated by an interior principle, he runs the risk of self-alienation, becoming a stranger to his original, deeper self, and thus losing his "Heavenly principle." Now it belongs to the function of music, together with the rites and ceremonies, to help maintain or restore man's inner harmony, which is, or ought to be, a reflection of the harmony between Heaven and Earth, and the source of all virtuous thoughts and behavior.

Harmony is the thing principally sought in music: it therein follows Heaven, and manifests the spirit-like expansive influence characteristic of it. Distinction is the thing principally sought in ceremonies: they therein follow Earth, and manifest the spirit-like retractive influence characteristic of it. Hence the sages made music in response to Heaven, and framed ceremonies in correspondence with Earth. In the wisdom and completeness of their ceremonies and music we see the directing power of Heaven and Earth.[20]

Emotional harmony and psychic equilibrium—the harmony of due proportion rather than the absence of passions—became the cornerstone of Confucian spirituality and the essence of Confucian meditation itself. However, is such meditation also "prayer"— does it bring the person in contact with the divine, with God? The question becomes more serious when we remember that the ritual texts owe much of their inspiration to the philosopher Hsün-tzu, the avowed atheist who gave a naturalist meaning to the word "Heaven." Certainly, such meditation could be called prayer only if it is open to the transcendent. Here, the Doctrine of the Mean may be of help. It speaks of two states of soul, the "pre-stirred" state, before the rise of emotions, and the "post-stirred" state. According to this Doctrine, the *Mean* lies in the *harmony* of emotions which have *arisen* resembling the equilibrium of the earlier state. It goes on to say that this harmony puts a person in touch with the processes of life and creativity in the universe.

> While there are no stirrings of pleasure, anger, sorrow or joy, the mind may be said to be in the state of equilibrium. When these emotions have been stirred, and act in their due degree, there ensues what may be called the state of harmony. This equilibrium is the great root of all under Heaven, and this harmony is the universal path of all under Heaven.
> Let the states of equilibrium and harmony exist in perfection, and a happy order will prevail throughout Heaven and Earth, and all things will be nourished and will flourish.[21]

There is no mention of God in this text, and the meaning of the word Heaven it contains is ambiguous. But there is a clear expression of the belief that emotional harmony opens man to something greater than himself. What this is, and how emotional harmony is to be acquired, remain unclear. Besides, another question arises: what has such emotional harmony to do with the study or reading of the Classics? Is Confucian meditation entirely independent of the texts, entirely subjective, where Christian meditation has so emphasized a reflective and prayerful reading of the Scriptures? An answer to these questions may enlighten us further regarding the nature of Confucian meditation itself, its later evolution and its own distinctive contribution to the subject of prayer and mysticism.

Certainly, the disciples of the sages read the Classics with attention and reverence, as did Confucius himself. Besides, such reading and study of these revered books remained an important part of Confucian self-cultivation. Chu Hsi's Recorded Conversations, for example, give abundant instructions on how such reading is to be made. But Confucian meditation, properly speaking, did not evolve out of reading Classics, as did the Christian's reading of the Scriptures. The Confucian word for meditation, "quiet-sitting" (*ching-tso;* 靜坐), suggests strong Taoist and Buddhist influences, associated with Chuang-tzu's *tso-wang* (忘; sitting and forgetting), and with Ch'an Buddhism and its practice of *dhyana* (meditation).[22] As we know, many of the Neo-Confucians of Sung and Ming China, of Yi Korea and Tokugawa Japan, had received some training and experience in Ch'an Buddhism. Even after their ideological rupture with the Buddhist religion, they continued to practice a simplified form of meditation, adapting freely from Ch'an practices of "sitting in meditation" (*tso-ch'an*; Japanese: *zazen*), "pondering upon riddles" (*kung-an*, 公案; Japanese: *koan*) and awaiting illumination or enlightenment (*wu*, 悟; Japanese: *satori*). The remote preparation for this exercise was, and is, a morally upright life; the immediate preparation remains an attitude of stillness. An erect sitting posture, whether on the chair, or, like the Buddhist, on the rush-mat, and in a lotus position, is usually recommended. Attention is also given to the control and regulation of breathing during the exercise.[23] Chu Hsi himself wrote a famous instruction on breath control, for which he recommends "watching the white on the nose", originally a Taoist technique. Control should also be exercised over the sensations in order to keep away external stimuli. The mind is to concentrate upon itself, to the exclusion of all distracting thought and for the sake of attaining unity and harmony between consciousness and the object of consciousness, which is one's own innermost self.

As it developed, Confucian quiet-sitting assumed a different character from Taoist and Buddhist meditation. Confucians place greater emphasis upon the knowledge of the moral self—of one's own strengths and weaknesses—in view of achieving self-improvement, of becoming more perfect in the practice of virtues and the elimination of vices. Confucians speak of developing or realizing the Heavenly principle (*T'ien-li*) within and of removing passions or "human desires" (*jen-yu;* 人欲), even sometimes of achieving "desirelessness' in stillness. But Confucian meditation is not just an examen of conscience. It is definitely oriented to a higher consciousness, through emptying of the self and its desires. Emotional harmony rather than dialogue remains its essence. As a form of inner concentration, Confucian meditation stands somewhere between two other forms: the intellectual concentration of discursive thought and the moral concentration of assuring that there is no thought. Confucian meditation seeks peace without doing violence to human nature. It does not require the attainment of a state of intellectual and emotional impassivity. Thoughts may come and go; they need not become distractions except when one pays attention to them.

Confucian meditation developed in a religious tradition that did not know monastic life. It represents essentially a *lay* spirituality. Confucian mysticism is the portion of the man who knows how to unite action and contemplation, the outer and the inner. The Confucian sees his outer activity as the authentic expression of his inner attitudes and of the fountainhead of his intentions. The Confucian does not seek enlightenment for its own sake. He is a mystic *for others*. Confucian mysticism enables the person to perceive the profoundly dynamic character of the Heavenly principle within—that by which birds fly, fishes swim, and human beings love virtue. This is the true meaning of man's oneness with Heaven and Earth and all things. It is at the same time a source of deep joy. For it is by nourishing oneself at the source of one's life that the person becomes most truly himself, radiating his inner vitality and energy. As Mencius has said: "All things are present and complete in me. There is no greater delight for me than to find, on self-examination, that I am true to myself. If one tries his best to treat others as he wishes to be treated himself, he will find that [his goal of] jen (perfect virtue) is very close." (7A:4.)

Confucian mystique is open to the other where Buddhist mystique tends to fall back upon the self.[24] Confucian mystique supports ethical values where Ch'an (Zen) Buddhist mystique tends toward moral ambivalence. The proposition that man is one with all things can and has been variously interpreted, for example, to infer a sense of ethical indifference stemming from a mystic's transcendence of the realm of good and evil, right and wrong.[25] In Confucianism, however, it has served to indicate a state of mind that is at the same time mystical and ethical. The Confucian achieves this transcendence of the differentiations between the self and the other by extending his practice of jen, of love, from himself and those near him to all others in the universe. Confucian mystique refers to the crowning accomplishment of virtue and of love, which put him in contact with the life and creativity of the universe. It bears a certain kinship to Pure Land Buddhism and its teachings of universal compassion. It also resembles Christian mysticism which does not lose sight of man's ethical responsibilities.

Indeed, Confucianism celebrates man's relationship to other men, and to the universe, as being also manifestation of what is greater than man. Confucian philosophy reaches for the transcendent through the immanent, the divine through the human. It is for these reasons that the Confucian term, jen, has become imbued with a richness of meaning which connotes virtue, life and creativity, and even the Absolute. For it is in and through human relationship that the Confucian has discovered the one reality in and behind Life itself, the Love that is the drive to Life, and the One explanation for manifold being. And then, Confucian mysticism once more leads the person back to human relationships and the daily practice of jen, in and through which one can discover, over and over again, the presence of the Absolute.

Activity and Passivity in Confucian Spirituality

The words "cultivation" (*hsiu;* 修) and "enlightenment" (*wu;*悟) will appear strange to those not acquainted with the Confucian tradition and with the Buddhist influence which transformed it. By "cultivation" I refer to such Chinese practices as "learning", that is, a process of intellectual and moral striving, described frequently in the Analects, in the Book of Mencius and in the Great Learning, and "character-forming," an important teaching of the Great Learning and the Doctrine of the Mean. The word "enlightenment," on the other hand, refers, in this context, not to any parallel development of the eighteenth century intellectual movement in Europe which is contrasted to the Dark Ages, but to inner illumination (*ming;* 明), as referred to in the Great Learning, the Doctrine of the Mean, *Hsün-tzu* and *Chuang-tzu,* to awakening (*chüeh;* 覚), found in Mencius and *Chuang-tzu,* as well as in the Buddhist texts, where it is equated with the Sanskrit *vidya* (knowledge, Buddha-wisdom)and *bodhi,* the awakening of the mind to the meaning of the truth. The "cultivation" *versus* "enlightenment" polarity was first experienced in Buddhist spirituality before it was reflected in the Neo-Confucian experience.[26] Evidently, cultivation has always been present in the Confucian consciousness while enlightenment, associated more with Taoism and Buddhism, gained importance much later, through the penetration of Taoist and Buddhist influence in Neo-Confucianism.

To a large extent, cultivation represents a more active or "voluntarist" sympathy while enlightenment stands for a more passive or mystical affinity. Superficially, the tension between the two may appear to resemble that of asceticism *versus* mysticism, of self-reliance *versus* surrender to grace. But the cultivation-enlightenment polarity represents also an inner tension in the mystical quest itself. The way of "cultivation" implies sometimes a basic attitude of faith and confidence, of readiness to wait for light, even of finding light in darkness and in waiting, thus implying some form of subconscious reliance upon a higher power (Japanese: *tariki;* 他力). The way of "enlightenment", on the other hand, may require the inducement of a sudden, psychic experience, through one's own efforts (Japanese: *jiriki*).[27] Besides, it is possible that faith

is present in both ways—of cultivation and enlightenment: faith
in the possibility of enlightenment and in the *meaning* of transcendence it signifies. And here lies the basic importance of such
spiritual experience—the opening up of a vast horizon of transcendence.

The cultivation *versus* enlightenment tension in Confucian
meditation and mysticism, like the Christian controversy between
"quietist" passivity and voluntarist activity, highlights a basic
problem encountered by all who seek for a higher perfection in
self-transcendence. It is a problem of "attachment" or "detachment"—attachment to God and detachment from self, or *vice
versa*, to use age-old language.[28] The difficulty regards the subtlety
of the spiritual experience which one encounters within the depths
of one's self. The Christian may question himself, whether the
attachment is really to God—or is it to perfection in itself, or
even to an *experience* of God? When perfection becomes the goal
in itself, the weight of selfishness returns to the soul. When
experience is sought after for itself, it may become emptied of
real content. The Confucian—and even more so, the Ch'an Buddhist—may wonder, whether he is more intent upon *acquiring* enlightenment, than *forgetting* himself. Attachment to enlightenment
can also fetter the soul, straining its efforts toward transcending
itself until self-preoccupation replaces any possible self-forgetfulness. For this reason, the great Buddhist and Confucian masters
have described all authentic self-cultivation as being akin to "non-
cultivation"—implying a necessary attitude of detachment from
one's own deepest desires. After all, the Heavenly principle (*T'ien-
li*) resides within the soul. It is both active and dynamic. The
disciple of the sages needs only be attentive to this presence, which
can eventually transform his life, from within to without, moving
from his heart to his exterior demeanour and instinctive reactions.
Such has been the experience of the great Confucians. Such is also
the teaching of the Christian mystics.

Indeed, the great mystics of *all* religions share a common experience of the mystical quest itself—the waiting, the frustration,
the joy. They also find a common meeting ground in their very
mystical experience, even if they differ sometimes with regard to
its precise theological interpretation. Certain Christian mystics, as

heirs to the Christian prophetic religion as well as to Neo-Platonist mystical philosophy, have served as apt interpreters of this common mystical experience, and of the dimensions of both immanence and transcendence encountered in it. St. Augustine is one of these. In his book on Western Mysticism, Dom Butler offers Augustine's description of mystical prayer: *Mens mea pervenit ad id quod est in ictu trepidantis aspectus* (My mind in the flash of a trembling glance came to that which is).[29] He infers from this statement the experiential perception of transcendental reality, the Absolute, which, for the Christian, is God. He also indicates certain effects of such an experience, particularly a rapturous joy. He remarks that while the language of the Scriptures and of Augustine, Gregory and Bernard, in the description of such an experience, is one of affirmation and plenitude, later generations—probably through the influence of pseudo-Dionysius—preferred a language of negation, using words as darkness, void or nothingness to represent both the experience and the Absolute. And so, on the one hand, mystical experience recalls God's immanence—the Divine within; on the other, it also communicates the sense of his transcendence and otherness, to be found also in the writings of Eckhart, Ruysbroeck, and John of the Cross.

Moreover, all mystics refer to a point of centrifugal recollection and concentration, where immanence is experienced and transcendence is perceived. This has been variously called the mind or the heart: *mens*. It is here that man meets that which is greater than himself, greater than his heart, and yet within his heart. It is here that he finds the spiritual mirror of the Absolute, the temple of God and his image. Karl Rahner has called the mystic especially the man of the heart:

> German mysticism often named as its ideal the man "of the heart" *(innig)*, the "collected" *(gesammelt)* man, that is, whose whole activity is an exhaustive expression of his innermost center and his innermost vital decision, and who therefore remains "collected" in this innermost center without being dispersed in anything alien to his decision.[30]

THE QUESTION OF RITUALS

Public rituals are an essential dimension of religious life, giving expression to communal beliefs. They are closely associated to prayer, meditation and even mysticism, whether in Confucianism or Christianity. Most of the prayers uttered by the Confucian sage-kings, and quoted earlier in this study, arose probably out of ritual contexts. Scriptural reading itself, as well as meditation on God's word, has always been associated with public worship—whether as integral part or as a prolongation of its spirit. And where mysticism is concerned, the word itself arose out of ritual context, even if the experience signified came to mean more and more something extremely personal and individual. All the same, especially in Christianity, it has been frequently asserted that mystical experience is born of faith in the "Mysteries"—the *Mysterium*—that is, the faith of the community, which expresses itself especially in rituals, above all, in the Eucharist.[31]

In many Christian churches, certain of the rituals are called "sacraments." The word comes not from New Testament Greek, but from a Latin word meaning a soldier's oath, or initiation. Perhaps, this had something to do with one of the "sacraments": Baptism, the sacrament of initiation into the Christian life. In any case, the word connotes today theologically certain officially sanctioned forms of communal worship. It is generally believed that the sacramental system is the means by which man's most profane actions, and those which express his entire dependence upon the material universe for support and nutrition, are consecrated to God, the creator of all life and matter.[32] For purposes of comparison with Confucian practices, I shall only mention those sacraments for which equivalent ceremonies can be found in Confucianism. I refer here to the Eucharist, Baptism—together with Confirmation—and Matrimony. But I shall also say some words on funeral rites and memorials to the dead, since these have a great importance in Confucianism, even though they are not regarded as "sacraments" in Christianity, but only as "sacramentals"—in the Catholic Church—that is, cultic prayers and actions related in some manner to the sacramental system.

The Chinese word "ritual" (*li;* 禮) designates etymologically cult or sacrificial offerings. The derived meanings are rituals and ceremonies, and the rules and prescriptions which govern these ceremonies.[33] By extension, it refers also to all the rules and prescriptions governing human behavior, especially in terms of the moral relationships, as well as the inner spirit which should inspire the persons who observe these rules and prescriptions. Confucius himself gave special emphasis to the importance of ritual, as well as to the virtue of "propriety" and decorum which is considered as related to ritual observance. Even the philosopher Hsün-tzu, who explicitly denied the existence of a supreme being, waxed eloquent on rites as an important component of a gentleman's life and education. The Confucian Classics include three ritual texts: the Institutes of Chou (*Chou-li*), an idealized account of ancient political institutions, the Ceremonials (*Yi-li*), or rules of conduct for princes and their ministers, also of the Chou dynasty, and the Book of Rites (*Li-chi*), with its extensive treatment of rituals touching on every aspect of life, together with some philosophical reflections.[34]

For a Christian approaching the subject of Chinese—Confucian Rites—, two very different problems would emerge. The first relates to the Rites as cultic offerings. The Christian would be quite satisfied had the Chinese only one cult, that paid to the supreme deity—the Cult of Heaven. The Christian is understandably perplexed with the existence of multiple cults, not only to Heaven, but also to a host of other spirits and deities, as well as to deceased ancestors. A possible reaction to such a discovery, the recorded historical reaction on the part of the Roman Papacy, was repugnance, even abhorrence.

Actually, an understanding of the meaning of the secondary cults—to various spiritual beings, including one's ancestors—comes with a careful study of the cult of Heaven itself. Here, one is informed that Heaven is regarded as supreme deity—over and above the host of other spirits, especially the ancestors. The cultic offerings to the spirits inferior to Heaven represent therefore veneration rather than worship.

The Doctrine of the Mean (Ch.19) attributes these words to Confucius himself: "The cult of Heaven and Earth are ordained to the service of the Lord-on-High; the cult of ancestors is ordained to the service of the deceased." In this way, it would appear that the school of Confucius clearly supports the primary and secondary cults as expressions of faith in a supreme God.

The second problem concerns the "ceremonies" rather than the cultic offerings. I refer here to the Confucian *rites de passage*—the adolescent "Capping" ceremony, marriage, funeral and the like. Are these rituals of any religious significance, or have they merely a social importance? This question becomes more serious when we remember that Hsün-tzu, an avowed atheist, was the chief author —of the letter and the spirit—of the Book of Rites, which offers detailed instructions for the performance of such ceremonies.

In this regard, I would admit that the Confucian *rites de passage* can be interpreted in a purely secular manner, as regulated expressions of human sentiments which arise out of certain decisive experiences in life. Such has been the considered opinion of Fung Yu-lan.[35] But I wish to point out their latent—if not also, at least sometimes, manifest—religiosity. The Confucian *rites de passage* are usually performed in the ancestral temple, a place considered sacred not merely in memory of the deceased, but especially because they are held to be in the presence of the Lord-on-High, enjoying with him their eternal reward. Thus, even though the ceremonies themselves seldom address direct prayers to God, they point to a need of divine blessings, through the intercession of the ancestors. At least, they would be so understood by those who performed the ceremonies—the majority of whom, like Confucius himself, believed in God.

The Confucian Liturgy: the Cult to Heaven

The word "eucharist" is derived from the Greek word for thanksgiving. The celebration of the Eucharist has as its beginning and model the thanksgiving action of Jesus at the Last Supper (Luke 22:19, 1 Cor. 11:24, Mark 14:23, Matt. 26:27). It has been defined as the "sacramental meal of the Church celebrated according to the example and instructions of Jesus," which is at the same time "an actualizing of the salvific reality" represented by Jesus, "through the words of thanksgiving uttered over bread and wine."[36]

For those Christian churches that celebrate the Eucharist, it remains the one central liturgy, a public proclamation of faith, that in which all believers may participate. When we turn to Confucianism, we find a different picture. The cult of Heaven is undoubtedly the highest collective expression of religious faith for Confucian China. But it resembled the Jewish Temple Sacrifice more than the Christian Eucharist in that it occurred only once a year. Besides, attendance was very limited—participation being forbidden to the populace in general. In a culture which knew no separation of the *imperium* and the *sacerdotium*, the sacrifice to Heaven was considered the unique duty and privilege of the emperor—Heaven's Son and Vicar in his political as well as religious functions. Where the Jewish temple worship represented, among other factors, the unity of a people considered as God's Elect, who alone worshipped the true God, the Confucian cult of Heaven was especially a proclamation of one man's claim to rule over a country considered as "all under Heaven." It was an expression of political legitimacy as well as religious duty.

The ritual surrounding the cult of Heaven developed very early, existing already at the time of Confucius, and remaining in many respects the main feature of Chinese religion until the early twentieth century. The temple of Heaven still stands today outside Peking, a monument to more than 600 years of recent history, when the cult was offered there, under those rulers who made Peking their capital city. Within the temple compound, the "Holy of Holies" has neither wall nor ceiling. It is an open altar of white marble, standing in the open under the sky, the hierophany of the deity called Heaven. The cult took place annually at the winter solstice. The emperor prepared himself for his high-priestly action by three days of fast and vigil, in which his assistants—the princes and officials—also took part. He then approached the open altar, rising in three circular terraces of impressive simplicity, to pray for himself and his people. The offering was an animal victim, a bullock of one color, without blemish, presented in a burnt sacrifice. The ritual was accompanied by other oblations and invocations as well as by solemn music. "The whole service was a *thanksgiving* to the Lord-on-High (*Shang-ti*) and to the great dynastic ancestors, and to the hosts of heaven, for the blessings bestowed from above during the year."[37]

Let us emphasize here that the keynote of the cult was *Eucharistein*, thanksgiving. The sacrificial oblation itself was performed out of thanksgiving and not propitiation. Indeed, the entire idea of propitiatory sacrifice appears alien to the Confucian cult. This is a fact which impressed many missionaries, including the great interpreter of Chinese culture, James Legge, who considered propitiation an essential feature of the Christian religion.

The cult of Heaven was an assertion of faith in one God. A multitude of celestial and terrestrial spirits—of the Sun and Moon, of Mountains and Rivers—was associated with Heaven, but always as his subordinates, his appointed officials. The imperial ancestors were also associated with this cult—as witnesses and participants, and not as deified figures. The imperial ancestors also merited their own cult—at the end of the year and at seasonal changes. To them, the emperor reported the successes and failures of his reign, in a spirit of filial unworthiness. This was a family ceremony, only carried out on a more grandiose scale than the ancestral cult of the average family.[38]

Where the cult to Heaven required a sacrifice of burnt offering, the ancestral cult was a memorial service, held at ancestral temples, or more frequently, at ancestral graves or at home, where tablets, engraved with the names of the ancestors, were—and in many places, still are—kept. Wine and food libations are usually offered; silent prostrations are then made in front of the tablets. And then, the whole family partakes of the meal—which the ancestors allegedly have already tasted. Like the Eucharist, therefore, the ancestral cult represents the religious celebration of a common meal—in which both living and dead take part, and the bond of clan and family is renewed and strengthened.[39]

The cult of Heaven has come to an end, with the establishment of a republic in China (1912). The ancestral cult lingers on—with difficulty. The People's Republic has turned its back to the past, and to the veneration of ancestors. The Chinese who left the mainland to settle in Hongkong, Taiwan and Southeast Asia have not usually brought with them their ancestral tablets, which are required for the continuance of the cult. But the consciousness of the cult and its significance remain in the living memory of the people, continuing to maintain and strengthen the family bonds. In this way also, Confucianism has become, even less than ever before, an organized religion, and more than ever before, a diffusion of religious sentiment, which takes place within the family.

The "Rites de passage"

The Confucian *rites de passage* emphasize the importance of family consciousness and family loyalties in the life of an individual. They demonstrate the *familial* orientation of Confucian religious practice, with its focus—for the vast majority of the population—upon the ancestral cult. They have been singled out for special treatment by the philosopher Chu Hsi himself in a treatise entitled "Family Rituals." These include the ceremonies surrounding the person's growth and maturity, the affirmation of the family principle by marriage, which is also a union of families, and the mourning and funerary rites.

The birth of a child is an important event in every family. But while Confucian teachings emphasize such preparations for this event as "embryo education," and customs provide for a variety of ceremonies, including a ritual bath three days after birth, there is no equivalent for Christian Baptism at this moment.[40] The naming ceremony takes place at the end of the third month after the child's birth, when he or she is also given a "tonsure," and the name is entered into a record. Confucian rites give greater importance to the celebration of the child's maturity. This takes place between the ages fifteen and twenty—by local calculation—and is called the "Capping" Ceremony, for the growing boy. By an impressive and ceremonial change of garments and bestowal of the "cap" of manhood, followed by a wine libation and the giving of a formal name, the youth is received into mature society and presented to his ancestors.[41] This ceremony resembles therefore Christian Baptism—the Christening—and Confirmation—the celebration of the young man's resolve to serve God or follow the ways of the sages.

For the Confucian, "the ceremony of marriage was intended to be a bond of love between two [families] . . with a view . . . to secure the services in the ancestral temple, and . . . the continuance of the family line."[42] Hence the good of the family is always put before the good of the individual. Hence also, marriage has been regarded not only as the natural, but also as the necessary part of life. The marriage ceremony itself expresses these intentions. It begins, so to speak, with the announcement to the ancestors in the temple, accompanied by a wine libation. The two spouses, after meeting—the young man having gone to fetch his bride—prostrate to each other before sharing a common meal, joining in sipping from the cups made of the same melon to show their union and affection.[43] But the words by which groom and bride express their matrimonial union show their obedience to the choice of their parents rather than to personal wishes. As the Book of Rites puts it:

> The respect, the caution, the importance, the attention to secure correctness in all the details, and then the [pledge of] mutual affection,—these were the great points in the ceremony, and served to establish the distinction to be observed between man and woman, and the righteousness to be maintained between husband and wife . . . . From that righteousness came the affection between father and son; and from that affection, the rectitude between ruler and minister. Whence it is said, 'The ceremony of marriage is the root of the other ceremonial observances'.[44]

Confucian ceremonies are said to begin with the Capping, to have their root in marriage, and to be most important in the rites of mourning and sacrifice. A considerable part—including many extensive chapters—of the Book of Rites is concerned with funerary and mourning ceremonies, the duration of mourning periods for the different degrees of kinship, and rituals surrounding the ancestral cult. Certainly, the Chinese and the Koreans paid meticulous attention in the past to doing the proper thing by their dead. Mourning is supposed to express the sorrow of departure from this life, but the veneration to the dead also implies a belief in the afterlife, as well as the continued mutual dependence of living and dead. This is a distinctive characteristic of Confucianism which bears some resemblance to the Christian memorial services—but goes far beyond it. It is interesting to observe that while the Confucian ethics is clearly oriented to life in this world, the Confucian follower spends much of his life in mourning, living near the grave of his deceased parents, and in retirement from social and political activity. In this respect, the Christian conscience, although "other-worldly" in its orientation, shows much less scruples.

The problem with rituals—both with cultic offerings and sacraments and ceremonies—is that they can become an end in themselves, instead of a means of self-transcendence, of pointing the way to God, as authentic expressions of communal faith. This is the reason for incessant efforts at liturgical renewal, at simplification of ritual and enriching of symbols. All this is done to prevent cultic and ritual practice becoming mere formalism, at which the heart is no longer present. This is important for all the world's religions. Confucius has asked: "Do rites refer merely to jade and silk . . . ? Does music refer merely to bells and drums?" (Analects 17:11.) And, "If a man is lacking in the virtue of humanity, what can the rites do for him?" (Analects 3:3.)

Conclusion

In concluding this comparative study of Confucianism and Christianity, especially through consideration of prayer and meditation, mysticism and ritual, one cannot but be struck by the real differences between early Confucianism, with its expressions of faith in a supreme, personal deity, and later Confucianism, where a greater mystical tendency tends to obscure this dimension of transcendence, while emphasizing the oneness between self and the universe. This same difference is also found between the Confucian cult—especially the cult to Heaven, which is a legacy of early Confucianism—and Confucian meditation or "quiet-sitting." In fact, as already mentioned, the prayers which sage-kings addressed to the Lord-on-High or Heaven arose most probably out of a cultic context. It is interesting to note, therefore, the continual, ritual adherence to a belief in the one God, supreme above all other spirits, Creator and Benefactor of all, and the divergence from this belief in personal religious piety. Of course, Confucian meditation and mysticism do not explicitly deny God's personhood and transcendence. But they give little importance to this faith.

The question, of course, is why. Why the divergence, and why the continued dichotomy between cult and meditation—or philosophy? Did the change come with Confucius himself, or later, and how?

Confucius himself has been variously designated as a believer in God or an agnostic. Certainly, his recorded dialogues, the Analects, do not offer much evidence of personal prayer. Any faith in one God, as personal deity and transcendent power, is more implicit than explicit. What is important, however, is that it is *implicit*. Even the contemporary Confucian philosopher, Fung Yu-lan, an advocate—at least before the days of the anti-Confucius Campaign—of Confucianism as philosophy rather than religion, acknowledged Confucius' faith in this personal God.

All the same, Confucius did initiate a change in orientation in the course of Chinese thought—less in the direction of formal religion, and more in the direction of a humanism based on the moral nature of man. His followers would further strengthen this humanistic orientation: Mencius, by introducing also a mystical dimension, emphasizing the oneness between self and the universe, and Hsün-tzu, by introducing the possibility of real agnosticism and even atheism, by his "demythologizing" of Heaven—reducing it to the physical emporyean—even if he continued to give importance to ritual matters, as education, moral restraint and decorum.

However, it is important to point out the impact and consequences of the ancient and continued association of rulership and Heaven, and the very restriction of the cult of Heaven to the ruler himself. The Confucian Classics give a record of prayers to God and conversation with God—but the human partners in this sacred dialogue are usually rulers. Now Confucius was no ruler; neither were the philosophers who followed him. In this way, the very "democratization" of Confucian religion and philosophy— the fact that commoners, rather than sage-kings, should have become interpreters of that ancient religious philosophy which came to be known in the West as "Confucianism"—led also to its increasing secularist focus, even if the religious dimension was never lost sight of.

And then, we cannot deny the syncretist influences of Taoism and Buddhism, from which Confucianism received a greater mystical orientation, especially with the rise of the great Neo-Confucian thinkers, from the ninth century on. Confucian "quiet-sitting", both as a method, and as a means directed toward the end of self-forgetfulness in self-transcendence and union with All, bears the strong imprint of Ch'an Buddhist influence. This development continued during a period of centuries, without however affecting the basic orientation of the Confucian cult—protected, as it has been, by its very exclusiveness, and by the very rituals which surround this formal act of prayer and worship.

I reach, therefore, a conclusion very similar to that of the Jesuit missionaries of the sixteenth and seventeenth centuries, of Matteo Ricci and his followers. I am persuaded that early Confucianism, indeed, the Chinese religion *before* Confucius, offers a real similarity to Christianity, in its life of prayer and cult as well as in the theology this implies. To use once more Friedrich Heiler's terminology, it came very close to being a "prophetic religion," based on a simple revelation which sage-kings received from God, a revelation which united ethics with politics, worship with rulership, a revelation in which God stands out as a supreme, personal deity, the source of all life and power. Through the influence of Taoism and Buddhism, however, later Confucianism assumed more and more the characteristics of "mysticism," and might have transformed itself into a mystical religion, had it not been for the continuance of a state cult to Heaven, a yearly reminder of God's transcendence.

Nevertheless, while agreeing with Matteo Ricci and other Jesuits regarding the greater resemblance between early Confucianism and Christianity, I do not therefore share their regret over the later evolution in Neo-Confucianism, a regret born of religious-apologetic zeal. I find this evolution interesting in itself, and a clear indication of certain *differences* between Confucianism and Christianity. Confucianism, even in its early form, only *came close* to being a prophetic religion. The simple "revelation" which the sage-kings claimed to have received did not have the importance of the revelation of Christ in the Christian religion, and did not lead to the development of any doctrine of faith or revelation. The idea of God as a supreme and personal deity never became a dominant problem for the Confucian tradition. Confucius himself, *the* great prophet of the tradition which he both inherited and developed, focused more and more attention upon an ethical humanism. Without ruling God out of the picture, he kept the idea of God itself at a safe and respectful—even reverential—distance, at least intellectually. Confucianism would never have its own theology. The later influences of Taoism and Buddhism deepened its spirituality and mysticism, while further obscuring the pristine belief in God.

I offer the above analysis as an explanation for certain divergences between the Confucian cult and its philosophy and spirituality. I think that the very unique manner in which prophetic and mystical factors became interrelated in the Confucian tradition is most meaningful. It shows us how the prophetic religion can learn much from the mystical—and the mystical from the prophetic, but always according to a specific cultural context, and within a peculiar cultural and religious community. Confucianism and Christianity each provide a different example of how such a learning process has taken place, and continues to take place. Confucianism and Christianity can also learn from each other— from what is common between them, as well as from what is different.

NOTES

1. Friedrich Heiler, *Das Gebet* (München, 1921), pp. 248–63, *passim*. See English translation by Samuel McComb, *Prayer: A Study in the History and Psychology of Religion* (London, 1932), ch. 6. This is not the place to discuss in detail the suitability of Heiler's categories for a study of Confucianism. I wish to emphasize that I am only singling out *certain features* in early Confucianism by calling it "prophetic religion," and even then, strictly within the limits of Heiler's categories. For this, I have the support of H. H. Rowley, who, without mentioning Heiler, has done so in his work *Prophecy and Religion in Ancient China* (London, 1956). See especially p. 120. Rowley made special mention also of the Book by E. R. Hughes and K. Hughes, *Religion in China* (1950), where the authors regarded Confucius as a prophet "such as we find in the Old Testament." (See Rowley, p. 2.)

Let it be said here also that I disagree with Max Weber's contention that "there had never been an ethical prophecy of a supramundane God who raised ethical demands." (*The Religion of China*, New York, 1964, pp. 229–30). I should say rather that there had been both ethical prophecies and a belief in a supramundane God, but that the Chinese prophets did not speak out *explicitly* in the name of such a God. An exception might be made, even here, of the philosopher Mo-tzu (fifth to fourth century B.C.).

2. Henri de Lubac, "Christliche Mystik in Begegnung mit den Weltreligionen," in Josef Sudbrack, ed., *Das Mysterium und die Mystik* (Würzburg, 1974), pp. 86–88. This is taken from deLubac's Preface to *La Mystique et les Mystiques*, ed. by A. Ravier, SJ (Paris, 1965).

3. See Josef Sudbrack's article in Karl Rahner *et al.*, ed., *Sacramentum Mundi*, English translation by C. Ernst *et al.* (New York, 1970), vol. 5, pp. 74–81; Louis Bouyer, *Introduction à la Vie spirituelle* (Paris, 1960), ch. 3; G. Ebeling, "Das Gebet," *Zeitschrift für Theologie und Kirche* 70(1973), pp. 206–25.

4. D. Howard Smith, *Chinese Religions* (New York, 1968), pp. 14–21.

5. James Legge, tr., *The Chinese Classics* (Oxford, 1893), vol. 4 (The Book of Poetry), p. 448. When using Legge, I usually offer adapted versions of his translations.

6. Ibid., p. 505.

7. Ibid., p. 599.

8. Ibid., p. 255–56.

9. Ibid., p. 340.

10. Ibid., p. 312.

11. Ibid., p. 534. Such complaints of the just man, in this case undoubtedly a king, may be compared to Job's complaints to God in his suffering (See Job 23–24). See Kierkegaard's comments on Job's complaints in *Wiederholung*, German translation by E. Hirsch (Düsseldorf, 1955), pp. 68–9; see also Ernst Bloch, *Atheismus im Christentum* (Frankfurt, 1968), pp. 148–59.

12. D. Howard Smith, *Chinese Religions*, pp. 37–40; H. G. Creel, *Confucius the Man and the Myth* (London, 1951), pp. 129–30; Herbert Fingarette, *Confucius—the Secular as Sacred* (New York, 1972). See also Smith's book on *Confucius* (New York, 1973), p. 61.

13. Smith, *Confucius*, pp. 44–59.

14. Louis Bouyer, "La Vie spirituelle et la Parole de Dieu," in *Introduction à la Vie spirituelle*, ch. 2.

15. Louis Bouyer, "Mystisch: zur Geschichte eines Wortes," in *Das Mysterium und die Mystik*, pp. 57–60.

16. Cuthbert Butler, *Western Mysticism* (New York, 1966), Prologue and pp. 181–86.

17. Heiler, *Das Gebet*, pp. 248–63.

18. Klemens Tilmann, *Die Führung zur Meditation* (Einsiedeln, 1972), p. 55.

19. English translation From D. C. Lau, *Mencius* (Baltimore, Md., 1970), p. 182.

20. See the chapter on Music in the Book of Rites. English translation by James Legge, *Li Ki* (Sacred Books of the East, edited by F. Max Müller, v. 28), (Oxford, 1885), p. 103.

21. Doctrine of the Mean, in J. Legge, tr., *The Chinese Classics*, v. 1, pp. 384–85.

22. For more information on Buddhist prayer and spirituality, see Heinrich Dumoulin, *Christianity Meets Buddhism* (LaSalle, Ill., 1974), ch. 4–5; H. M. Enomiya Lassalle, *Zen Meditation for Christians* (LaSalle 1974).

23. See Okada Takehiko, *Zazen to seiza* (Nagasaki, 1965), pp. 19–20. This

small work is almost unique in its treatment of Zen Buddhist and Confucian meditations. It exists only in Japanese.

24.   Fung Yu-lan speaks of Confucian mysticism as inspiring a "Work of love" where Buddhist mysticism tends to remain introverted. See *A History of Chinese Philosophy*, English translation by Derk Bodde (Princeton, 1952), vol. 2, 492.

25.   On this point, see R. C. Zaehner, *Our Savage God* (London, 1974), Introduction and ch. 3 and 4. He makes mention of Confucianism especially on p. 197, for approaching God in a way that is "both human and humane."

26.   On this subject, Julia Ching, *To Acquire Wisdom: the Way of Wang Yang-ming* (New York, 1976), ch. 7; see also W. T. deBary, ed., *The Unfolding of Neo-Confucianism* (New York, 1975), pp. 141–84. I wish to mention here what J. A. Cuttat has said: that extreme interiority calls for a transcendence, as the base of an edifice is ordained to its summit, by preparing for a meeting with God. See *La Rencontre des Religions* (Paris, 1957), pp. 41–46.

27.   On the concepts *jiriki* and *tariki*, which are taken from Japanese Buddhism, see Heinrich Dumoulin, "Grace and Freedom in the Way of Salvation in Japanese Buddhism," in R. J. Zwi Werblowski and C. J. Bleeker, ed., *Types of Redemption* (Leiden, 1970), pp. 98–104.

28.   For attachment and detachment in Buddhist cultivation, see Fung Yu-lan, *A History of Chinese Philosophy*. vol. 2, pp. 393–406.

29.   The reference is to Augustine's Confessions, vii, 23; quoted in Butler, *Western Mysticism*, 47.

30.   Karl Rahner, "The Theological Concept of Concupiscentia," *Theological Investigations*, tr. by C. Ernst (Baltimore, 1960), vol. 1, p. 374.

31.   Josef Sudbrack, *Das Mysterium und die Mystik*, Foreword by Otto Knoch and Friedrich Wulf S. J., p. 6.

32.   See *Neues Glaubensbuch: Der gemeinsame christliche Glaube*, ed. by J. Feiner and L. Vischer. (Freiburg 1973), pp. 379–81, 88–89; English translation in *The Common Catechism: A Book of Christian Faith* (New York, 1975), pp. 365–68, 375–76.

33.   See J. Shih, "I riti nella Religione Chinese," *Studia Missionalia* 23(1974), p. 145.

34.   For Hsün-tzu, see "A Discussion of Rites," in Burton Watson, tr., *Hsün Tzu: Basic Writings* (New York, 1963), pp. 89–111.

35.   See Fung Yu-lan, "Ju-chia tui-yu hun-shang chi-li chih li-lun," (The Confucian Theories of Marriage, Funerals and Sacrificial Rites), *Yen-ching hsüeh-pao* 3 (1928), pp. 356–58.

36.   See Johannes Metz' article on the Eucharist, in *Sacramentum Mundi*, vol. 2, 257.

37.   W. E. Soothill, *The Three Religions of China* (Oxford, 1923), p. 232. See also the chapter on the Meaning of Sacrifices, in the Book of Rites, ch. 21, English translation by James Legge, *Li Ki*, vol. 2, pp. 210–20.

38.   D. Howard Smith, *Chinese Religions*, pp. 140–45; James Legge, *The Religions of China*, 44–51.

39.   For ancestral sacrifices, see Book of Rites, ch. 21–22, in Legge, tr., *Li Ki*, vol. 2, pp. 226–35, 236–54. See also Chu Hsi's Family Ritual, French translation by Charles de Harlez, *Kia-li* (Paris, 1889), pp. 18–27, 146–48. See Martin Buber, "China and Us," in *A Believing Humanism* (New York, 1967), p. 188.

Buber says that the Chinese ancestral cult "signifies an attitude of the receiving principle; it means that the generation that lives after receives from the dead. This ancestor cult is thus only possible in a culture where familiarity with the dead prevails." He goes on to say that he judges such to be alien to the Western mentality.

40.   For the ritual bath, see P. H. Dore, SJ, *Manuel des Superstitions Chinoises* (Paris-Hongkong, 1970), p. 8. For the child's "tonsure," see *Li Ki*, vol. 1, p. 473.

41.   For the Capping Ceremony, see Chu Hsi, *Kia-li*, tr. by de Harlez, ch. 4. and *Li Ki*, vol. 1, pp. 437–38. For the girls, there is a ceremony by which they are given their adult hair-pin at the time of their betrothal. See *Kia-li*, ch. 5.

42.   Book of Rites, 41, in *Li Ki*, vol. 2, p. 428.

43.   *Kia-li*, ch. 7; Book of Rites, 41 (in *Li Ki*, vol. 2, pp. 428–34).

44.   *Li Ki*, vol. 2, p. 434.

Chapter Six

THE PROBLEM OF POLITICAL RELEVANCE

Introduction

Politics and political involvement have always presented problems to Christian thinking, and in many ways, more than to Confucian philosophy. In the first place, the precise political import of the authentic teachings of Jesus Christ remains today an open and debatable question. With Confucius and his teachings, the problem is different, on account of his open and continual preoccupation with political *praxis* in the society of his own time, as he travelled about from one state to another, seeking a ruler who might use his counsel. He was concerned with the establishment of a just society—or better still, the restoration of a lost order— based on moral leadership and persuasion. In the case of Jesus Christ, the known historical data give us quite a different picture. On the one hand, he was no man of the socio-political, or even religious Establishment. A Jew born and bred in a Roman colony, his only aristocratic claim was through the Davidian line which had long ago lost its throne. He did not toady to the Roman authorities as did the Herodian party or the Sadducees. Neither was he a member of the priestly hierarchy or of the learned scribes and elders. On the other hand, he also kept a distance from the patriotic Zealot movement, and the injustice of his death lay especially in the fact of the political mistrial—false accusations and hasty condemnation. He was no socio-political revolutionary. This does not mean that his teachings lack a social and political dimension. Rather, like the earlier Jewish prophets and going beyond them, Jesus preached not only against cultic formalism but also against all injustice, privilege, oppression and narrow nationalism.[1]

Indeed, positive political teachings are difficult to derive from the Gospels. Jesus Christ teaches a "kingdom which is not of this world." He has explicitly acknowledged the coexistence of two authorities: that of Caesar and that of God (Matt. 22:16–22), thus emphasizing the need of civil obedience, in his case, to a foreign power exercising dominion in Palestine. St. Paul has followed this example in preaching obedience to human authority, while emphasizing that Christian hope is to be placed in God, since "our City is in heaven" (Phil. 3:20). And, in 1 Peter 2:16, we find an explicit statement with regard to temporal power, to "honor the king." For all power is ultimately derived from God, and deserves due respect.

This faith in God as the source of all power and authority led to the development of a dualism of power in the context of Western European history. Many early disputes were over questions of religious *versus* civil authority, representing the division of the *sacerdotium* and the *imperium*. Conflicts of jurisdiction led to claims and counter-claims, the development of jurisprudence as well as a careful codification of laws. Thus, it is said sometimes that this dualism of authority has contributed to the growth of political freedom—a freedom under law.

> The Church is not the *regnum* Christi, but the sign of this *regnum* . . . . Equally, for the ruler there is no sovereignty in the full sense, except that of God. On each side the view of power is that it is exercised by those who act in the name and with the authority of God; but they are vicars, delegates, substitutes, representatives.[2]

Confucius was also the scion of a former noble line linked to a fallen dynasty. But he clearly identified himself with the cause of the ruling dynasty of his day, out of no sense of betrayal, but rather on account of his membership in and belonging to a society which has already attained a high degree of cultural and ethnic harmony. Confucius was never clearly a man of the Establishment, although he probably served a brief term as minister of justice in his native state. But he had obvious ambitions of entering into the political Establishment, while desiring to keep intact his moral principles, and indeed, to make these principles the foundation for reforming the social order. He thus displayed an open and continual preoccupation with political *praxis* in the society of his own times.[3]

Instead of speculating upon life after death, Confucius kept his eyes fixed firmly on this life and this world, especially the social and political. Active political service was, according to him, an inherent human responsibility, and any departure from this norm could be tolerated only when undertaken itself as a form of social protest—as with the sage-hermits of legendary antiquity. Confucian involvement in society was intended as a mission of self-transcendence, both for the individual so engaged, and for the "salvation" of the social order. But the very political concern of Confucian philosophy led to the risk of its becoming subservient to political authority and its being transformed into political ideology. Such a subservience and transformation was never total or entire. Even after Confucius and Mencius, the Confucian tradition continued to produce thinkers who were critical of the social and political *status quo*, and called for reform in the name of a return to the ancient moral order. But such process did take place, especially in a culture and society that knew no dual power—of church and state. In the Han dynasty especially, Confucianism became exalted as a state philosophy—sometimes called a state religion—at the cost of accepting into its own system ideas coming from a correlative metaphysics based on *yin-yang* philosophy as well as from a Legalist doctrine of power. This helped to give justification to the new monarchical order and its universal authority. To some extent, it represented a development parallel to the ideas and efforts of Eusebius of Caesarea, the fourth-century Christian bishop under Emperor Constantine, who projected a "political theology" of one God, one Logos, one Emperor, one World—an application of philosophical monotheism to a monarchical order.[4] In the case of Confucian philosophy, however, the idea of Heaven as supreme deity suffered some setback with the emphasis on the dual power of Heaven-and-Earth. But the recognition of the Emperor as the mediator and high priest between Heaven and Earth safeguarded the dimension of transcendence inherited from the past in both religious thinking and cultic observance. All the same, it must be said that, in some ways, Confucianism became subjugated to the state in China somewhat as the Byzantine church would become subject to the Eastern Roman Emperor.

The problem of authority was formulated in terms of the ruler-subject relationship in the Confucian tradition. This is itself worthy of attention. The Western notion of authority is defined in juridical terms, but in the Far East, law has been regarded mainly in its penal aspects, while personal relationship dominates the understanding of political society and the mutual obligations of ruler and the ruled. This was true even in the Chinese feudal (*feng-chien;* 封建) system, where lord-vassal relationships were based more on kinship and other personal ties than on the idea of contract and the fealty this called for.

The Latin notion of *auctoritas* has no precise correspondent in Hebrew or Greek in the Scriptures. For the Romans, it had reference to their duties toward Emperor and Senate, as well as to writings of philosophers regarded as teachers of truth. The fundamental question of God's authority is a strange one, relating to the *freedom* of man's response to revelation. It is usually presumed that since man's whole being has been called into existence by God's creative word, he is to answer this divine call with his entire life, saying with Samuel, "Speak, Lord, for Thy servant heareth" (1 Sam. 3:10). In the New Testament, Jesus Christ is presented as a model for obedience to God's will (John 14:31), through which he has become the cause of man's salvation (Rom. 5:19, Heb. 5:8f). Thus, Christian obedience presupposes and is itself a response to faith in God and in Jesus' revelation. But this partnership of obedience and authority between Man and God, begun in religious dialogue, runs many risks when expressed through institutional channels. The problems regard both the authenticity of such claims and the correctness of exercise of this authority. True, the belief remains that all power and authority come from God. Human beings can serve only as God's delegates—exercising a *vicarious* authority. Thus, in the Christian context, no authority, whether that of pope or prince, could ever claim to be completely "absolute." And the New Testament emphasizes that authority itself is ordained to service (*diakonia*) of the community (Luke 22:24–27, 2 Cor. 4:5).[5]

There are certain difficulties underlying any comparative study of political relevance in Confucianism and Christianity, stemming from the different character of the two traditions. After all, Confucianism is not a religion in the precise sense in which Christianity is understood to be. Confucianism has always had a strongly secular orientation where Christianity has emphasized the primary importance of an "absolute future"—of God and the afterlife. Flowing from these basic differences, Western political theory has developed very much out of Church-State tensions that have no clear parallel in the Far East. Even where Buddhism and Taoism are concerned, their essentially other-worldly orientations have forestalled the development of authentic political philosophy in spite of periods of conflict between their "churches" and the state. On the other hand, Confucianism could hardly have been termed a church, save in a modified sense. Confucianism had its ideal leader: the king, regarded as a paradigmatic individual and bearer of Heaven's Mandate. But the institutionalization of dynastic kingship increased the distance between the ideal and the real, leading to a growing idealization of the role of the minister: the Confucian scholar-official who assisted his ruler in exercising the responsibilities of government. Together, they pledged to work for the fulfilment of a political vision: the restoration of a Golden Past. Grave failures on their part might hasten the dynasty's end, since the theory of the Mandate of Heaven provided also for a justification of rebellion against the tyrant who no longer deserved to be called Heaven's Son.

It is my intention to discuss the problem of political relevance by comparing Confucian ideas of kingship and government, of an ideal society, of rebellion and revolution, to certain Christian ideas of Messianism, political eschatology and liberation. I shall do so with a clear recognition of the differences between the two traditions as well as of certain areas of common ground. It is my contention here that while Christianity has an important political dimension, it is not to be reduced to a political religion. On the other hand, Confucianism has always been much more closely associated with politics and government. The Confucian ruler and minister are both political persons. And the critical distance between the minister and his ruler has served a function at once different from and similar to that between the priest and the king in the West.

THE CONFUCIAN KING

Earlier I mentioned how every Confucian man was regarded as king—real or potential, since the ideal of kingship was associated with charisma and merit. In actuality, of course, the ideal was never attained—except by the sage-kings of legendary antiquity. But the ideal continued to exert a real influence: that every man may be king is after all a logical conclusion of the doctrine of human perfectibility. It served therefore as a powerful reminder to the actual monarch to strive after the ideal, to remember that government remained a stewardship, that the kingdom was a trust, not a personal possession.

Confucian China shares with Christian Europe the idea of vicarious authority. Unlike ancient Egypt, or even Japan, China never entertained the idea of a God-ruler. At the same time, China did not experience the tension of conflict between the *sacerdotium* and the *imperium*, as this was known to Europe. According to the Confucian conception, the political ruler was regarded as bearer of Heaven's Mandate, Son of Heaven and father and teacher to the people. Indeed, such was the sacred aura surrounding the ruler's office that the all-wise and all-humane qualities of the sage —qualities of a charismatic personality—came gradually to be attributed to the ruling sovereign in the court rhetoric and etiquette, even if his moral and intellectual mediocrity was known to all, including himself.[6]

A Paradigmatic Individual

The charisma surrounding the ideal king, the sage, and his office, was such that the king was considered as a paradigmatic individual, the *one man* of the Chinese Classics, a term made famous by Hegel, although it was not intended to refer to his being the only free man of the realm.[7] According to the Confucian Classics, the king is the *one man*, because he is Son of Heaven, mediator between the powers above and the people below, in a unique manner. He governs by Heaven's Mandate; his actions are carried out according to

Heaven's wishes. On the one hand, his exalted position and awe-some responsibilities make him a *solitary* man. On the other hand, he alone is guilty of fault whenever his people have offended Heaven; he is, in some sense, the *collective* man. He alone must offer prayer and reparation to the Lord-on-High in time of natural disaster, regarded as a sign of divine displeasure.[8]

Fundamental to the concept of charismatic kingship is the well-known theory of the Mandate of Heaven. This theory was apparently developed during the Chou dynasty (1111—249 B.C.) to justify the successful overthrow of the Shang dynasty by the Chou house. It is recorded in several Confucian Classics, in particular the Book of Documents and the Book of Odes. According to this theory, the ruler's authority is based upon a Mandate bestowed on him by Heaven—the Lord-on-High—and is to be used for the good of his subjects. If the ruler sins against Heaven by personal transgressions and by misrule, he may forfeit the Mandate, which will then be given to someone else with the proper virtues. The founder of the Chou dynasty claims to have received the Mandate to crush the power of a vicious tyrant and save the people from oppression.

> We do not presume to know and say that the lords of Yin (Shang) received Heaven's Mandate for so many years; we do not know and say that it could not have been prolonged. But they did not reverently attend to their virtue and so prematurely threw away their Mandate . . . . Now our king has succeeded to and received their Mandate . . . . Being king, his position will be that of a leader in virtue . . . May those above and below (the king and his servants) labor and be anxiously careful.[9]

It is interesting to note here that the Chinese term for political revolution remains that of *pien-t'ien* (変天; changing Heaven), or more formally, *ko-ming* (革命; removing or changing the Mandate).

The doctrine of the Rectification of Names, as enunciated by Confucius himself, has contributed to the understanding of the Mandate of Heaven theory. Confucius insists that the "ruler be ruler, the minister (or subject) minister (or subject), the father be father, the son a son" (Analects 12:11). It has at times been misinterpreted as a defense of the *status quo*, an objection to social change and mobility. The truth is rather the contrary. Confucius sees the need for *good* government: the ruler must be a *good* ruler, the minister a *good* minister, and so on—that names may conform to the ethical ideals they represent. Confucius' great follower, Mencius, has certainly understood the teaching in this way. When asked by King Hsüan of Ch'i whether a minister may murder his king, Mencius replied, referring to the successful overthrow of the Shang house by the Chou, that the last Shang ruler had forfeited his rulership by his vices: "I have heard of the killing of a mere fellow (the former king), but I have not heard of murdering a ruler" (1B:8).

In the Han dynasty, the Confucian world-view grew more and more immanent through the influence of ideas coming from the *yin-yang* school. The powers of Heaven and Earth increasingly replaced the notion of Heaven as a supreme being. Man is regarded especially as forming a kind of triad with Heaven and Earth, on account of his special dignity and his resemblance to these powers.

If Man forms a triad with Heaven and Earth, it is especially in the person of the King. He remains in an important sense the *one man*, who alone is responsible for all that passes in the natural and social orders. Tung Chung-shu offers his own hermeneutic of the Chinese word, "king," by saying:

> Those who in ancient times invented writing drew three lines and connected them through the middle, calling the character "king" (*wang*; 王). The three lines are Heaven, Earth and Man, and that which passes through the middle joins the principles of all three. Occupying the center of Heaven, Earth and Man, passing through and joining all three—if he is not a king, who can do this?[10]

The King is at the same time God's vicar to the people as well as the people's representative before God. He is the ruler as well as the exemplar. His position is an exalted, but not always an enviable one. He is King, not for himself, but for the people. As Mencius has put it: "The people are of supreme importance; the altars of the Earth and Grain come next, and the Ruler comes last" (7B:14).

This should cause no wonder if we are once more reminded that the office of ruler belonged rightfully to the sage: the man who lived, not for himself, but for others. Mencius had also been pained by the absence of any sage-king after seven hundred years of Chou rule. And the Han scholars were puzzled by the fact that Confucius, the sage par excellence, should never have been king. In order to lend more credence to the belief in the sage as ruler, they gave Confucius the unique honor of having been an "uncrowned king" (素王; su-wang), even making him founder of a fictitious dynasty. They proclaimed him as governing the world, through the judgments he made over history in his writings. It has indeed been the irony of history itself that no king or emperor of the Han dynasty and after should have been a sage, even if every dynasty sought to provide itself with fictitious ancestral lines claiming descendance from some sage-king of antiquity.[11]

The Confucian belief in the periodic appearance of sage-rulers bears some resemblance to the Jewish expectation of a political Messiah, who is to usher in a reign of peace and justice. It is not based on an alleged divine promise, as is the case with the Jews, but remains all the same, a manifestation of trust in the divine guidance of history, which permits cyclical alternation of good rule and disorder. Besides, the Confucian teaching that every man can become a sage, assures the dimension of freedom in history, and encourages aspirations to sagehood itself. The Confucian Messiah is thus an Elect One, not only of God, but also of Man—with the people confirming the divine choice. And the consciousness of a Golden Past remains always an essential component of such Messianism, as it behooves the political savior to restore a former state of bliss. Mencius has given expression to this belief in the following passage:

A true king should arise every 500 years, and during the course of this time, other illustrious men should also appear. From the beginning of the Chou dynasty till now, more than 700 years have elapsed. Numerically speaking, the date is already overdue. And judging from our times, such men should be already making their appearance. However, Heaven does not seem to wish that the world should have peace and good government. If Heaven did wish it, who is there besides me, today, in the world, to bring it about? (2B:13)[12]

A Doctrine of Rebellion

Authority is meaningless except in dialectical relationship to some form of obedience and loyalty. Here, the rule which determines the bearer of authority and the extent of this authority also determines where and in what respect obedience is to be given. Is the command just and reasonable, that obedience becomes pleasing to God, or is it otherwise? Is authority being exercised rightfully, in the interest of service to the community? The human person remains morally free—to obey or disobey, to obey actively or passively, or to rebel against the commands of a given authority, be that personal or juridical.

For both Christian Europe and Confucian China, the idea of a justified rebellion is incipient in the very notion of delegated authority. In Europe, a doctrine of rebellion against authority was associated with certain religious-apocalyptic beliefs. Karl Mannheim mentions specifically Thomas Münzer, the leader of the peasant rebellion against the Lutheran princes.[13] In this regard, the notion of rebellion may be said to derive from the linear view of history itself—as the rebels believed themselves to be contributing to the realization of a historical *parousia*.

As already mentioned, religious-apocalyptic ideas associated with Taoism and Buddhism had also inspired various political rebellions in Chinese history. However, they did not lead to a clear formulation of a doctrine of rebellion as such. This was rather inferred from the Confucian theory of power itself—from the "Mandate of Heaven" theory.

Mencius insists upon the reciprocity of the ruler-minister relationship. In his words: "If a ruler regards his ministers as his hands and feet, then his ministers will regard him as their belly and heart. If a ruler regards his ministers as dogs and horses, the ministers will regard him as any other man. If a ruler regards his ministers as dirt and grass, the ministers will regard him as a bandit and an enemy" (4B:3).

Mencius' approval of tyrannicide had a decisive influence on Chinese history. Generations of rebels—and dynastic founders—had appealed to this doctrine. In this regard, Confucian China experienced many dynastic changes, justifiable according to its own political ethics. Japan, on the other hand, witnessed a different political evolution. Although the Japanese accepted Confucianism, they interpreted its teachings somewhat differently, and would not tolerate any rebellion against their God-ruler.

A theory of tyrannicide developed much later in Christian Europe than in Confucian China, being associated with the Church-State political conflicts, and with the Protestant Reforms. John of Salisbury wrote of the permissibility for the people to act as God's instruments in putting a tyrant to death—in extreme circumstances. This was in the twelfth century. In the late sixteenth century, these ideas were more clearly enunciated by the anonymous Huguenot author of *Vindiciae contra Tyrannos* (1579) and by the Spanish Jesuit, Luis Mariana, author of *De Rege et regis institutione* (1598–99). The former work was publicly burned in England and the latter was condemned by the Gallican Parliament.[14]

But tyrannicide is not equivalent to social and political revolution, even if a justification of tyrannicide clears the ground for some of the problems posed by the necessity for a revolution. As understood today, the word revolution refers to a *complete change* in the political, social, economic or technological order, bringing about important consequences for the whole of human life. The events in the People's Republic of China of the last decade have also brought into vogue the term "Cultural Revolution," which implies a change on many levels of social life *at the same time*. Revolution is usually understood as a swift and sudden event, its political models being the French Revolution of 1789, the Russian Revolution of 1917, and the Chinese Communist Revolution of 1949, each of which involved also violence and bloodshed. Revolution differs therefore from rebellions and revolts, which may be merely anarchist, or which may aim merely at a change in leadership on the political level without bringing about wide-ranging changes in the social order. In this sense, it has been asserted that Chinese history knew no revolution until the twentieth century, although there have been countless rebellions and many changes of dynasties.

The Confucian Minister

Where the Confucian king had his sage-models in the persons of the legendary Yao and Shun of remote antiquity,[15] the Confucian minister looked up to more historical forerunners: whether Yi-yin, of the Shang dynasty, or the Duke of Chou, Confucius' own favorite sage. This fact alone may teach a subtle lesson: that Yao and Shun, who yielded the throne to the worthy rather than to their own sons, had less need of sagely ministers than the later dynastic founders, who wanted to secure the Mandate of Heaven for their family as well as for themselves. Following the example of the Duke of Chou, Confucius never aspired personally after kingship, but sought everywhere for a ruler who was willing to use his services. History yielded the verdict that he was more worthy of the throne than anyone else of his time. His exaltation as "uncrowned king" made him a model at once for both the real king and his real minister. Both must strive to imitate him in virtue. Each could claim to succeed him as teacher for the realm. And, where the king is teacher of all under Heaven, the minister participates in this responsibility in a special way, not only by teaching the people under their rule, but also and especially by acting as the king's advisor—his mentor.

The minister's duty as the king's *critical* advisor raises an interesting problem: that of political loyalty (*chung*; 忠). How must he act toward the unworthy monarch, who turns a deaf ear to his advice, and plunges the kingdom in chaos, the people in misery? Should he take upon himself the duty of starting a rebellion, especially when he sees himself or some other man as a more worthy ruler? Should he rather try his best even when he recognizes the dynasty's coming end, and die for or with the ruler?

I propose to examine the idea of the Confucian minister in terms of his duty of loyalty to the ruler and the corollary notion of political protest. I wish to emphasize that the Confucian idea of loyalty means first and foremost loyalty to one's own conscience—over and above the person of the ruler. Implicit in this notion is the common duty—the king's and minister's—of loyalty to Heaven who whispers its commands in the conscience. But if, in theory, the Confucian minister is entitled to rebel against a tyrant, in practice, he usually prefers to articulate protest rather than take up arms and risk a violent revolution.

The Meaning of Loyalty

The Confucian response to the problem of political authority has usually been articulated in terms of loyalty. It differs from the more Western notion of obedience. For obedience has an impersonal aspect, and may be applied internally to the conscience and externally to laws. Loyalty on the other hand, remains deeply personal, whether directed to a cause—in the name of moral conviction—or to another person, or group of persons.[16]

The notion of loyalty, understood as the virtue which governs the duty of the subject or minister toward the ruler or sovereign, had actually a much broader meaning in the early Confucian Classics. In the Annals or Tso, loyalty is defined for the ruler as "benefitting the people." In the Analects, Tseng-tzu speaks of it in reference to oneself, as "being true to one's own nature," and in association with reciprocity (shu; 恕) which governs one's relationship to others. He also describes it in terms of devotedness, to both superiors and equals, in carrying out one's duties. Confucius himself mentions loyalty most often in conjunction with faithfulness (hsin; 信) which governs one's relationship with oneself or with others, regardless of social rank. He speaks of faithfulness to the ruler, who must show parental devotion to the people under him in order to win their loyalty. One of Confucius' heroes is Kuan Chung (d. 645 B.C.) who had abandoned his first lord in order to serve a rival, the Duke of Ch'i. In the Great Learning and the Doctrine of the Mean, the word "loyalty" usually occurs in connection with "faithfulness," and on one occasion, refers to the ruler's devotedness to the subjects. In the Book of Mencius, it refers almost always to being true to one's own mind and nature, and to teaching others to be good. Even Hsü Shen (c. A.D. 30–124) defines this word in his lexicon as "devoting one's mind (to something or someone)" without limiting it to the ruler-subject relationship. And Cheng Hsüan (A.D. 127–200), commenting on the Rites of Chou, speaks of "loyalty" as "keeping the mind or heart in the middle position," that is, being devoted, impartial and balanced in one's judgments and actions.[17]

In the course of history, with the increasing centralization of political power, the meaning of loyalty became distorted, to refer to mere passive devotion to a ruler or to his dynasty. This was encouraged by the appearance of a forged classic, the so-called Classic of Loyalty, a short treatise modelled upon the Classic of Filial Piety, attributed to Confucius' disciple Tseng-tzu. It was allegedly written by Ma Jung (A.D. 79–166), but is now universally recognized as a forgery, which probably appeared for the first time in the Sung dynasty. It exalted loyalty as an absolute virtue, centered upon respect for, and devotion to the person of the ruler, whose duty was defined as "serving Heaven above and Earth below, and the ancestral temple in the middle, in order to face [and govern] the people." His ministers must "forget themselves in the service of the ruler, forget their families in the service of the country, remain upright and direct in their speech, and even give up their lives in fidelity [to the ruler] at a time of calamity."[18]

And so, the opinion became prevalent that the ruler's duty was primarily to serve the spiritual powers of the universe and of his own ancestors, to whom he owed the good fortune of sitting on the throne. The minister's duty, on the other hand, was to remain absolutely faithful to the person of the ruler and his dynasty, pre- ferring loyalty to filial piety. But the welfare of the people, who, according to Mencius, came before the gods of the Earth and Grain and even the ruler himself, was relegated to a secondary position. They now exist only to be governed.

The philosophers of Neo-Confucianism stayed with the earlier understanding of political "loyalty" while remaining also favora- bly inclined to a less centralized state.[19] In the words of Ch'eng Yi, the word *chung* means to "exert all one's energy" and "freedom from falsehood." Chu Hsi said the same thing, identifying *chung* with *shu* (reciprocity). For him, *chung* means being faithful to one's own convictions, while *shu* means extending this faithfulness to one's dealings with others. In whatever regards the ruler-subject relationship, these philosophers usually showed themselves anxious to assert the subject's dignity and limit the ruler's authority. They stood for the absolute value of eternal truths which transcend the control of political authority. They took upon themselves the duty enjoined by Mencius—to set the ruler's mind and heart aright. The Ch'eng brothers and Chu Hsi all wrote memorials to the throne which resemble moral lectures. They sought to elucidate for their sovereigns the basic distinction between kingliness and tyranny. They spoke of the need for the ruler to rectify his own mind, to order well his family—the harem and the palace personnel, and to select carefully competent officials to assist him in the government of the state. As Ch'eng Yi once said, in the presence of his pupil, the boy emperor, Che-tsung (r.1085–99): "The sovereign need not fear that his dignity is not being upheld. He should rather fear that the subjects exalt it excessively, to the point of causing his pride to augment."[20]

Loyalty and Protest[21]

If loyalty means essentially personal integrity, the source and principle of all faithfulness, whether to persons or to a cause, how should a loyal minister behave toward an undeserving ruler? Do the Classics offer any instruction to help him make his moral decisions in times of difficulty and stress? Mencius has considered these questions already in his time. He speaks, for example, of three kinds of nobility, of rank, age and virtue. If rank receives primordial regard in the feudal courts, age holds the first place in the villages, while virtue produces the most effect in the government of men. He who possesses one of the three kinds of nobility should not therefore despise others who might possess the other kinds. In this way, the philosopher argues that his own conduct, in not responding to the summons of a feudal king, is quite correct (2B:2).

Mencius also speaks of two kinds of chief ministers: those related to the ruler by bonds of kinship, bearing the same surname as he, and those having a different surname. When the ruler is at fault, his kinsmen ought to remonstrate with him, and, after having done so repeatedly without obtaining any result, they ought to remove him from the throne. The others, in a similar situation, should rather leave the service of the state (5B:9).

Mencius' teaching has not passed without criticism. The Sung statesman Ssu-ma Kuang (1019–86) was probably the best exponent of a minister's duty of strict loyalty and respect. He criticized the doctrine of "revolution" which would enhance the danger of imperial relatives competing for power:

> Ministers, whether imperial relatives or those of a different surname, are all subjects. The duty of a subject obliges him to offer good counsel to the ruler. If he is not listened to, he may either leave the imperial service or die [as a martyr]. But how dare he supplant the ruler in his position, just because he may be an imperial relative?[22]

As a minister himself, Ssu-ma Kuang was devoted to the common people whose welfare he sought to secure. But he was always emphatic about maintaining the ruler's dignity. He was also a Taoist by preference, advocating a policy of non-interference and opposing the reforms of Wang An-shih (1021–86). It is an example of historical irony that Ssu-ma Kuang, the ultra-loyalist, should later on suffer the consequences of a ruler's caprices. In 1101, under the instigation of a latter-day disciple of Wang An-shih, a stone tablet was erected in an attempt to defame those who opposed reform. The name of Ssu-ma Kuang headed the blacklist.

With the increasing centralization of power and exaltation of the ruler's position, the minister seeking to correct the ruler's abuses of power attempted to do so more and more by accusing himself, *instead of* the ruler, of the alleged abuses. An example in the Ming dynasty was a memorial submitted by Wang Yang-ming whose efforts to rehabilitate the people of Kiangsi after a war were being thwarted by a pleasure-loving sovereign. Wang begged for removal from office, enumerating four crimes of which he regarded himself as being guilty—including that of failure to persuade the emperor to mend his ways(!) He concluded by saying:

> Any official, with only one of these crimes, would be suf-

ficiently guilty to give rise to a calamity and to a rebellion. So much the more would be the case of someone guilty of all these crimes. . . . I beg Your Majesty to take compassion on the great calamity that has taken place, remove your servant from his office, select another worthy man to take his place. Even should your servant be executed, as an example to the world, your servant should consider himself fortunate.[23]

An expression of irony and protest this document certainly was. But it represented also a futile effort, a desperate act undertaken with the hope of moving the heart of the ruler, the really guilty party. And then, when we recall to mind the practice of the ancient rulers to accuse themselves of the crimes committed by their people, we perceive also an added significance: that the Confucian minister has stepped into the moral vacuum left behind by the irresponsible ruler. As a faithful disciple of the sages, he has become a kind of paradigmatic individual himself.

Contrary, therefore, to the conventional impression of the Neo-Confucian philosophers as the loyal supporters of the ruler's dignity and absolute authority and the zealous preachers of the subject's duty of unchanging loyalty to the ruling sovereign and his dynasty, these thinkers of the Sung and Ming dynasties considered themselves rather as the rulers' teachers and judges, either through word or action. Their profound awareness of the unity which should exist between ethics and politics made of them the conscious bearers and spokesmen of the Confucian conscience, the "prophets," who, like Confucius and Mencius before them, had received the charismatic mission from Heaven, to stand up to the kings, to offer them counsel and criticisms, on behalf of the people for whom the state existed. These men saw clearly the important position of the ruler in the absolute imperial system. Although they did not directly criticize the system itself—Huang Tsung-hsi (1610–95), the direct heir of the Ming thinkers, would do this also —they were volatile in their praises of the Golden Past, when rulers were sages who governed by moral persuasion rather than by the force of their will made into law. They were also persevering and courageous in their repeated efforts, in and out of office, to convert the ruler's mind and heart, to make him into a true sage-king. If the ruler-subject relationship implies a mutual obligation, it would seem that the philosophers regarded the ruler's responsibility of loving the people to be infinitely heavier than the subject's duty to show loyalty—a duty which is besides only conditional to the ruler's merits and virtues.[24]

The Confucian Society

It is important to remark that Jewish and Christian hopes for an ideal state of affairs, whether in the form of a Promised Land for the Jews, or of the expectations of the Messiah and his reign, which have played a significant role in the shaping of a Christian consciousness, nourished particularly in the hopes of a future Millennium (Rev. 20),[25] are usually founded upon an alleged *promise* of God. This is characteristic of revealed religions based on faith in God as Creator, Providence, and Lord of history. For the believer, political desires have always had religious premises and presuppositions, and expressed themselves in Biblical images. Besides, the *eschatological* dimension of Christian Millenarianism brings an unmistakably *linear* orientation—linear in the sense of a straight line. The ideal society is regarded as the *final* fulfilment of man's dreams regarding his earthly abode and existence, even if it is to come within time and history, as a prelude to the new Heaven and the new Earth located beyond the limits of time and history.

The work of St. Augustine contributed further to this linear orientation in a Christian philosophy of history, as is obvious in his book, the *City of God* (A.D. 427).[26] Augustine did not identify Church and State with his heavenly and earthly cities. According to him the earthly city is made up of those whose behavior is governed by love of self, while the heavenly city is the community of the elect, whose hearts are dominated by love of God. Indeed, the "City of God" is to become fully revealed only at the end of time. This apocalyptic impulse is intended, not as escape into a dream world, but as a theme of action for all who will, to fight and struggle for a new Promised Land—built upon a foundation of peace and justice.

Considerations of peace and justice dominated also Thomas

More's classic, the *Utopia* (1516),[27] the best-known and perhaps normative work for the Western mentality. More wrote as a humanist and a prophet, decrying the social inequalities and religious intolerance of his time. His "happy island" is a non-Christian society. More used it to criticize the selfishness, divisions and strifes of the Christian Europe he knew. It also sent out echoes of geographical discoveries—then being made outside of Europe, often in the illusory hope of finding an ideal society, a "promised land." It represents another example of a dynamic, linear interpretation of history. But then, More's Christian inspiration led him to project the image of a paradise on earth—a society which did not yet know the Gospel message, and a state of original human innocence. It is therefore an example also of the *cyclical* dimension which never completely vanished from the horizon of Christian social imagination. The "Golden Past" is, independently, a Christian heritage as well as a Confucian one.

And so, we turn now to the Confucian tradition, to discover its ideal social order, and the similarities and differences this offers with reference to the Christian model.[28]

Once more, one should mention the difficulty of the sources. The Chinese philosophical tradition has never known the separation of politics from ethics. The only exception has been with the evolution of teachings of applied statecraft, closely associated with the amoral philosophy of Legalism, and written down in treatises that may be aptly described as "rulers' manuals." Such was the treatise of *Han Fei Tzu* (third century B.C.), which bears resemblances to a much later work, Machiavelli's *Prince* (1512–13). Both manifest a cold and calculated rationality which reckons with only one concern: the interest of the man in power. Chinese philosophy produced no "utopian" treatise that may be compared to Plato's *Republic* or to More's classic, with a clear analysis of the principles of government of the ideal society. Premodern Chinese sources can only offer a few scattered chapters and passages, taken from classical texts, which evoke "utopian" sentiments.

The Ideal Polity

The utopias of the Taoist intellectuals bear greatest resemblance to that described by Thomas More's classic. They include Chuang-tzu's fanciful Chien-te (Virtue Established), placed by him in the southern regions (Nan Yüeh), and Lieh-tzu's countries of Hua-hsü shih and Chung-pei. All these are presented in naturalistic terms. Their inhabitants live a simple and blissful life, away from civilization and its artificial distinctions of social and political hierarchy, its virtues of righteousness and propriety, its preoccupation with life and death. Such are the products of the daydreams of recluse-philosophers dissatisfied with the social order, who had neither the inclination nor the intention of starting a rebellion or a revolution.[29]

The utopian dreams of a more religious and apocalyptic nature, fall into a different category, since these had frequently promoted attempts to bring about violent social or political change. There had been, for example, the vision of the Great Peace presented by *T'ai-p'ing ching* (Classic of Great Peace) which contributed to the Yellow Turban rebellions of the late second century A.D. There had also been messianic dreams of Maitreya, the Buddha of the Future, in the sixth century and after, culminating in the successful revolution of Chu Yüan-chang (r.1368–98), the dynastic founder of Ming, who began his career as a supporter of Han Lin-erh, the purported reincarnation of the Buddha of the Future.[30]

Confucian utopian theories differ from both the peaceful dreams of earthly paradises in which the naturalist philosophers indulged and the religious-apocalyptic visions of popular rebels. Confucian utopias tended to be of time rather than of place. They have strong moral connotations, representing the state of affairs as it should be and can be, provided the correct measures are undertaken to effect such a transformation. Nearly every successful rebel or dynastic founder had sought, in some way or other, to justify his action by appropriating to himself the Confucian vision of a just society as his avowed aim, and that for which Heaven conferred on him the great Mandate. Confucian ideas influenced in part the Meiji reforms of nineteenth century Japan, as well as the 1911 Republican revolution in China.

In the chapter on the Evolution of Rites in the Book of Rites, the Confucian Golden Age is described as comprising both the age of Great Unity (*Ta-t'ung;* 大同) of early antiquity as well as of the subsequent age of Lesser Tranquillity (*Hsiao-k'ang;* 小康), identified as that of the Three Dynasties (Hsia, Shang and Chou). Attributing the words to Confucius, this chapter presents the Great Unity as a time when "the world belonged to all:"

> When the Great Way was practiced, the world was shared by all alike. The worthy and the able were promoted to office and men practiced good faith and lived in affection. Therefore, they did not regard as parents only their own parents, or as sons only their own sons. The aged found a fitting close to their lives, the robust their proper employment; the young were provided with an upbringing and the widow and widower, the orphaned and the sick, with proper care. Men had their tasks and women their hearths. . . . This was the age of Great Unity (*Ta-t'ung*).[31]

But the age of "Great Unity" did not last long. A collective fall somehow took place in antiquity, giving rise to strong leaders, who assured order by governing the people with ritual laws drawn from man's social nature. The five moral relationships became institutionalized. The world, which used to "belong to all," became the "possession of private families." Each of the Three Dynasties was founded by a sage-ruler, but each chose to pass the throne to his own descendants rather than to another, selected on the basis of merit alone, as did the legendary Yao and Shun. Moreover, each dynasty decayed in the course of time. The emergence of "rites and righteousness" was thus a necessary evil, to prevent and control selfishness and intrigue.

> Now the Great Way has become hid and the world is the possession of private families. Each regards as parents only his own parents, as sons only his own sons; goods and labor are employed for selfish ends. Hereditary offices and titles are granted by ritual law while walls and moats must provide security. Ritual and righteousness are used to regulate the relationship between ruler and subject, to insure affection between father and son, peace between brothers, and harmony between husband and wife. . . . This is the period of Lesser Tranquillity.[32]

The earlier fellowship or *Gemeinschaft* gave way to a society, the *Gesellschaft*. Rites, however, rested on moral foundations, and so differ from "laws," which in the Chinese conception, would be simply expressions of the ruler's will. Thus, even the age of Lesser Tranquillity (*Hsiao-k'ang*) presented conditions that were much more desirable than those of subsequent ages. The sage-emperors, aided by their sage-ministers, were "constantly attentive to the rites, manifested righteousness and acted in good faith." Of how many later rulers can this be said?

Despite Taoist overtones, the two stages of the Golden Past, as given in the "Evolution of Rites," provided inspiration for Confucian and Neo-Confucian scholars who found their ideals outlined in this chapter. As the conditions of the age of Great Unity seemed in practice nearly unattainable, the age of Lesser Tranquillity, identified historically especially with the early Chou Dynasty—the age of the Duke of Chou—became the *model* age for later generations. Throughout Chinese history, scholars expressed their desire to see re-established in their own times such institutions as the well-field system of land distribution and even political feudalism itself. Time and again, the cry was raised that the pre-Ch'in conditions should be restored and that the way of tyrants (*pa;* 霸) should again yield to the gentle way of kings (*wang;*王).

The identification of the Confucian "utopia" with the Golden Past, which was to remain a model for the present and future, became definitive especially with the emergence of the Neo-Confucian philosophers of the Sung and Ming dynasties. A reformist drive appeared in those days which was seldom found earlier. The philosopher Chu Hsi provided a metaphysical interpretation of history, describing the age of remote antiquity as having been dominated by the heavenly principle (*T'ien-li*), a time when men lived according to Heaven-endowed virtues of humanity, righteousness, propriety and wisdom, under the governance of sage-rulers like Yao and Shun. Unfortunately, the Golden Past gave way to another age, dominated by human desires (*jen-yü*), as self-interest became rule rather than exception, the moving power of despots who usurped the kingly title. Chu placed the key to the restoration of the Golden Past in moral education, and in the careful selection of rulers.[33]

Neo-Confucian philosophers have sometimes been represented as conservatives supporting a social-political *status quo*, and in frequent opposition to reform measures. The facts, however, were not so simple. Frequently, where the practical politicians, whether conservative or reformist, were interested only in pragmatic policies, the philosophers preached moral regeneration, paying as much attention to the morality of means as well as of ends. They also maintained a position of greater independence with regard to political power, advocating some limit to the exercise of absolutism through moral suasion, where the politicians—especially those in high places—attempted to strengthen the ruler's dignity and authority for the sake of carrying out measures of practical policy. Thus it is the philosophers' merit to have upheld a utopian vision as safeguard of ethical ideals in political life.

To locate an ideal society in the order of time rather than of place indicates some self-satisfaction on the part of Confucian China, center of its own geographical world, and with little desire to explore beyond its known frontiers. To situate it in a Golden Past considered possible of restoration indicates also a strongly *cyclical* notion of time, as contrasted with the more *linear* view associated with Christianity and its millenarianist dreams. But the Confucian utopian mentality has also its own linear dimension, shown in an allegorical interpretation of the Classic, the Spring-Autumn Annals. This came with the Han dynasty, when Tung Chung-shu spoke of the Three Ages revealed in that text—those years personally witnessed by Confucius, those he heard of through oral testimony, and those he heard of through transmitted records. This was in reversed chronological order. But the Kung-yang school of allegorical interpretation, through its representative Ho Hsiu, arranged these Three Ages in a successive order, describing them as those of Disorder (*chü-luan;* 據亂), Approaching Peace (*sheng-p'ing;* 升平) and Great Peace (*t'ai-p'ing;* 太平), while also proclaiming their disclosure of a pattern for good government in the historical present and future.[34] A certain parallel between the Approaching Peace and the Great Peace mentioned here and the Lesser Tranquillity and Great Unity of the Book of Rites may be discerned, even if the "Evolution of Rites" proposes a devolution rather than an evolution. In the late Ch'ing dynasty, K'ang Yu-wei revived the Kung-yang interpretations, making explicit these parallels in his own utopian treatise, the Book of the Great Unity. K'ang Yu-wei was exposed to utopian ideas coming from the West. But the combination of the Book of Rites and the Spring-Autumn Annals provides a view of time and history which may be described as spiral—a cyclical progression of human society. Yet it must be admitted that for most of Chinese history, the utopian vision had been identified with the restoration of a Golden Past, with the belief in its historical facticity lending faith in the possibility of recapturing it—provided the proper sage-rulers would appear.

Mention has already been made that even in the Western utopian mentality, a nostalgia for a lost past remains present, even if the quest for an ideal future dominates. This is true not merely with the preoccupation over an original state of human innocence and bliss in the "Garden of Eden," but also with the description of early community sharing in the Acts of the Apostles. It can be found even in Marxism, with its claim of a primitive communist society in the remote past, vaguely resembling the utopia of the future. Generally speaking, however, it may be said that the *linear* view of history dominates the Western utopian mentality in spite of certain cyclical vestiges.

Still, if the Western—and especially Christian—utopian mentality displays more linear features while the Confucian dreams appear more cyclically oriented, the two agree in one common assumption: that it is the human being who makes history. It is man who seeks to bring about a future that suits his fancies, be these associated with a coming Golden Age, or with restoring the Past. To both Christians and Confucians, man and history have a great importance, and with them, society and state as well. Here, Christianity and Confucianism differ from those religions originating in India, whether Hinduism or Buddhism, with its disdain for the temporal, the secular, the social and political.

The Situation Today

How much can one still discern of Confucianism in today's China—the People's Republic? In which ways have the old ideals survived in the new political vision, as well as in the new social structure this has inspired? These are hard questions, especially after an intensive anti-Confucius Campaign following upon the Great Proletarian Cultural Revolution of 1964 and afterward.

Ostensibly, today's China aims at a total eradication of Confucian influences from all forms of life and thought. As the People's Daily of January 10, 1967, puts it:

> In our Socialist new China, there is absolutely no room for Confucian concepts and capitalist and revisionist ideas which serve the exploiting classes. If these ideas are not uprooted, it will be impossible to consolidate the dictatorship of the proletariat and build socialism and communism. In the Great Proletarian Cultural Revolution, one of our important tasks is to pull down the rigid feudal corpse of Confucius and eradicate thoroughly the completely reactionary Confucian concepts.[35]

And the goal of such eradication is clearly known: to make possible the establishment of the "absolute authority" of Mao Tsetung's thought.[36]

Interestingly enough, the commitment to a new cultural and political vision brings to mind a clearly *dialectical* correlation between Confucianism and the new state ideology. Like the Confucian *Tao* of old and replacing it, Dialectical Materialism is now taught and revered as infallible doctrine, the norm for all philosophy, logic, history and even "eschatology." In place of the "philosopher-king" myth, we have now the reality of a Party Chairman, the political ruler as well as the guardian and exponent of the new ideology, and father and mother to the people. The goal of Chinese society is a New Socialism—a universal vision with strong resonances of the Confucian ideal society, formulated as a world "belonging to all" (*ta-t'ung*).[37]

Chinese communism differs from classical Marxism on an essential point: the substitution of "the people" for "the proletariat." The People—the "masses"—have been made the vanguard of the revolution, the source of all truth and wisdom. This has its roots also in the Confucian—and Mencian—emphasis on the people as being of "supreme importance." For "Heaven sees as my People sees; Heaven hears as my People hears."[38] Chinese communism has clearly articulated a doctrine of the ruler's responsibility before the People. As Chairman Mao himself said:[39]

> When we say "We are sons of the People," China understands it as she understood the phrase "Son of Heaven." The People has taken the place of the ancestors.

The People has taken the place of the ancestors in the sense that the People deserves the veneration formerly reserved for one's forebears. The People has indeed taken the place of Heaven itself. Chairman Mao is claiming a Mandate bestowed upon him by the new God—the People.

The dialectical correlation between Chinese communism and Confucianism is so strong as to lead one writer to comment in the following words:

> What Mao has done has been to establish himself as a new Confucius, a counter-Confucius; this was implicitly stated in the Cultural Revolution and in the famous collection of *Quotations from Chairman Mao Tse-tung*. Mao wishes to do for the new age what Confucius did for the traditional Chinese society. To do this he must establish an absolute barrier . . . between the old and the new. . . .
>
> But while Mao has set himself squarely against the Confucian virtues as well as against the entire social context in which they were expressed, he has only reestablished these same virtues within another context. The revolutionary struggle itself, with its constant self-examination, is nothing other than a transposed version of the traditional Chinese effort at inner personal renewal each day. . . . The willingness to serve others, to submit to the community . . . is a manifestation, in a new context, of the traditional virtue of *jen*. . . . The key to understanding Mao is in recognizing in him a counter-Confucius, whose greatest historical mission, in spite of himself, is to evoke a renewal of the Confucian tradition.[40]

Of course, the correlation remains a dialectical one. If the ultimate social goal offers resemblances to the Confucian vision of the "Great Unity"—one may even say, the "Great Equality"—

the *way* of attaining this goal is defined in terms very dissimilar to the traditional ones. We hear not of a restoration of the past and of social harmony, but rather of class struggle and socialist revolution—even a permanent revolution. Perhaps, the contours of the new collective society, as those of the new ideology, present certain points of continuity with those of the Confucian clan society. But the social focus as well as the content of ideas has radically changed. The total philosophical orientation is no longer in the direction of harmony, but rather of struggle, of contradiction, of revolution. An extremist doctrine has replaced that of moderation.

And yet, for those who prefer to dwell on the continuities more than on the discontinuities, the following words could offer some clue for the future:

> Confucius will one day be recognized as the colossus of Chinese tradition who challenged Mao as consistently as Mao challenged him. Confucius can even now be seen as the hidden anxiety of Mao, as the judge of his deeds, the one against whom Mao was struggling throughout the entire course of the Cultural Revolution. . . . Until this day, Confucius remains both the inspiration and the indestructible nemesis of Mao. . . . Just how long the present chasm can be maintained between the old and the new is problematic . . . Lao Tzu tells us that the movement of the Tao is to return, to turn back upon itself. The broken lines of the I Ching hexagrams tend to join while the unbroken lines tend to separate. So we can expect the Chinese revolution in some manner to turn and recover its past, not to deny but to preserve the remarkable achievements of the present.[41]

CONCLUSION

Christians today are beginning to discover more and more the political import of the original Christian message and the responsibility this calls forth on the part of believers with regard to social and political problems, and in the quest of a more just society. On the other hand, Confucianism, being more a "diffused" than "organized" religion, and suffering itself from the results of revolutionary social and political change in the whole of East Asia, has not been able to confront adequately the problems posed by such change, in spite of the essential political character of its own teachings. In fact, Confucianism remains passive, being used by political powers in such states as South Korea and Taiwan as a theoretical justification for a paternalistic and authoritarian government, which can be and has been, intellectually and politically repressive. In the People's Republic of China, and in North Korea, it has been officially discarded, in an effort to assure the total dominance of Marxist political ideology, as interpreted by the governments in power.

What future is there for Christians and Confucians to learn politically from each other's traditions? What are the contradictions present within the Christian's quest for political meaning in his faith, and how can the Confucian insights and experiences both serve as a source of reference for Christianity, as well as a starting point for transformation and new relevance for Confucianism itself?

As already mentioned, leading Christian thinkers as well as many thoughtful believers have shown themselves able to learn politically from dialogues with Marxists. They have been ready to accept certain elements in the Marxist view of man, society and history that are not entirely antagonistic to Christian belief, discerning in these a religious sense of commitment and purpose that responds to their own inner stirrings. They have therefore set an example for Confucians to emulate. This is not the time for polarization, but for authentic reflection in the light of self-criticism. For Confucian scholars—except those in the People's Republic, where they have no option, and where, indeed, they have been obliged, under pressure, to renounce Confucianism itself— have largely neglected the study of Marxism, preferring to live in an unreal intellectual atmosphere associated romantically with the past glories of a tradition which is facing a radical challenge.

In seeking to learn from each other as well as from Marxist theories and from the Critical theorists, Christians and Confucians must first of all be able to discern between the *essentials* of the Christian or Confucian teachings and the peripheral. This will give them a basis from which they can evaluate the merits of their own past as well as the possibilities for future growth. This will also assist them to evaluate the validity of Marxist and other social theories, without abandoning their own basic positions. For Christians, the irony is that the recent history of the missions has been largely one of alliance with political and military powers—with Western imperialism. This is the principal reason for a rejection of Christianity today by the socialist governments in East Asia and elsewhere. Besides, there has been also a sense of racial, cultural and religious superiority—the result of ignorance of other traditions and their own self-image, as well as of a triumphalist dogmatic orientation: the conversion of infidels. It is here that Christian missions have actually contributed to the birth of socialist China, by helping to pull the old "feudal" society quickly through a bourgeois-capitalist phase and on to a socialist present.[42]

Besides, there is yet another problem, that of the *transcendence of politics*. To say that theology, starting from man's self-understanding, needs to become politically conscious in order to be true to itself and to the message it bears, does not mean that theology must deal exclusively with problems of social and political relevance. After all, we have witnessed the developments of theologies of hope, protest, revolution and liberation, and have learned from them the Christian's inherent responsibilities regarding serious injustices. But we need to point out that certain important problems remain unresolved: violence in revolution, and how that may be controlled or "contained," for example. And we may perhaps question whether themes of hope, revolution and protest and liberation can embrace the *whole* of theology. Does social and political responsibility imply a complete *immersion* into this world and its problems, or should the Christian not practise here, as in his spiritual life of prayer and meditation, a certain *detachment* in spirit from his secular engagements, as well as a definite *attachment* to the values of social justice and political equity? Otherwise, is there not the risk of forgetting the real meaning of hope, of a real eschatology, and the *religious* nature of the revolution and liberation achieved by Jesus Christ, who alone can be his model?

A theologian writing from India about its difficult social situation as well as its multi-variegated religious landscape, has made some comments on the importance of the *praxis* of Christian social ethics in that country. He has also pointed out the equal importance of keeping in the Christian consciousness, a sense of attachment to and detachment from the world, since, he says, the Church is *in* the world but not *of* the world. He tells his Christian readers that the Hindus and Buddhists in India tend to regard Christian concern for social and political relevance as naive and this-worldly, in comparison with their quest for Brahman-ātman or *nirvāna*.[43]

From these words, one may infer that Christianity holds a certain *middle* position in its attitude on social and political concerns—somewhere between Hindus and Buddhists, who are too detached, and Confucians, who may sometimes appear too attached. It all depends on one's own perspective, therefore, whether Christianity should be considered as "this-worldly" or "otherworldly."

To refer once more to the words of J. Russell Chandran:

The Church understands itself as the new creation of God in Christ and not simply as an agent of society. It is a community brought into being as the Body of Christ, sharing the ultimate concerns of God and . . [waiting] for the fulfillment of the new humanity and the summing up of all things in Christ.[44]

For the Christian, the ultimate meaning of Christianity is found in the Cross and Resurrection of Jesus Christ, because of which he will always be "in the world but not of the world."

Notes

1.   For the political background of Jesus Christ, see Hans Küng, *Christsein*, (München, 1974), 169–80, Gustavo Gutierrez, *A Theology of Liberation*, tr. by Sr. C. Inda and J. Engleton (New York, 1973), pp. 225–31.
2.   See J. M. Cameron, *Images of Authority: A Consideration of the Concepts of Regnum and Sacerdotium* (New Haven, 1966), p. 2.
3.   For Confucius' political position, see H. G. Creel, *Confucius, the Man and the Myth* (New York, 1949), pp. 25–55.
4.   See Jürgen Moltmann, "The Cross and Civil Religion," in Moltmann *et al., Religion and Political Society*, ed. and tr. in the Institute of Christian Thought (New York, 1974), pp. 24–25. Moltmann quotes in this regard E. Peterson's treatise, "Monotheism as a Political Problem" (1935).
5.   J. M. Cameron, op. cit., ch. 1.

6.   For the charismatic qualities of kingship in Confucian China, see Max We-ber, *The Religion of China*. tr. by Hans H. Gerth, with an Introduction by C. K. Yang (New York, 1964), pp. 30–32.

7.   See Hegel's *Philosophy of History*, English translation by J. Sibree (New York, 1956), Introduction, p. 18.

8.   References are to the Book of Documents. See J. Legge, tr., *The Chinese Classics*, vol. 3, pp. 175, 185, 288, 292, 379.

9.   Book of Documents (Announcement of Duke of Shao), English translation adapted from Legge, op. cit., vol. 3, p. 430.

10.   See Tung Chung-shu's *Ch'un-ch'iu fan-lu* (Luxuriant Gems of Spring-Autum Annals), English translation in W. T. deBary, ed., *Source Book of Chinese Tradition* (New York, 1964), vol. 1, p. 163.

11.   Fung Yu-lan, *A History of Chinese Philosophy*, English translation by Derk Bodde (Princeton, 1953), pp. 71, 129–30.

12.   English translation adapted from D. C. Lau, *Mencius*, p. 94.

13.   Karl Mannheim, *Ideology and Utopia*, tr. by L. Wirth and E. Shils. (New York, 1936), p. 212. Mannheim cites especially Ernst Bloch's work, *Thomas Münzer als Theologe der Revolution* (Munich, 1921).

14.   Touchard, op. cit., vol. 1, pp. 283–84.

15.   I must acknowledge here that Shun serves also as model for the minister, since he was such before rising to the position of king. See Mencius 4A:2.

16.   See Josiah Royce, *The Philosophy of Loyalty* (New York, 1909), pp. 16–17, 162, 357ff.

17.   The references are to *Tso-chuan* (Annals of Tso), sixth year of Duke Huan, Analects 4:15, 1:4, 9:24, 12:10, 15:5, 2:20, 3:19, 14:17–18, Great Learning 10, 18, Doctrine of the Mean 20, Book of Mencius 1A:5, 3A:4, 4B:28, 31, 6A: 16, 7A:32 and 7B:37. See also *Shuo-wen chieh-tzu* (Taipei edition, 1964), p. 507. The Chinese word for "loyalty" (忠) is made up of two components signifying "middle" (中) and "heart" (心).

18.   See my article, "Neo-Confucian Utopian Theories and Political Ethics," *Monumenta Serica* 30 (1972–73), part 2, p. 40.

19.   Ibid., p. 54.

20.   This is given in Chu Hsi's chronological biography of Ch'eng Yi. See also Hsiao Kung-ch'üan, *Chung-kuo cheng-chih ssu-hsiang shih* (History of Political Thought in China) (Taipei, 1954), vol. 4.

21.   "Neo-Confucian Utopian Theories," part 2, op. cit.

22.   *Ssu-ma Kuang wen-chi* (Collected Writings of Ssu-ma Kung), SPTK ed., 73:12a–b.

23.   *Wang Wen-ch'eng kung ch'üan-shu* (Complete Writings of Wang Yang-ming), SPTK double-page lithograph ed., 13:391. See translation by Chang Yu-ch'üan in his article, "Wang Shou-jen as a Statesman," *Chinese Social and Political Science Review* 23 (1939–40), pp. 221–22. (Wang Shou-jen was Wang Yang-ming's formal name).

24.   "Neo-Confucian Utopian Theories," part 2.

25.   Jean Servier, *Histoire de l'utopie* (1967), pp. 47–60, 74–86.

26.   See especially St. Augustine, *City of God*, Book VI, ch. 12.

27.   Thomas More, *Utopia* (London and New York, 1955).

28.   See Julia Ching, "Neo-Confucian Utopian Theories and Political Ethics," in *Monumenta Serica* 30 (1972–73), part 1, p. 3.

29.   Ibid., the references are to *Chuang-tzu* 20, *Lieh-tzu* 2 and 5.

30.   The *T'ai-p'ing ching* was allegedly written in the second century AD and attributed to Yü Chi. See also *Hsin Yüan-shih* (New Dynastic History of Yüan), (K'ai-ming edition, 1935), 225:431 ff., for the background of the Ming dynastic founder.

31.   This English translation is adapted from W. T. deBary, ed., *Sources of Chinese Tradition* (New York, 1960), vol. 1, pp. 175–76.

32.   Ibid., p. 176.

33.   "Neo-Confucian Utopian Theories," 18.

34.   Ibid., p. 22.

35.   Donald E. MacInnis, *Religious Policy and Practice in Communist China: A Documentary History* (New York, 1972), p. 294.

36.   Ibid.

37.   Dai Sheng-yu, *Mao Tse-tung and Confucianism* (Unpublished doctoral dissertation, University of Pennsylvania, 1953), Stuart R. Schram, *The Political Thought of Mao Tse-tung* (London, 1963), pp. 46–55.

38.   James Legge, tr., *The Chinese Classics*, vol. 3, p. 292 (taken from the Book of Documents, The Great Declaration, pt. 2).

39.   Mao to André Malraux, quoted in MacInnis, op. cit., p. 17.

40.   Thomas Berry, "Mao Tse-tung: The Long March," *Theological Implications of the New China* (Geneva and Brussels, 1974), p. 67.

41.   Ibid., p. 68.

42.   See my reflections on the Louvain Conference held on the subject of Christian Faith and the Chinese Experience, in the article entitled "The Christian Way and the Chinese Wall," *America* vol. 131, No. 14 (November 9, 1974), pp. 275–78. The Conference took place in September, 1974, after a preparatory meeting in Bastad, Sweden (January, 1974).

43.   See J. Russell Chandran, "Where Other Religions Dominate," in John Bennett, ed., *Christian Social Ethics in a Changing World* (New York, 1966), p. 230.

44.   Ibid.

EPILOGUE

The time has come for a summing up of this study. I wish to recall to mind the general goals which I set forth in the Introduction. There I spoke of my reasons for writing this book. I spoke of a desire to promote intercultural and interreligious dialogue, to make Confucianism better known and understood among those who are Christians or have knowledge of Christianity. I mentioned also how a deepened knowledge of another tradition could contribute to a better and enriched knowledge of one's own, in the light of wider perspectives. I have labored, throughout these chapters, to make possible a better and fuller knowledge of Confucian teachings. It is also my hope that an examination of certain important themes present in the Confucian tradition and analyzed against the perspective of Christian teachings would contribute to the theological self-understanding of Christianity. This is important in two ways: for the ecumenically minded Christians of the West, who desire to realize a more authentic "catholicity," as well as for the "newer" Christians of East Asia, who are searching for more genuine forms of theological expressions which take into account their own cultural heritages. In this epilogue, I wish to speak more on the issue of Asian Christianity, and of the theological challenges involved in the shaping of its future.

In the time of Matteo Ricci and his immediate successors in the missions of the Far East, the task of adapting Christianity to local cultures meant especially a readiness to learn from that form of traditional wisdom known today to the world as Confucianism. But the intellectual orientation has since changed. Today, a much more living dialogue is taking place between Christianity and Buddhism in its varied forms. This dialogue is being encouraged by institutional churches, and has evoked a great interest among a larger public all over the world.[1] Confucianism appears to have been largely neglected or even forgotten. This is not the place to discuss the reasons for this changed orientation. I do not consider it entirely mistaken. Indeed, where earlier missionaries in China and Japan had ignored and criticized the Buddhist religion, today, a newer generation of Christian intellectuals and missionaries have manifested a much more positive attitude, showing themselves ready to learn as much as possible from Buddhist metaphysics and spirituality. This is very much to be commended. But I recommend that Confucianism also not be overlooked, especially on account of its greater inner compatibility with Christianity. This is all the more important as the fundamental outlook of harmony and nonduality present at the heart of East Asian cultures[2] has permitted much interaction between Confucianism, Buddhism and Taoism—or Shinto in Japan. It is therefore impossible to understand the East Asian without some knowledge of each of these traditions, as well as the ways in which they have learned from one another.

In East Asia, both Catholics and Protestants have said much about the development of indigenous theologies. In this respect, the Japanese Protestants have made the most contributions.[3] The best-known Japanese theologian is Kazō Kitamori, who has placed special importance on the relation between the Christian message and the *inner* dimension of Japanese culture. His own advocacy of a theology of the Pain of God has been recognized as a truly creative effort to think Christianity theologically in a Japanese manner. It shows more Buddhistic overtones than Confucian ones. But the very demand of *interior* knowledge of native culture as a theological prerequisite is most important in any effort of creative theological thinking.

Chinese Christians have lagged behind in the task of theological thinking, although real, if halting, efforts have been made, and here, especially by Christian converts—including second-generation "converts"—who remain attached to Confucian values. One needs only to read the writings of Dom Lu Cheng-hsiang, John C. H. Wu and others to see how they regard the road from Confucius to Christ as a smooth one—with no real rupture necessary for someone with a Confucian past.[4] The Protestant T. C. Tsao has especially outlined the conditions for a Chinese theology built upon the common ground between Christianity and Confucianism. He spoke of "purifying" institutional Christianity and those dogmas that have little relevance for life, and of concentrating upon the central teaching, that "God is Love"—a teaching which Confucians, educated on *jen*, should be quite ready to accept.[5]

Christians in China, Japan and Korea, have all shown a great sense of social responsibility, paying particular attention to the social message of Christianity—an obvious influence of Confucian social ethics.[6] True, with the rise of socialism and the triumph of socialist regimes in a large part of East Asia, many Christians—including T. C. Tsao, so it seems—have decided to embrace Marxist social theories or at least adapt them to Christian beliefs. Some of them have expressed difficulties in reconciling love and violence. Others have found it hard to remain Christian. Their efforts and examples should serve as a useful lesson for the political theologians of the West today. Theology, after all, cannot be constructed upon an experiential vacuum. It can only be the product of the believer's reflections over his confrontation with life, both individually and socially.

But Asian theologies are emerging with difficulty, not only because of the churches' attachment to positions of "dogmatic orthodoxy"—coupled with a fear of "heresy"—but also because Asian Christianity remains young and somewhat insecure, both with regard to its European or American mentors in theology and *vis-à-vis* the non-Christian majority. A Christian tends to move within a social and intellectual ghetto—be this a local village mission or an educated, Westernized élite society. He has feelings of self-alienation as he knows himself to be surrounded by compatriots who do not share his religious beliefs, and by an entire cultural ambiance which remains largely unknown to his Western and missionary friends. He seems to have a perpetual identity crisis. Endo Shusaku's novel, *Silence*,[7] gives strong witness to this sense of lost identity. Must a Christian apostatize, in order to become once more Japanese, Chinese or Korean?

The question posed here is a grave one, calling into question, as it does, the whole problem of Christian humanism—as well as the adaptation of Christianity to different cultures. If Christianity means a better human*ity*, it should also mean a better

Chinese, or Japanese, or Korean human*ity*: a better and a happier humanity. The message of conflict, which the Gospel introduces into Asia, must somehow pave the way to a new harmony between man and himself, man and the universe and his fellow men, to become acceptable, to become indeed, Asian.

It is with this in mind that I have written this book. Conflict and tension, so experience tells us, can be the *locus* of cultural and spiritual fermentation, of an enriched future. One must, however, have consciousness of the value of such conflict and tension, in order to be able to draw out the dialectical results in philosophical and theological expressions. Christian and Confucian humanisms: what and how much can one learn from the other? What are the positive, and negative lessons? What are the chances for survival, and for transformation? These remain the basic questions, upon which depends much of the future.[8]

There are also other considerations. There is yet much that the West has to learn from the East, and Western Christians especially from the non-Christians of the East. In this book, we have discussed the problem of man and of his self-transcendence, pointing out the Confucian theories of human nature, conscience, and community. We have treated the problem of God—the personal God of the Christian Scriptures and the Confucian Classics as well as the metaphysical Absolute of the mystic-philosophers. We have also gone into the *praxis* of self-transcendence in prayer, mysticism and cult, noting how early Confucianism, with its belief in a personal God, offers evidence also of prayer as dialogue with God, while later Confucianism, with its philosophical orientations, produces a greater interiority as well as a mysticism that is open to others. We have also discussed the problem of political relevance, of the Confucian doctrine of kingship and rebellion, and the modern implications of such teachings. The whole spectrum of comparative study offered here represents the entire drama of life—of the desires, tensions, and possibilities of human life. And the Confucian and Christian have much to learn from each other— from the teachings of the Classics and scriptures, from the collective wisdom of tradition, as well as from the felt needs of the present.

In a few words of brief summary, one may say that Confucianism has kept its focus throughout the centuries on the moral, religious and even cosmic significance of the virtue of *jen*, discerning the transcendent in the experience of intersubjectivity, of man's relationship with man. Christianity, on the other hand, has always declared its central teaching, that which sums up the entire revelation of Jesus Christ, in the statement, "God is Love." Let us therefore conclude this book on the note of love, of *jen*. With Confucius, let us hope that we may "meet friends on the basis of culture (*wen;* 文), and allow friendship to serve the growth of *jen*" (Analects 13:24).[9]

Notes

1. For Buddhism in the world today, see especially Heinrich Dumoulin, ed., *Buddhismus der Gegenwart* (Freiburg, 1970); see also his *Christianity Meets Buddhism* (LaSalle, 1974), ch. 2.

2. See O'Hyun Park, *Oriental Ideas in Recent Religious Thought* (Lakemont, 1974), ch. 2. Park also points out how difficult it is for the Western mind to understand the East Asian's multiple religious identities and loyalties. W. E. Hocking appreciates this too. See *Living Religions and a World Faith* (New York, 1940), 77.

3. See Carl Michaelson, *Japanese Contributions to Christian Theology* (Philadelphia, 1960); Charles H. Germany, *Protestant Theologies in Modern Japan* (Tokyo, 1965).

4. See Dom Pierre-Celestin Lu Tseng-tsiang, *Souvenirs et Pensées* (Bruges, 1945), John C. H. Wu, *Beyond East and West* (New York, 1951), and *Chinese Humanism and Christian Spirituality* (New York, 1965); and Paul K. T. Sih, *From Confucius to Christ* (New York, 1952). To prove that there is no need of a rupture with one's Confucian past, to show that he did not have to turn his back upon his Confucian beliefs, Dom Lu speaks of his "vocation" to Christianity and Catholic monasticism rather than of a "conversion." John Wu and Paul Sih both speak well of their Confucian pasts. But the tendency in the writing of converts has been to see Confucianism as a philosophical preparation for the religious revelation of Christianity. I wish to maintain here that Confucianism also has a claim to independent and separate existence and development, even though in contact and dialogue with Christianity and other traditions. This is not denied in the converts' writings, but it has not been emphasized either.

5. See Ng Lee-ming, "An Evaluation of T. C. Tsao's Thought," *Ching-feng* 14 (1971), pp. 21–35. Ng has also published "A Study of Y. T. Wu," *Ching-feng* 15 (1972), pp. 5–54, and "Wang Ming-tao: An Evaluation of His Thought and Action," *Ching-feng* 16 (1973), pp. 51–80. Of these three men studied, T. C. Tsao has the most theological import.

6. On this point, see Ng's articles, ibid., and S. Wu's "Confucianism and its Significance to Christianity in China," *Ching-feng* 12 (1969), pp. 4–23. On the Japanese side, see especially Masaharu Anesaki, *History of Japanese Religion* (Tokyo, 1968), pp. 360–65.

7. See the English translation by William Johnston (Tokyo, 1969). Even today, Asian members of Catholic religious institutes continue to feel that they are treated as "second-class" members in their own countries, while being "culturally alienated" from their fellow countrymen through a "foreign" formation and education. See the SVD survey, "Pluralism and Pluriformity in Religious Life: A Case Study," *Pro Mundi Vita Bulletin* No. 47 (1973), pp. 29–33.

8. In this regard, see also the article in *Ming-pao* written by a group of Chinese Christian students at the Chinese University of Hongkong. The article is entitled, "'Wo-men Chi-tu-t'u tui shih-tai yü wen-hua wen-t'i chih k'an-fa" (Our Christian View of the Times and the Problem of Culture), *Ming-pao Monthly*, No. 102 (June 1974), pp. 41–47, No. 104 (August, 1974), pp. 37–38. The latter part is especially concerned with the relationship between Christianity and Confucianism.

9. Analects 12–24. The English translation is my own.

Chronological Table
(Important dates for *Confucianism and Christianity*)

CHINA

Shang Dynasty
Pre-classical Religion

Chou dynasty c. 1111–249 B.C. Spring-Autumn Period:
722–481 B.C. (Age of Prophets in Israel)
Warring-States Period: 403–221 B.C.
The Age of Philosophers (in China as well as Greece)
Confucius 551–479 B.C.
Mo-tzu c. 468–c. 376 B.C.
Lao-tzu
Mencius c. 371–289 B.C.
Chuang-tzu c. 369–c. 286 B.C.
Hsün-tzu c. 298–c. 238 B.C.
Han Fei Tzu d. 233 B.C.

Ch'in Dynasty 221–207 B.C.
The Imperial Age (Burning of Books: 213 B.C.)

Han Dynasty 207 B.C.–A.D. 220 (Introduction of Buddhism)
Tung Chung-shu 179?–104? B.C. (Birth of Christ: 6 B.C.)
Wang Ch'ung A.D. 27–c. 100 (Destruction of Jerusalem:
A.D. 70)

Three Kingdoms A.D. 220–280

Chin Dynasty A.D. 280–420
Neo-Taoism and Buddhism

Northern and Southern Dynasties A.D. 421–589

Sui Dynasty A.D. 589–618

T'ang Dynasty A.D. 618–906
  Buddhism: Prosperity and Decline
  Confucian Revival
    Han Yü A.D. 786–824
    (Nestorians in China)

Five Dynasties: Age of Disorder A.D. 907–959

Sung Dynasty A.D. 960–1279
  Neo-Confucianism
    Chou Tun-yi 1017–73
    Ch'eng Hao 1032–85
    Ch'eng Yi 1033–1107
    Chu Hsi 1130–1200
    Lu Chiu-yüan 1139–92

Yüan Dynasty (Mongols) 1260–1367
  (Franciscan Missionaries in China)
Ming Dynasty 1368–1644
  Wang Yang-ming 1472–1529
  Wang Ken 1483–1514
  (Matteo Ricci in China)

Ch'ing Dynasty (Manchus) 1644–1912

Republican Period: 1912—present
  People's Republic: 1949 to present (Chinese Marxism)
  (Missionaries expelled)

Selected Bibliography

This is a selected list of books on comparative philosophy and religion as well as Confucianism and Christianity; some have been mentioned in the notes. Specialized studies and monographs are not given here since they can be found in the notes.

General Works: Anthologies and Comparative Studies

Chan, W. T. *et al. The Great Eastern Religions: An Anthology.* New York, Macmillan, 1968.

Eliade, M. *Patterns in Comparative Religion.* New York, New American Library, 1974.

—— and Kitagawa, J. M. *The History of Religions: Essays in Methodology.* Chicago, University of Chicago Press, 1959.

Hartshorne, C. *et al. Philosophers Speak of God.* Chicago, University of Chicago Press, 1953.

Heiler, F. In *Prayer*, ed. by Samuel McComb. London, Oxford U. P., 1932.

Hocking, W. E. *Living Religions and a World Faith.* New York, Macmillan, 1940.

Kaplan, A. *The New World of Philosophy.* New York, Vintage Books, 1961.

Kitagawa, J. M. *Religions of the East.* Philadelphia, Westminster, 1963.

Nakamura, H. *Parallel Developments: A Comparative History of Ideas.* New York/Tokyo, Kodansha International, 1975.

Otto. R. *The Idea of the Holy*, trans. by J. W. Harvey. Oxford U. P., 1923.

Smith, W. C. *The Faith of Other Men.* New York, New American Library, 1965.

Smart, N. *The Religious Experience of Mankind.* London, Collins, 1970.

Tillich, P. *Christianity and the Encounter of World Religions.* New York, Columbia U.P., 1961.

Toynbee, A. *Mankind and Mother Earth.* London, Oxford U.P., 1976.

Special Works: Confucianism and Related Subjects
a. Classics and Philosophers in Translation and Anthologies of
Translations
Legge, J. *The Chinese Classics.* Oxford, Clarendon, 1893– ,
5 vols. (The four books are reprinted in *Confucius,* New
York, Dover, 1971.)
Lau, D. C. *Lao-tzu: Tao-te ching.* London, Penguin Classics,
1963.
_____. *Mencius.* London, Penguin Classics, 1970.
Waley, A. *The Analects of Confucius.* London, Allen & Unwin,
1939.
Watson, B. *Chuang-tzu: Basic Writings.* New York, Columbia
U.P., 1964.
_____. *Han Fei Tzu: Basic Writings.* New York, Columbia U.P.,
1964.
_____. *Hsün-tzu: Basic Writings.* New York, Columbia U.P.,
1963.
_____. *Mo-tzu: Basic Writings.* New York, Columbia U.P.,
1963.
Anthologies
Chan, W. T. *A Source Book in Chinese Philosophy.* Princeton,
Princeton U.P.
deBary, W. T. *Sources of Chinese Tradition.* New York, Columbia
U.P.
b. Other Works
Chan, W. T. *Religious Trends in Modern China.* New York,
Columbia U.P., 1953.
Creel, H. G. *Chinese Thought from Confucius to Mao-Tse-tung.*
Chicago, University of Chicago Press, 1955.
_____. *Confucius the Man and the Myth.* New York, John Day,
1949.
Fingarette, H. *Confucius: the Secular as Sacred.* New York, Harper
Torchbook, 1972.
Fung Yu-lan. *A History of Chinese Philosophy,* trans. by Derk
Bodde. Princeton, Princeton U.P., 1952–3, 2 vols.
_____. *A Short History of Chinese Philosophy.* New York, Mac-
millan, 1948.
Jaspers, K. *The Great Philosophers: the Foundations.* New York,

Harcourt & Brace, 1962. (Paradigmatic Individuals: on Confucius.)

Smith, D. H. *Confucius.* New York, Holt, Rinehart, 1973.

———. *Chinese Religions.* New York, Holt, Rinehart, 1968.

Waley, A. *Three Ways of Thought in Ancient China.* London, Allen & Unwin, 1939.

Weber, M. *The Religion of China.* New York, Free Press, 1964.

Special Works: Christianity

The Holy Bible. Revised Standard Version (Catholic Edition). London, Catholic Truth Society, 1966.

Bonhoeffer, D. *The Cost of Discipleship.* New York, Macmillan, 1959.

Bultmann, R. *Theology of the New Testament.* New York, Scribner, 1968–70.

The Common Catechism: A Christian Book of Faith, ed. by F. Feiner and L. Vischer. London & New York, Seabury, 1975.

Conzelmann, H. *Outline of the Theology of the New Testament.* New York, Harper & Row, 1969.

Documents of Vatican II, ed. by Walter M. Abbott, S. J. New York, Corpus, 1966.

Häring, B. *The Law of Christ.* Paramus, Newman Press, 1961, 2 vols.

Küng, H. *On Being a Christian. (Christsein).* New York, Doubleday, 1976.

Rahner, K. *et al., Sacramentum Mundi. An Encyclopaedia of Theology.* London, Burns & Oates, 1968, 6 vols.

Rahner, K. *Theological Investigations.* Baltimore, Helicon Press, 1961–9, 13 vols.

Schnackenburg, R. *The Moral Teaching of the New Testament.* New York, Herder, 1971.

Theological Dictionary of the New Testament, ed. by G. Kittel and G. Friedrich. Grand Rapids, 1971ff, 10 vols.

Tillich, P. *Systematic Theology.* Chicago, Chicago U.P., 1964–6, 3 vols.

Index